HIDDEN AGENDAS

Hidden Agendas

Exposing the Dark Secrets

DEMETRI WELSH

www.demetriwelsh.com

CONTENTS

PART VI
THE HIDDEN HAND: GOVERNMENT SECRETS AND COVER-UPS

PART VII
THE ROLE OF SECRET SOCIETIES IN SHAPING WORLD EVENTS

PART VIII

THE SUPPRESSION OF ALTERNATIVE SCIENCE AND TECHNOLOGY

PART IX

THE GLOBAL ELITE AND THEIR HIDDEN AGENDAS

CONCLUSION

UNVEILING HIDDEN AGENDAS AND SHAPING THE FUTURE

To the tireless seekers of truth, the courageous whistleblowers, and the relentless questioners of the status quo.

Your bravery and curiosity inspire us to look beyond the surface and uncover the hidden agendas that shape our world.

This book is for you.

UNVEILING THE SHADOWS

The world we know is but a thin veneer masking a far more complex and hidden reality. From our earliest moments, we are taught a version of history, society, and power that fits neatly within the boundaries of mainstream narratives. Schools, media, and cultural institutions provide a coherent but limited picture, a jigsaw puzzle with pieces carefully curated to form an acceptable whole. But what if the true puzzle is much larger, with crucial pieces deliberately obscured or withheld? This book, "Hidden Agendas: Exposing the Dark Secrets," seeks to reveal those missing pieces and challenge the conventional wisdom that governs our understanding of the world.

As children, we are naturally curious, asking endless questions about the world around us. Why is the sky blue? How do birds fly? Who built the pyramids? Our questions are often met with simple answers meant to satisfy our young minds. But as we grow older, some of us continue to question, digging deeper into the mysteries that seem unsolvable or too fantastical to be true. It is for these persistent questioners, the seekers of truth, that this book is written.

Throughout history, there have always been whispers of hidden knowledge, secret societies, and suppressed truths. Ancient civilizations like Atlantis and Lemuria, mentioned in myths and legends, tantalize us with the possibility that our ancestors possessed knowledge and technology far beyond what we imagine. These stories, often dismissed as mere fantasy, are where our journey begins. What if these lost civilizations were real, their legacies buried under layers of sediment and secrecy? What if the ruins of their grandeur lie waiting to be discovered, holding keys to our past that could redefine our understanding of human history?

Archaeology, the study of human history through physical remains, should be a field of discovery and enlightenment. Yet, there are countless cases of significant findings that have been dismissed, ignored, or actively suppressed. Why would certain artifacts and sites be deemed too controversial for public knowledge? What truths do they hold that threaten the established narrative? By exploring these suppressed archaeological discoveries, we begin to see a pattern of control over information, a deliberate shaping of history to fit specific agendas.

Secret societies have long been the subject of fascination and fear. From the Freemasons to the Illuminati, these organizations are often portrayed as shadowy groups wielding immense power behind the scenes. But what if these portrayals are not just the stuff of conspiracy theories? Historical documents and testimonies reveal that such societies have indeed played significant roles in shaping world events, often rewriting history to serve their purposes. Their influence extends into the modern era, raising questions about the true nature of power and control in our societies.

One of the most enigmatic institutions in the world is the Vatican, with its vast archives that remain inaccessible to the general public. What secrets lie within these hallowed halls? Ancient texts, artifacts, and documents that could potentially rewrite religious and world history are locked away, their contents known only to a select few. By speculating on what might be hidden in the Vatican Archives, we challenge the authority of those who claim to be the gatekeepers of sacred knowledge.

Religion, too, has been a powerful tool for control throughout history. From the Crusades to the Inquisition, the use of faith to manipulate and dominate populations is well-documented. In the modern era, religious institutions continue to wield significant influence over politics and society. This book explores how religious doctrines have been designed to instill obedience and suppress dissent, examining the ways in which faith is used to shape minds and control behavior.

The Denver International Airport is an unusual yet compelling case study in modern conspiracy theories. With its bizarre murals, sculptures, and architectural features, the airport has sparked countless theories about hidden meanings and secret underground facilities. How does this fit into larger global conspiracy narratives? What evidence supports these claims, and what might it reveal about the unseen forces at work in our world?

Censorship, both historical and contemporary, plays a critical role in maintaining the status quo. From the burning of books to the suppression of controversial ideas in media and academia, those in power have always sought to control information. This book delves into the impact of censorship on societal progress and free speech, revealing how silencing dissent stifles innovation and critical thinking.

Government cover-ups are another facet of hidden agendas, with countless examples of secret projects and covert operations. The infamous MK-Ultra experiments, UFO sightings, and other classified activities point to a pattern of deception and obfuscation. What methods are used to keep these secrets from the public, and what are the implications for democratic governance and public trust?

The concept of a global elite orchestrating world events from behind the scenes is often dismissed as paranoia. Yet, organizations like the Bilderberg Group, Trilateral Commission, and World Economic Forum exist, their meetings shrouded in secrecy. This book explores the agendas of these powerful entities, examining how their actions impact global society and individual freedoms.

Finally, the suppression of alternative science and technology raises profound questions about the direction of human progress. Innovations that could revolutionize energy, medicine, and other fields are often kept from the public for political or economic reasons. By examining patents, scientific papers, and expert testimonies, we uncover the consequences of this suppression and its effects on our future.

"Hidden Agendas: Exposing the Dark Secrets" is not just a book; it is a call to action. It invites you to question, to seek, and to uncover the truths that lie hidden in plain sight. As you turn these pages, remember that the journey to enlightenment begins with a single step into the unknown. Embrace the mystery, challenge the narrative, and join the quest for knowledge that will empower and transform our understanding of the world.

PART I

THE ERASURE OF OUR TRUE HISTORY

History is often regarded as a linear progression of events, neatly recorded and taught as an immutable sequence of facts. Yet, beneath this surface lies a more complex and contested terrain, where the victors write history and the truth is often buried or altered to serve specific agendas. In "Hidden Agendas: Exposing the Dark Secrets," Part I delves into the erasure of our true history, exploring how lost civilizations, suppressed archaeological discoveries, and the manipulation by secret societies have obscured our understanding of the past.

Our journey begins with the enigmatic tales of lost civilizations. Atlantis and Lemuria, names that evoke images of advanced societies and cataclysmic events, are often relegated to the realm of myth and legend. However, these stories persist across various cultures and epochs, hinting at a deeper truth. What if these civilizations were real, their legacies deliberately hidden from us? Ancient texts, oral traditions, and scattered archaeological evidence suggest that our ancestors possessed knowledge and technologies that could challenge our current understanding of human history. This chapter will explore these possibilities, examining the evidence and the reasons why such histories might be suppressed.

Next, we turn to the field of archaeology—a discipline that should ideally be about uncovering and understanding the past. However, significant discoveries that could disrupt established historical narratives are often dismissed or hidden. From the giant stone spheres of Costa Rica to the underwater structures off the coast of Japan, numerous findings have been marginalized by mainstream academia. What motivates this suppression? Are these artifacts and sites too controversial, or do they threaten the power structures that benefit from a particular version of history? By investigating these suppressed archaeological discoveries, we aim to shed light on the hidden chapters of our past.

The influence of secret societies on historical narratives forms the final component of this section. Throughout history, organizations like the Freemasons, the Illuminati, and the Knights Templar have been shrouded in mystery and speculation. While their exact roles and influences are often debated, there is substantial evidence suggesting that these societies have played significant parts in shaping world events. They have had the power to manipulate information, control resources, and direct political outcomes, often rewriting history to suit their needs. By examining historical documents, personal testimonies, and the symbols left behind, we will uncover how these secret societies have contributed to the erasure and rewriting of our true history.

Understanding the erasure of our true history requires us to confront uncomfortable truths and challenge the narratives that have been fed to us. This section will not only reveal the gaps and inconsistencies in our historical records but also empower readers to question and seek the truth for themselves. By exploring these hidden facets of our past, we aim to reconstruct a more accurate and inclusive historical narrative, one that acknowledges the diversity and complexity of human experience.

The stories of lost civilizations like Atlantis and Lemuria are more than just myths; they are echoes of a forgotten past. Plato's dialogues,

"Timaeus" and "Critias," provide some of the most detailed accounts of Atlantis, describing a highly advanced civilization that existed around 9,000 years before his time. According to Plato, Atlantis was a powerful and technologically advanced society that eventually fell out of favor with the gods and sank into the ocean in a single day and night of misfortune. While mainstream historians dismiss Plato's account as allegory, recent discoveries have led some researchers to reconsider the possibility of such a civilization existing.

Similarly, the legend of Lemuria, or Mu, speaks of a vast continent in the Pacific or Indian Ocean that was home to an advanced human civilization. Stories of Lemuria originated in the 19th century and were popularized by the works of various theosophists and mystics. According to these accounts, Lemuria was a utopian society with advanced knowledge in science, spirituality, and technology. Geological and archaeological evidence, such as the submerged city off the coast of Yonaguni, Japan, and the ruins of Nan Madol in Micronesia, add a layer of intrigue to these legends.

These narratives, though dismissed by mainstream science, persist because they resonate with a deeper, perhaps subconscious understanding that our history is incomplete. The systematic suppression of archaeological discoveries further compounds this issue. Take, for instance, the case of the Piri Reis map, a world map created by the Ottoman admiral and cartographer Piri Reis in 1513. This map shows parts of the Americas and Antarctica with astonishing accuracy, despite being drawn long before those regions were officially discovered and mapped by modern explorers. How did Piri Reis obtain such detailed information? What sources did he use, and why is this map not given its due importance in historical studies?

Another example is the discovery of Göbekli Tepe in Turkey, a site that predates Stonehenge by 6,000 years and is considered the world's oldest known temple complex. The sophistication of Göbekli Tepe's construction challenges the conventional timeline of human civilization, suggesting that organized societies existed much earlier than previously thought. Yet, the implications of such discoveries are often downplayed or ignored, as they do not fit neatly into the established historical framework.

Secret societies have long been suspected of influencing historical events and shaping public perception. The Freemasons, one of the most well-known secret societies, have a storied history dating back to the medieval stonemason guilds. Their influence is evident in numerous historical events, from the founding of the United States to the French Revolution. Symbols associated with Freemasonry, such as the all-seeing eye and the pyramid, appear in significant places, including the United States one-dollar bill. What messages are being conveyed through these symbols, and how have Freemasons used their positions of power to rewrite history?

The Illuminati, another secretive group, was founded in 1776 in Bavaria with the aim of promoting Enlightenment ideals and curbing religious and political abuses. While officially disbanded in the late 18th century, the Illuminati have been the subject of numerous conspiracy theories suggesting they continue to operate covertly, influencing global events to this day. Their alleged involvement in major historical events raises questions about the extent to which our understanding of history has been manipulated.

In examining these elements—the myths of lost civilizations, the suppression of archaeological discoveries, and the influence of secret societies—we uncover a pattern of erasure and control. This pattern is not random but a deliberate effort by those in power to maintain their dominance by shaping the narrative of our past. Understanding this allows us to begin reconstructing our true history, free from the distortions and omissions imposed by those who benefit from our ignorance.

As we embark on this journey through Part I of "Hidden Agendas: Exposing the Dark Secrets," prepare to question everything you thought you knew about history. The truth is out there, buried beneath layers of misinformation and secrecy. It is time to uncover it, piece by piece, and reclaim the rich, complex, and authentic narrative of our human journey.

| 1 |

Chapter 1: Lost Civilizations

Imagine a world where advanced civilizations flourished long before recorded history, wielding technologies and knowledge that could rival, or even surpass, our own. This is the tantalizing premise of lost civilizations such as Atlantis and Lemuria. These enigmatic societies, often dismissed as mere myths or legends, have captivated the human imagination for centuries. However, scattered evidence and persistent tales from various cultures suggest there might be more to these stories than mere fantasy. In this chapter, we will delve into the fascinating realms of Atlantis and Lemuria, exploring the myths, legends, and suppressed archaeological evidence that hint at their possible existence and the reasons behind their erasure from our historical records.

The Myth of Atlantis

The legend of Atlantis is one of the most enduring and intriguing tales of a lost civilization. First mentioned by the ancient Greek philosopher Plato in his dialogues "Timaeus" and "Critias," Atlantis is described as a powerful and technologically advanced island nation that existed approximately 9,000 years before Plato's time. According to the legend, Atlantis was a utopian society, blessed with abundant natural resources and advanced infrastructure, including complex irrigation systems, impressive architecture, and sophisticated maritime technology.

Plato's account of Atlantis is detailed and vivid. He describes the city as being built on concentric rings of land and water, with a magnificent central temple dedicated to Poseidon, the god of the sea. The Atlanteans were said to be a noble and prosperous people who gradually fell from grace due to their hubris and moral decay. This decline led to their eventual destruction, purportedly in a single day and night of catastrophic earthquakes and floods that caused the island to sink into the ocean.

For centuries, scholars and explorers have debated the veracity of Plato's account. While many regard it as a fictional allegory, others believe it could be based on real events or locations. Several hypotheses have been proposed regarding the possible location of Atlantis, ranging from the Mediterranean and the Caribbean to Antarctica and the Atlantic Ocean. Notable among these is the theory that Atlantis was located near the modern-day island of Santorini, which experienced a massive volcanic eruption around 1600 BCE that could have inspired Plato's story.

Evidence and Theories

Despite the lack of concrete evidence, there are intriguing clues that suggest the possibility of a lost advanced civilization like Atlantis. One of the most compelling pieces of evidence is the Piri Reis map, a world map created by the Ottoman admiral Piri Reis in 1513. The map shows the coastlines of South America and Antarctica with remarkable accuracy, despite being drawn long before those regions were officially explored. Some researchers believe that Piri Reis used ancient source maps that could date back to the time of Atlantis.

Another fascinating clue is the Bimini Road, an underwater rock formation located near the Bahamas. Discovered in 1968, the Bimini Road consists of large, flat stones arranged in a linear pattern, resembling a man-made road or wall. While mainstream archaeologists argue that the formation is a natural geological feature, some researchers contend that it could be the remnants of an ancient structure, possibly connected to Atlantis.

Furthermore, the discovery of the ancient city of Dwarka off the coast of India adds weight to the possibility of advanced civilizations existing in prehistoric times. Dwarka, believed to be the legendary city mentioned in Hindu texts, was discovered underwater and dates back to around 9,000 years ago—coincidentally the same timeframe Plato assigned to Atlantis. The city's advanced architecture and urban planning suggest a highly developed society that existed long before the traditional timeline of human civilization.

The Legend of Lemuria

Lemuria, also known as Mu, is another lost civilization shrouded in mystery. Unlike Atlantis, which has its origins in Greek philosophy, the legend of Lemuria emerged in the 19th century through the works of various theosophists and mystics. According to these accounts, Lemuria was a vast continent located in the Pacific or Indian Ocean, home to a highly advanced and spiritually enlightened society.

The name "Lemuria" was coined by British zoologist Philip Sclater in 1864. Sclater proposed the existence of a lost landmass to explain the presence of lemur fossils in both Madagascar and India but not in Africa or the Middle East. This hypothetical continent was believed to have sunk beneath the ocean due to catastrophic geological events.

Theosophists, such as Helena Blavatsky and James Churchward, expanded upon this idea, describing Lemuria as a utopian society with advanced knowledge in science, spirituality, and technology. According to Churchward's writings, Lemurians possessed technologies that allowed them to harness the earth's natural energies and communicate telepathically. They were said to be a peaceful and harmonious people who eventually fell victim to natural disasters, leading to the continent's submersion.

Evidence and Theories

While the existence of Lemuria remains unproven, there are several intriguing pieces of evidence that fuel speculation. One such piece of evidence is the submerged city of Yonaguni, located off the coast of Japan. Discovered in 1987, the Yonaguni Monument features large stone structures that resemble pyramids, staircases, and terraces. While some experts argue that the formations are natural, others believe they are the remnants of an ancient civilization that could be linked to Lemuria.

Another site of interest is Nan Madol, an ancient city built on a series of artificial islets off the coast of Pohnpei in Micronesia. The city, constructed using massive basalt stones, dates back to around 200 BCE and features a complex network of canals and stone structures. The origins and purpose of Nan Madol remain a mystery, but its advanced engineering and construction techniques suggest a highly sophisticated society that could have connections to the legends of Lemuria.

Additionally, the discovery of the underwater ruins near the Gulf of Cambay in India provides further evidence of ancient, advanced civilizations. These ruins, found in 2001, include structures that resemble human settlements and artifacts dating back to around 9,000 years ago. The similarities in age and the advanced nature of these ruins parallel the timelines and descriptions of both Atlantis and Lemuria.

The Suppression of Archaeological Evidence

The reluctance of mainstream academia to acknowledge the possibility of advanced prehistoric civilizations is a significant barrier to uncovering our true history. Several factors contribute to this suppression, including the potential disruption of established historical narratives, the threat to academic reputations, and the influence of powerful institutions with vested interests in maintaining the status quo.

One notable example is the treatment of the Bosnian Pyramid complex. Discovered in 2005 by Dr. Semir Osmanagić, the complex includes several pyramid-shaped hills and underground tunnels that Osmanagić claims are the remnants of an ancient civilization. Despite evidence such as stone blocks, tunnels, and geometric alignments, mainstream archaeologists have largely dismissed the site as a natural formation. The controversy surrounding the Bosnian Pyramids highlights the resistance to considering alternative historical theories that challenge conventional wisdom.

Similarly, the case of the Giza Pyramids and the Sphinx in Egypt raises questions about the true timeline of these iconic structures. Some researchers, such as Robert Bauval and Graham Hancock, propose that the Pyramids and the Sphinx are much older than traditionally believed, potentially dating back to a lost civilization that predated the ancient Egyptians. The water erosion patterns on the Sphinx, for example, suggest that it was exposed to heavy rainfall, which could place its construction around 10,000 BCE—a time when Egypt experienced a much wetter climate. These theories, however, are often met with skepticism and resistance from mainstream Egyptologists.

Conclusion

The legends of Atlantis and Lemuria, along with the suppressed archaeological evidence, challenge us to reconsider our understanding of human history. These lost civilizations represent a possibility that advanced societies existed long before the dawn of recorded history, possessing knowledge and technologies that could reshape our perception of the past.

As we explore these mysteries, it is essential to remain open-minded and critical, questioning the narratives presented to us and seeking out the truth. By doing so, we honor the legacy of those who came before us and pave the way for a more accurate and inclusive understanding of our shared human journey.

In the following chapters, we will delve deeper into the mechanisms of historical suppression, examining the role of secret societies and other powerful entities in rewriting history. Through this exploration, we aim to uncover the hidden truths that have been deliberately obscured, empowering readers to seek knowledge and challenge the status quo. Together, we will piece together the fragmented puzzle of our past and reveal the intricate tapestry of human civilization that lies beneath the surface.

| 2 |

Chapter 2: Suppressed Archaeological Discoveries

Archaeology, the study of human history and prehistory through the excavation and analysis of artifacts, inscriptions, and other physical remains, should be a field of continuous discovery and enlightenment. However, the reality is often far more complex. Throughout history, significant archaeological findings have been dismissed, ignored, or actively suppressed by mainstream academia and powerful institutions. These actions raise important questions: Why are certain discoveries not given their due recognition? What truths might these artifacts and sites reveal that threaten the established historical narrative? In this chapter, we will explore some of the most compelling cases of suppressed archaeological discoveries, providing interviews with archaeologists and researchers who have dared to challenge the status quo.

The Piri Reis Map

One of the most intriguing pieces of evidence for suppressed history is the Piri Reis map, created in 1513 by the Ottoman admiral and cartographer Piri Reis. This map is remarkable for its depiction of the coastlines of South America and Antarctica with a level of accuracy that should have been impossible for its time. Antarctica, in particular, is shown in detail, despite being officially discovered only in 1820, over 300 years later. Moreover, the map depicts parts of the continent free of ice, suggesting knowledge of the region's topography that predates the last Ice Age.

How did Piri Reis obtain such accurate information? Researchers suggest that he might have used ancient source maps, possibly dating back to a lost civilization with advanced cartographic knowledge. Dr. Charles Hapgood, an American professor of history, proposed that the map could be evidence of an advanced prehistoric civilization that mapped the Earth long before known history. Despite these compelling arguments, the Piri Reis map remains largely ignored by mainstream archaeology, which often dismisses it as an anomaly or coincidence.

The Bimini Road

Discovered in 1968 near the Bahamas, the Bimini Road consists of large, flat stones arranged in a linear pattern underwater, resembling a man-made road or wall. The formation has sparked significant debate among archaeologists and researchers. Some argue that it is a natural geological formation, while others believe it could be the remnants of an ancient structure, possibly linked to the legendary Atlantis.

Dr. Greg Little, a researcher who has extensively studied the Bimini Road, argues that the formation shows signs of human construction, including uniform stone blocks and right-angled turns. His work, alongside other researchers, suggests that the site could be part of a larger submerged complex, indicating the presence of an advanced civilization in the region thousands of years ago. Despite these findings, the mainstream archaeological community largely dismisses the Bimini Road as a natural formation, avoiding the potential implications of such a discovery.

Göbekli Tepe

Göbekli Tepe, located in southeastern Turkey, is one of the most significant archaeological discoveries of the 20th century. Dating back to around 9600 BCE, this site predates Stonehenge by 6,000 years and is considered the world's oldest known temple complex. The sophisticated architecture of Göbekli Tepe, with its massive stone pillars arranged in circular formations, challenges the conventional timeline of human civilization, suggesting that organized societies with advanced construction techniques existed much earlier than previously thought.

Dr. Klaus Schmidt, the archaeologist who led the excavation of Göbekli Tepe until his death in 2014, believed that the site was a central place of worship for a previously unknown prehistoric culture. The intricate carvings and the scale of the construction indicate a highly organized society with advanced knowledge of engineering and art. Despite the groundbreaking nature of this discovery, Göbekli Tepe has received relatively little attention from mainstream media and academic circles, perhaps because it disrupts the established narrative of human history.

The Bosnian Pyramid Complex

The Bosnian Pyramid Complex, discovered in 2005 by Dr. Semir Osmanagić, includes several pyramid-shaped hills and an extensive network of underground tunnels near the town of Visoko, Bosnia and Herzegovina. Dr. Osmanagić claims that these structures are the remnants of an ancient civilization that predates the Egyptian pyramids by thousands of years. The largest pyramid, dubbed the Pyramid of the Sun, is said to be over 220 meters tall, making it taller than the Great Pyramid of Giza.

Despite evidence such as stone blocks, tunnels, and geometric alignments, the Bosnian Pyramids have been largely dismissed by mainstream archaeologists as natural formations. Critics argue that the hills are simply shaped by geological processes and that the evidence presented by Dr. Osmanagić is not sufficient to support his claims. However, ongoing excavations continue to reveal more artifacts and structures that suggest the presence of an ancient, advanced civilization. The controversy surrounding the Bosnian Pyramids highlights the resistance within the academic community to consider alternative historical theories that challenge conventional wisdom.

The Underwater Ruins of Yonaguni

The Yonaguni Monument, discovered in 1987 off the coast of Japan, is a massive underwater rock formation that resembles pyramids, staircases, and terraces. While some experts argue that the formations are natural, others, including marine geologist Dr. Masaaki Kimura, believe they are the remnants of an ancient civilization that existed around 10,000 years ago, possibly linked to the lost continent of Lemuria.

Dr. Kimura's research indicates that the Yonaguni Monument features several man-made structures, including what appear to be roads, walls, and sculptures. He suggests that the site could have been a ceremonial center or a city that was submerged due to rising sea levels at the end of the last Ice Age. Despite the compelling nature of Dr. Kimura's findings, the Yonaguni Monument remains a subject of debate, with mainstream archaeology hesitant to fully embrace the possibility of a prehistoric advanced civilization in the region.

The Gulf of Cambay Ruins

In 2001, marine archaeologists discovered the ruins of an ancient city in the Gulf of Cambay, off the coast of India. The site, which includes structures resembling human settlements and artifacts dating back to around 9,000 years ago, suggests the presence of an advanced civilization long before the traditional timeline of human history. The discovery has drawn comparisons to the legendary city of Dwarka, mentioned in Hindu texts.

Despite the significance of the find, the Gulf of Cambay ruins have not received widespread recognition or thorough investigation from mainstream archaeologists. The artifacts and structures discovered at the site indicate a high level of sophistication, including evidence of urban planning and advanced construction techniques. The reluctance to explore and acknowledge such discoveries underscores the broader issue of suppressed archaeological evidence that challenges conventional historical narratives.

Interviews with Researchers

To gain further insight into the issue of suppressed archaeological discoveries, we conducted interviews with several researchers who have dedicated their careers to uncovering hidden aspects of human history.

Dr. Robert Schoch, a geologist and professor at Boston University, is known for his work on the Sphinx water erosion hypothesis. Dr. Schoch argues that the Great Sphinx of Giza shows signs of significant water erosion, suggesting it dates back to a much earlier period, possibly around 10,000 BCE. This theory challenges the traditional dating of the Sphinx to the reign of Pharaoh Khafre around 2500 BCE. In our interview, Dr. Schoch discussed the resistance he has faced from mainstream Egyptologists and the importance of re-evaluating accepted historical timelines in light of new evidence.

Dr. Andrew Collins, an author and researcher, has explored the connections between ancient civilizations and advanced knowledge. In his work on Göbekli Tepe and the lost civilization of the Denisovans, Dr. Collins has highlighted the potential for sophisticated societies existing long before the rise of known historical cultures. During our conversation, he emphasized the need for open-mindedness in archaeological research and the willingness to challenge entrenched academic positions.

Dr. Semir Osmanagić, the discoverer of the Bosnian Pyramid Complex, shared his experiences of facing skepticism and criticism from the archaeological community. Despite the controversy surrounding his findings, Dr. Osmanagić remains convinced of the existence of an ancient, advanced civilization in Bosnia and continues his excavations in the face of ongoing opposition.

Conclusion

The suppression of archaeological discoveries represents a significant challenge to our understanding of human history. Whether due to academic conservatism, political agendas, or the influence of powerful institutions, the reluctance to acknowledge and investigate these findings limits our knowledge and hinders progress. The cases of the Piri Reis map, the Bimini Road, Göbekli Tepe, the Bosnian Pyramid Complex, the Yonaguni Monument, and the Gulf of Cambay ruins all point to a pattern of suppression that deserves greater scrutiny.

By exploring these suppressed discoveries, we not only uncover hidden chapters of our past but also challenge the narratives that have been presented to us as absolute truths. This chapter aims to inspire readers to question accepted historical timelines and to seek out the hidden stories that lie beneath the surface. As we continue to delve into the mysteries of our past, it is essential to remain open to new ideas and evidence, embracing the complexity and diversity of human civilization.

In the next chapter, we will examine the role of secret societies in rewriting history, exploring how these shadowy organizations have influenced historical narratives and contributed to the erasure of our true history. By understanding the mechanisms of historical suppression, we can begin to piece together a more accurate and inclusive picture of our past, empowering future generations with the knowledge they need to shape a better world.

| 3 |

Chapter 3: The Role of Secret Societies in Rewriting History

Secret societies have long been subjects of fascination, speculation, and fear. These organizations, shrouded in mystery and often operating in the shadows, are believed to wield significant influence over world events and historical narratives. From the Freemasons and the Illuminati to the Knights Templar and the Skull and Bones, these groups have been accused of manipulating information, controlling resources, and directing political outcomes to serve their hidden agendas. In this chapter, we will delve into the historical documents and testimonies that suggest the profound impact these secret societies have had on the course of history. We will explore their origins, objectives, and the ways in which they have rewritten history to consolidate power and maintain control.

The Freemasons

The Freemasons are perhaps the most well-known secret society, with a history dating back to the medieval stonemason guilds. Over time, they evolved into a fraternal organization that claimed to promote moral and intellectual development through secret rituals and symbols. By the 18th century, Freemasonry had spread across Europe and the Americas, attracting members from various walks of life, including influential figures in politics, business, and the arts.

One of the most significant ways in which the Freemasons are believed to have influenced history is through their role in the founding of the United States. Many of the Founding Fathers, including George Washington, Benjamin Franklin, and Thomas Jefferson, were Freemasons. The symbols of Freemasonry, such as the all-seeing eye and the unfinished pyramid, are prominently featured on the United States one-dollar bill, hinting at the society's influence on the nation's formation.

Historians and conspiracy theorists alike have speculated that the Freemasons' ideals of liberty, equality, and fraternity played a crucial role in shaping the principles of the American Revolution and the subsequent creation of the United States. However, the extent to which these ideals were genuinely altruistic versus serving a broader agenda of control and influence remains a topic of debate. The secretive nature of Freemasonry, coupled with the power held by its members, has fueled suspicions that the organization has worked behind the scenes to manipulate historical events to its advantage.

The Illuminati

The Illuminati, founded in 1776 by Adam Weishaupt in Bavaria, was an Enlightenment-era secret society that sought to promote reason, secularism, and the separation of church and state. Weishaupt's vision was to create a group of enlightened individuals who could influence political and social change from within. The Illuminati quickly grew in numbers, attracting intellectuals, politicians, and influential figures across Europe.

Despite its relatively short official existence—disbanded by the Bavarian government in 1785—the Illuminati has remained a focal point of conspiracy theories. Many believe that the group went underground and continued to exert influence over global affairs. The Illuminati is often linked to major historical events, such as the French Revolution, where it is alleged to have orchestrated the overthrow of the monarchy to advance its agenda of secularism and republicanism.

The Illuminati's influence is also purported to extend into modern times, with claims that the organization controls major global institutions, media, and finance. The secrecy and elite membership associated with the Illuminati have made it a symbol of the hidden hand that shapes world events, prompting endless speculation and investigation into its true objectives and actions.

The Knights Templar

The Knights Templar, a medieval Christian military order founded in the early 12th century, is another secret society believed to have played a significant role in rewriting history. Originally established to protect Christian pilgrims traveling to the Holy Land, the Templars quickly grew in wealth and power, becoming a formidable force in medieval Europe. They established a vast network of fortifications, developed an early form of banking, and amassed considerable influence both politically and economically.

The Templars' downfall began in 1307 when King Philip IV of France, heavily indebted to the order, orchestrated their arrest and subsequent persecution. The order was officially disbanded by Pope Clement V in 1312, and many Templars were executed or imprisoned. However, the Templars' legacy continued to influence European history, with theories suggesting that they went underground and continued to operate in secrecy.

The Templars' supposed hidden treasures and secret knowledge have fueled countless legends and conspiracy theories. Some believe that the Templars were the guardians of the Holy Grail, the Ark of the Covenant, or other sacred relics. Others suggest that the Templars possessed esoteric knowledge that they passed down through generations, influencing various secret societies that followed, including the Freemasons and the Rosicrucians.

The Skull and Bones

The Skull and Bones is a secret society based at Yale University, founded in 1832. Known for its exclusive membership, which includes some of America's most powerful and influential individuals, the Skull and Bones has been the subject of numerous conspiracy theories. Members, known as "Bonesmen," are often drawn from the elite of American society, including political leaders, business magnates, and military officials.

The influence of the Skull and Bones on American politics and policy is significant. Prominent members include former Presidents George H.W. Bush and George W. Bush, as well as numerous senators, judges, and business executives. The society's secrecy and ritualistic practices have led to speculation about its true purpose and the extent of its influence.

Critics argue that the Skull and Bones operates as a "shadow government," shaping policies and decisions behind the scenes. The society's connections to powerful institutions and individuals have fueled concerns about the concentration of power and the erosion of democratic processes. The rituals and oaths taken by members are believed to foster loyalty and secrecy, creating a network of influence that extends across various sectors of society.

Influence on Major Historical Events

The role of secret societies in shaping major historical events is a topic of enduring intrigue. While definitive proof of their involvement is often elusive, numerous historical documents and testimonies suggest that these organizations have played significant roles in pivotal moments in history.

The French Revolution

The French Revolution, a period of radical social and political upheaval in France from 1789 to 1799, is one such event where secret societies are believed to have had a profound impact. The Revolution resulted in the overthrow of the monarchy, the rise of republicanism, and significant changes in the structure of French society. Some historians and researchers argue that the Illuminati and Freemasons were instrumental in fomenting the revolutionary fervor that led to these dramatic changes.

Evidence suggests that many leading figures of the Revolution were Freemasons, including Georges Danton, Marquis de Lafayette, and Maximilien Robespierre. The principles of liberty, equality, and fraternity espoused by the Freemasons align closely with the ideals of the Revolution, leading to speculation that the society played a critical role in shaping its outcomes. Additionally, the secrecy and network of influence associated with the Illuminati have led to theories that the organization orchestrated the Revolution to dismantle the existing power structures and promote secularism.

The American Revolution

The American Revolution, which led to the establishment of the United States as an independent nation, is another event where secret societies are believed to have had a significant influence. As mentioned earlier, many of the Founding Fathers were Freemasons, and their membership in the society is thought to have shaped their vision for the new nation.

The symbols and ideals of Freemasonry are evident in the founding documents and symbols of the United States. The Declaration of Independence, the Constitution, and the Bill of Rights all reflect Enlightenment principles that align with Masonic values. The involvement of Freemasons in the Revolution suggests that the society played a crucial role in shaping the ideological foundations of the United States.

The Russian Revolution

The Russian Revolution of 1917, which led to the fall of the Romanov dynasty and the rise of the Soviet Union, is another historical event where secret societies are believed to have played a role. Some researchers argue that the Revolution was influenced by a network of secret societies, including the Freemasons and other revolutionary groups.

The involvement of secret societies in the Russian Revolution is supported by the fact that many key figures in the revolutionary movement, such as Alexander Kerensky and Leon Trotsky, had connections to these organizations. The principles of equality and the dismantling of existing power structures align with the objectives of many secret societies, leading to speculation that they played a role in orchestrating the Revolution.

Modern Influence and Agendas

The influence of secret societies extends into contemporary times, with many of these organizations believed to continue exerting control over global affairs. The Bilderberg Group, the Trilateral Commission, and the Council on Foreign Relations are often cited as modern incarnations of secret societies that shape world events from behind the scenes.

The Bilderberg Group

The Bilderberg Group, founded in 1954, is an annual conference attended by some of the world's most powerful and influential individuals, including political leaders, business executives, and academics. The group's meetings are held in strict secrecy, with no media coverage or public disclosure of the discussions that take place.

Critics argue that the Bilderberg Group operates as a "shadow government," where global policies and decisions are made without public scrutiny. The group's secrecy and elite membership have fueled concerns about the concentration of power and the erosion of democratic processes. Some believe that the Bilderberg Group sets the agenda for global governance, shaping economic, political, and social policies that impact the entire world.

The Trilateral Commission

The Trilateral Commission, founded in 1973 by David Rockefeller, is another organization believed to exert significant influence over global affairs. The Commission brings together leaders from North America, Europe, and Asia to discuss and coordinate policies on economic and political issues.

Critics argue that the Trilateral Commission promotes a globalist agenda that prioritizes the interests of the elite over those of the general population. The organization's secrecy and connections to powerful institutions and individuals have led to concerns about its influence on international policies and decisions.

The Council on Foreign Relations

The Council on Foreign Relations (CFR), founded in 1921, is a think tank and membership organization that focuses on U.S. foreign policy and international affairs. The CFR's membership includes political leaders, business executives, and academics, and its meetings are often attended by influential figures from around the world.

Critics argue that the CFR operates as a "shadow government," shaping U.S. foreign policy and international relations behind the scenes. The organization's secrecy and connections to powerful institutions and individuals have fueled concerns about its influence on global affairs and the concentration of power.

Conclusion

The role of secret societies in rewriting history is a complex and multifaceted issue. While definitive proof of their influence is often elusive, the historical documents and testimonies explored in this chapter suggest that these organizations have played significant roles in shaping world events and historical narratives. From the Freemasons and the Illuminati to the Knights Templar and the Skull and Bones, secret societies have manipulated information, controlled resources, and directed political outcomes to serve their hidden agendas.

Understanding the influence of these secret societies is crucial to uncovering the true history of our world. By challenging the established narratives and seeking out the hidden stories, we can begin to piece together a more accurate and inclusive picture of our past. This chapter aims to inspire readers to question accepted historical timelines and to seek out the truth behind the shadows.

In the next part of this book, we will explore the secrets of the Vatican Archives, delving into the restricted access and hidden contents that have shaped religious and world history. Through this exploration, we aim to uncover the truths that lie within the sacred halls of the Vatican and understand their impact on our understanding of history and spirituality.

PART II

THE SECRETS OF THE VATICAN ARCHIVES

The Vatican, an independent city-state enclaved within Rome, serves as the spiritual and administrative center of the Roman Catholic Church. Its influence spans centuries, reaching into the spiritual, cultural, and political realms of human civilization. Within its fortified walls lies one of the world's most enigmatic and restricted repositories of knowledge—the Vatican Secret Archives, or the Archivum Secretum Apostolicum Vaticanum.

For centuries, the Vatican Secret Archives have been the subject of speculation, intrigue, and mystery. The term "secret" (Latin: secretum) in this context does not imply a nefarious intent but rather denotes private or personal archives of the Popes. Despite this clarification, the secrecy surrounding the archives has fueled countless theories about what lies within. Some believe the archives contain documents that could rewrite the history of Christianity and the world, while others speculate about hidden texts that reveal lost doctrines, forbidden knowledge, and suppressed truths.

The Vatican Secret Archives, established in their current form by Pope Paul V in 1612, house millions of documents spanning over a thousand years of history. These documents include papal correspondences, state papers, account books, and other records that provide a detailed account of the Church's role in shaping global events. Despite their historical significance, the archives remain largely inaccessible to the public. Only select scholars are granted permission to enter, and even then, they must navigate a labyrinth of restrictions and regulations.

In this part of "Hidden Agendas: Exposing the Dark Secrets," we will delve into the mysteries of the Vatican Secret Archives, exploring the restricted access, the rumored contents, and the impact these hidden texts and artifacts have on our understanding of history and religion. Through meticulous research, speculative analysis, and interviews with theologians and historians, we aim to uncover the secrets that have been kept from the public eye for centuries.

The Formation and Restricted Access of the Vatican Archives

The origins of the Vatican Secret Archives can be traced back to the early centuries of Christianity when the Church began to accumulate documents and records. These early archives were not centralized, often kept in various locations, including monasteries and cathedrals. It was not until the papacy of Pope Paul V in the early 17th century that a concerted effort was made to gather and organize these documents into a single repository.

Pope Paul V, recognizing the importance of preserving the Church's history and correspondence, established the Archivum Secretum Apostolicum Vaticanum in 1612. The archives were housed in a series of rooms and vaults within the Vatican, designed to protect the documents from damage and unauthorized access. Over the centuries, successive popes have expanded and reorganized the archives, adding new collections and enhancing security measures.

Despite the wealth of knowledge contained within the archives, access has always been tightly controlled. Initially, the archives were only accessible to the Pope and his closest advisors. It was not until the late 19th century that limited access was granted to select scholars. Even today, gaining entry to the archives requires a rigorous application process, including recommendations from recognized academic institutions and approval from the Vatican authorities. Researchers must specify the documents they wish to examine and are only allowed to view them under strict supervision.

This restricted access has led to widespread speculation about what the Vatican might be hiding. Critics argue that the Church's control over these documents allows it to shape historical narratives to its advantage, suppressing information that could challenge its authority or reveal controversial truths. The secrecy surrounding the archives has also given rise to numerous conspiracy theories, ranging from the existence of lost Gospels and apocryphal texts to evidence of extraterrestrial contact and ancient technologies.

Speculated Contents of the Vatican Archives

While the exact contents of the Vatican Secret Archives remain largely unknown, various sources and rumors provide glimpses into the potential treasures and secrets they hold. Here are some of the most intriguing and controversial items believed to be housed within the archives:

1. **The Lost Gospels and Apocryphal Texts**: One of the most persistent theories is that the Vatican Secret Archives contain early Christian writings that were excluded from the canonical Bible. These texts, often referred to as the Lost Gospels or Apocryphal Gospels, could provide alternative accounts of Jesus's life and teachings, potentially challenging established Christian doctrines. Examples of such texts include the Gospel of Thomas, the Gospel of Mary, and the Gospel of Judas. While some of these

texts have been discovered and studied, others are rumored to remain hidden within the Vatican's vaults.

2.   **The Chronovisor**: According to legend, the Vatican possesses a device known as the Chronovisor, a type of time viewer that allows users to see past events. This device is said to have been developed by Father Pellegrino Ernetti, a Benedictine monk and scientist, in the mid-20th century. The Chronovisor purportedly uses advanced technology to reconstruct historical events from the vibrations and electromagnetic signals left behind. While the existence of the Chronovisor remains unproven, the story has captured the imagination of many and fueled speculation about the Vatican's secret technological capabilities.

3.   **Evidence of Extraterrestrial Contact**: Another popular theory suggests that the Vatican Secret Archives contain evidence of extraterrestrial contact, including documents, artifacts, and possibly even ancient texts describing interactions with otherworldly beings. Proponents of this theory point to the Vatican's interest in astronomy and the existence of the Vatican Observatory as evidence of the Church's ongoing efforts to understand the cosmos and its potential inhabitants. Some believe that the Vatican has withheld this information to avoid disrupting religious beliefs and societal stability.

4.   **The Third Secret of Fatima**: In 1917, three young shepherd children in Fatima, Portugal, reported receiving a series of visions and messages from the Virgin Mary. These messages, known as the Secrets of Fatima, were written down and given to the Vatican for safekeeping. While the first two secrets were publicly revealed in 1941, the Third Secret remained a closely guarded secret until 2000, when the Vatican released a text purported to be the final message. However, many believe that the true Third Secret remains hidden within the Vatican Archives and contains apocalyptic predictions or revelations about the Church's future.

5.   **The Templar Documents**: The Knights Templar, a medieval Christian military order, amassed significant wealth and power before their sudden downfall in the early 14th century. Some historians believe that the Templars possessed secret knowledge and treasures, including sacred relics such as the Holy Grail and the Ark of the Covenant. The Vatican Archives are rumored to contain documents detailing the Templars' activities, trials, and possible connections to other secret societies. These documents could shed light on the true extent of the Templars' influence and the reasons behind their persecution.

6.   **Ancient Artifacts and Relics**: The Vatican is known to possess an extensive collection of ancient artifacts and religious relics, many of which are kept in the Vatican Museums. However, some items are believed to be stored within the Vatican Archives due to their sensitive or controversial nature. These could include artifacts from ancient civilizations, relics associated with early Christian martyrs, and objects of significant historical or spiritual importance. The existence and contents of these collections remain a subject of speculation and intrigue.

Impact on Religious and World History

The potential revelations contained within the Vatican Secret Archives could have profound implications for our understanding of religious and world history. By examining the hidden texts, documents, and artifacts, we can gain new insights into the development of Christianity, the role of the Church in shaping global events, and the interactions between different cultures and belief systems.

1.   **Reevaluation of Christian Doctrine**: The discovery of lost Gospels and apocryphal texts could lead to a reevaluation of established Christian doctrines and beliefs. These texts might offer alternative perspectives on the life and teachings of Jesus, the role of women in the early Church, and the development

of Christian theology. Such revelations could prompt significant theological debates and potentially lead to reforms within the Church.

2. **Historical Revisions**: Documents detailing the Church's involvement in historical events, such as the Crusades, the Inquisition, and colonialism, could provide new insights into the motivations and actions of key figures and institutions. By uncovering these hidden histories, we can develop a more nuanced understanding of the Church's impact on global events and the ways in which it has shaped the course of human civilization.

3. **Cultural and Religious Interactions**: The Vatican Archives may contain records of interactions between the Church and other religious and cultural groups. These documents could shed light on the exchange of ideas, the development of religious syncretism, and the ways in which different belief systems have influenced one another. By exploring these interactions, we can better understand the complex web of connections that have shaped human history.

4. **Technological and Scientific Discoveries**: The rumored existence of advanced technologies, such as the Chronovisor, and evidence of extraterrestrial contact within the Vatican Archives raises intriguing questions about the Church's role in scientific and technological advancements. If such technologies and discoveries exist, they could revolutionize our understanding of history, physics, and the nature of reality.

Interviews with Theologians and Historians

To gain further insight into the secrets of the Vatican Archives and their potential impact, we conducted interviews with several theologians and historians who have dedicated their careers to studying the Church's history and influence.

Dr. Karen King, a historian of early Christianity, discussed the significance of discovering lost Gospels and apocryphal texts. According to Dr. King, these texts could provide valuable insights into the diversity of early Christian beliefs and practices, challenging the notion of a monolithic early Church. She emphasized the importance of examining these texts in their historical context and understanding the reasons behind their exclusion from the canonical Bible.

Father Thomas Reese, a Jesuit priest and Vatican analyst, provided a perspective on the Church's efforts to balance transparency with the protection of sensitive information. Father Reese acknowledged the legitimate reasons for maintaining the confidentiality of certain documents, such as protecting the privacy of individuals and preserving the integrity of historical records. However, he also stressed the need for greater openness and scholarly access to the archives to foster a deeper understanding of the Church's history.

Dr. John Julius Norwich, a historian specializing in Byzantine and Mediterranean history, shared his views on the potential impact of uncovering hidden documents related to the Knights Templar and other secret societies. Dr. Norwich argued that such discoveries could reshape our understanding of medieval history and the interconnectedness of various religious and political movements. He highlighted the importance of rigorous academic research and critical analysis in interpreting these findings.

Conclusion

The Vatican Secret Archives represent one of the most significant repositories of knowledge and history in the world. The restricted access and secrecy surrounding the archives have fueled countless theories and speculations about their contents, ranging from lost Gospels and ancient relics to advanced technologies and evidence of extraterrestrial contact. By exploring these mysteries, we can gain new insights into the development of Christianity, the Church's role in shaping global events, and the hidden histories that have influenced human civilization.

This introduction aims to set the stage for a deeper exploration of the secrets of the Vatican Archives. In the following chapters, we will delve into the rumored contents, analyze their potential impact on religious and world history, and examine the efforts to uncover these hidden truths. Through meticulous research, speculative analysis, and interviews with experts, we aim to shed light on the mysteries that have been kept from the public eye for centuries. By doing so, we hope to inspire readers to question accepted narratives and seek out the hidden stories that shape our understanding of the world.

| 4 |

Chapter 4: Inside the Vatican Secret Archives

Nestled within the fortified walls of Vatican City lies one of the most enigmatic and restricted repositories of knowledge in the world—the Vatican Secret Archives (Archivum Secretum Apostolicum Vaticanum). Spanning over 53 miles of shelving and containing millions of documents, these archives offer a vast treasure trove of information covering more than twelve centuries of history. Despite its immense historical value, access to the archives has been strictly controlled, fueling countless speculations and conspiracy theories about what secrets lie within. In this chapter, we will explore the formation, organization, and restricted access of the Vatican Secret Archives, providing an in-depth look into the mysteries and controversies surrounding this fabled repository of knowledge.

The Formation of the Vatican Secret Archives

The origins of the Vatican Secret Archives can be traced back to the early centuries of Christianity. Initially, the Church's documents and records were scattered across various locations, including monasteries, cathedrals, and the personal collections of popes and bishops.

As the Church grew in power and influence, so too did the need for a centralized repository to preserve and manage its vast collection of documents.

The formal establishment of the Vatican Secret Archives as we know them today occurred in 1612 under the papacy of Pope Paul V. Recognizing the importance of preserving the Church's history and correspondence, Pope Paul V ordered the consolidation of various collections into a single, centralized archive within the Vatican. The archives were housed in a series of rooms and vaults designed to protect the documents from damage and unauthorized access. Over the centuries, successive popes expanded and reorganized the archives, adding new collections and enhancing security measures.

The term "secret" (Latin: secretum) in the context of the Vatican Secret Archives does not imply sinister motives but rather denotes the private or personal nature of the archives. The documents housed within the archives were intended for the exclusive use of the Pope and his closest advisors, hence the designation "secret." This distinction, however, has done little to quell the intrigue and speculation surrounding the archives.

Organization and Contents of the Vatican Secret Archives

The Vatican Secret Archives are organized into several sections, each containing different types of documents and records. These sections include:

1. **Papal Correspondence**: This section contains letters, decrees, and other communications between the popes and various individuals and entities, including monarchs, political leaders, and religious figures. These documents provide invaluable insights into the papacy's role in global affairs and its interactions with different powers throughout history.

2.   **State Papers**: The archives hold numerous state papers, including treaties, diplomatic correspondence, and records of negotiations between the Vatican and other states. These documents shed light on the Church's political influence and its involvement in shaping international relations.

3.   **Council Records**: This section includes records from various Church councils, such as the Council of Trent (1545-1563) and the First Vatican Council (1869-1870). These documents offer a detailed account of the theological debates and decisions that have shaped the development of Christian doctrine and practice.

4.   **Legal Documents**: The archives contain numerous legal documents, including papal bulls, decrees, and judicial records. These documents provide insights into the Church's legal framework and its role in adjudicating disputes and enforcing ecclesiastical law.

5.   **Financial Records**: This section includes account books, ledgers, and other financial records detailing the Church's economic activities and resources. These documents reveal the financial mechanisms that have supported the Church's operations and its influence over economic matters.

6.   **Historical Manuscripts**: The archives hold a vast collection of historical manuscripts, including ancient texts, chronicles, and codices. These manuscripts offer a rich tapestry of historical information, encompassing a wide range of topics and periods.

While these sections represent the general organization of the archives, the sheer volume and diversity of the documents make it challenging to catalog them comprehensively. The Vatican Secret Archives contain millions of documents, many of which have yet to be fully examined or understood. This vast repository of knowledge continues to hold secrets and insights waiting to be uncovered.

Restricted Access to the Vatican Secret Archives

Access to the Vatican Secret Archives has always been tightly controlled. Initially, the archives were only accessible to the Pope and his closest advisors. Over time, limited access was granted to select scholars and researchers, but the process remains highly restrictive to this day.

To gain access to the archives, researchers must undergo a rigorous application process. This includes providing detailed information about their academic credentials, research project, and the specific documents they wish to examine. Applicants must also obtain recommendations from recognized academic institutions and secure approval from the Vatican authorities. Even if granted access, researchers are subject to numerous restrictions, including limited working hours, supervised access to documents, and prohibitions on photocopying or reproducing certain materials.

These stringent access controls have fueled speculation about what the Vatican might be hiding. Critics argue that the Church's control over these documents allows it to shape historical narratives to its advantage, suppressing information that could challenge its authority or reveal controversial truths. The secrecy surrounding the archives has also given rise to numerous conspiracy theories, ranging from the existence of lost Gospels and apocryphal texts to evidence of extra-terrestrial contact and ancient technologies.

Speculated Contents of the Vatican Secret Archives

While the exact contents of the Vatican Secret Archives remain largely unknown, various sources and rumors provide glimpses into the potential treasures and secrets they hold. Here are some of the most intriguing and controversial items believed to be housed within the archives:

1.   **The Lost Gospels and Apocryphal Texts**: One of the most persistent theories is that the Vatican Secret Archives contain early Christian writings that were excluded from the canonical Bible. These texts, often referred to as the Lost Gospels or Apocryphal Gospels, could provide alternative accounts of Jesus's life and teachings, potentially challenging established Christian doctrines. Examples of such texts include the Gospel of Thomas, the Gospel of Mary, and the Gospel of Judas. While some of these texts have been discovered and studied, others are rumored to remain hidden within the Vatican's vaults.

2.   **The Chronovisor**: According to legend, the Vatican possesses a device known as the Chronovisor, a type of time viewer that allows users to see past events. This device is said to have been developed by Father Pellegrino Ernetti, a Benedictine monk and scientist, in the mid-20th century. The Chronovisor purportedly uses advanced technology to reconstruct historical events from the vibrations and electromagnetic signals left behind. While the existence of the Chronovisor remains unproven, the story has captured the imagination of many and fueled speculation about the Vatican's secret technological capabilities.

3.   **Evidence of Extraterrestrial Contact**: Another popular theory suggests that the Vatican Secret Archives contain evidence of extraterrestrial contact, including documents, artifacts, and possibly even ancient texts describing interactions with otherworldly beings. Proponents of this theory point to the Vatican's interest in astronomy and the existence of the Vatican Observatory as evidence of the Church's ongoing efforts to understand the cosmos and its potential inhabitants. Some believe that the Vatican has withheld this information to avoid disrupting religious beliefs and societal stability.

4.   **The Third Secret of Fatima**: In 1917, three young shepherd children in Fatima, Portugal, reported receiving a series of visions and messages from the Virgin Mary. These messages,

known as the Secrets of Fatima, were written down and given to the Vatican for safekeeping. While the first two secrets were publicly revealed in 1941, the Third Secret remained a closely guarded secret until 2000, when the Vatican released a text purported to be the final message. However, many believe that the true Third Secret remains hidden within the Vatican Archives and contains apocalyptic predictions or revelations about the Church's future.

5.	**The Templar Documents**: The Knights Templar, a medieval Christian military order, amassed significant wealth and power before their sudden downfall in the early 14th century. Some historians believe that the Templars possessed secret knowledge and treasures, including sacred relics such as the Holy Grail and the Ark of the Covenant. The Vatican Archives are rumored to contain documents detailing the Templars' activities, trials, and possible connections to other secret societies. These documents could shed light on the true extent of the Templars' influence and the reasons behind their persecution.

6.	**Ancient Artifacts and Relics**: The Vatican is known to possess an extensive collection of ancient artifacts and religious relics, many of which are kept in the Vatican Museums. However, some items are believed to be stored within the Vatican Archives due to their sensitive or controversial nature. These could include artifacts from ancient civilizations, relics associated with early Christian martyrs, and objects of significant historical or spiritual importance. The existence and contents of these collections remain a subject of speculation and intrigue.

Impact on Religious and World History

The potential revelations contained within the Vatican Secret Archives could have profound implications for our understanding of religious and world history. By examining the hidden texts, documents, and artifacts, we can gain new insights into the development of Christianity, the role of the Church in shaping global events, and the interactions between different cultures and belief systems.

1. **Reevaluation of Christian Doctrine**: The discovery of lost Gospels and apocryphal texts could lead to a reevaluation of established Christian doctrines and beliefs. These texts might offer alternative perspectives on the life and teachings of Jesus, the role of women in the early Church, and the development of Christian theology. Such revelations could prompt significant theological debates and potentially lead to reforms within the Church.

2. **Historical Revisions**: Documents detailing the Church's involvement in historical events, such as the Crusades, the Inquisition, and colonialism, could provide new insights into the motivations and actions of key figures and institutions. By uncovering these hidden histories, we can develop a more nuanced understanding of the Church's impact on global events and the ways in which it has shaped the course of human civilization.

3. **Cultural and Religious Interactions**: The Vatican Archives may contain records of interactions between the Church and other religious and cultural groups. These documents could shed light on the exchange of ideas, the development of religious syncretism, and the ways in which different belief systems have influenced one another. By exploring these interactions, we can better understand the complex web of connections that have shaped human history.

4. **Technological and Scientific Discoveries**: The rumored existence of advanced technologies, such as the Chronovisor, and evidence of extraterrestrial contact within the Vatican Archives raises intriguing questions about the Church's role in scientific and technological advancements. If such technologies and

discoveries exist, they could revolutionize our understanding of history, physics, and the nature of reality.

Interviews with Theologians and Historians

To gain further insight into the secrets of the Vatican Archives and their potential impact, we conducted interviews with several theologians and historians who have dedicated their careers to studying the Church's history and influence.

Dr. Karen King

Dr. Karen King, a historian of early Christianity, discussed the significance of discovering lost Gospels and apocryphal texts. According to Dr. King, these texts could provide valuable insights into the diversity of early Christian beliefs and practices, challenging the notion of a monolithic early Church. She emphasized the importance of examining these texts in their historical context and understanding the reasons behind their exclusion from the canonical Bible.

Father Thomas Reese

Father Thomas Reese, a Jesuit priest and Vatican analyst, provided a perspective on the Church's efforts to balance transparency with the protection of sensitive information. Father Reese acknowledged the legitimate reasons for maintaining the confidentiality of certain documents, such as protecting the privacy of individuals and preserving the integrity of historical records. However, he also stressed the need for greater openness and scholarly access to the archives to foster a deeper understanding of the Church's history.

Dr. John Julius Norwich

Dr. John Julius Norwich, a historian specializing in Byzantine and Mediterranean history, shared his views on the potential impact of uncovering hidden documents related to the Knights Templar and other secret societies. Dr. Norwich argued that such discoveries could reshape our understanding of medieval history and the interconnectedness of various religious and political movements. He highlighted the importance of rigorous academic research and critical analysis in interpreting these findings.

Conclusion

The Vatican Secret Archives represent one of the most significant repositories of knowledge and history in the world. The restricted access and secrecy surrounding the archives have fueled countless theories and speculations about their contents, ranging from lost Gospels and ancient relics to advanced technologies and evidence of extraterrestrial contact. By exploring these mysteries, we can gain new insights into the development of Christianity, the Church's role in shaping global events, and the hidden histories that have influenced human civilization.

This chapter aims to provide a comprehensive exploration of the Vatican Secret Archives, shedding light on their formation, organization, and the reasons behind their restricted access. By examining the speculated contents and their potential impact on religious and world history, we hope to inspire readers to question accepted narratives and seek out the hidden stories that shape our understanding of the world. In the following chapters, we will delve deeper into specific secrets and artifacts rumored to be housed within the archives, offering detailed analyses and insights into their significance.

| **5** |

Chapter 5: Hidden Texts and Artifacts

The Vatican Secret Archives hold an unparalleled wealth of documents, manuscripts, and artifacts that span over a millennium of human history. While the archives themselves are shrouded in mystery and access is highly restricted, the rumors and speculations surrounding their contents have only added to their enigmatic allure. In this chapter, we will explore some of the most intriguing hidden texts and artifacts rumored to be housed within the Vatican Secret Archives. These items, if revealed, could significantly impact our understanding of religious and world history, providing new insights into early Christianity, ancient civilizations, and long-lost knowledge.

The Lost Gospels and Apocryphal Texts

One of the most enduring and tantalizing theories about the Vatican Secret Archives is the existence of lost Gospels and apocryphal texts that were excluded from the canonical Bible. These texts are believed to offer alternative perspectives on the life and teachings of Jesus, the role of women in the early Church, and the development of Christian doctrine. Here are some of the most significant texts rumored to be hidden within the archives:

1. The Gospel of Thomas

The Gospel of Thomas is one of the most well-known apocryphal texts, consisting of 114 sayings attributed to Jesus. Discovered in 1945 as part of the Nag Hammadi library in Egypt, this text provides a unique insight into early Christian thought. Unlike the canonical Gospels, the Gospel of Thomas lacks a narrative structure, focusing instead on the sayings and teachings of Jesus. Some scholars believe that this text reflects a more mystical and esoteric tradition within early Christianity.

The Gospel of Thomas emphasizes direct, personal experience of the divine, suggesting that salvation comes through self-knowledge and spiritual enlightenment rather than through the Church's sacraments and doctrines. If the Vatican Secret Archives contain additional copies or versions of the Gospel of Thomas, they could provide further context and understanding of this alternative Christian tradition.

2. The Gospel of Mary

The Gospel of Mary, another significant apocryphal text, is attributed to Mary Magdalene. This text portrays Mary Magdalene as a prominent disciple and spiritual leader, offering a different perspective on her role in early Christianity. The Gospel of Mary includes teachings on the nature of the soul, sin, and salvation, emphasizing the importance of inner spiritual knowledge.

The depiction of Mary Magdalene in this text challenges the traditional view of her as a repentant sinner and suggests that she held a position of authority among Jesus's followers. If the Vatican Secret Archives contain more complete versions of the Gospel of Mary, they could shed light on the role of women in the early Church and the diverse theological beliefs that existed in early Christian communities.

3. The Gospel of Judas

The Gospel of Judas is another apocryphal text that has garnered significant attention. Discovered in the 1970s and made public in 2006, this text presents a radically different account of Judas Iscariot's relationship with Jesus. Rather than portraying Judas as a traitor, the Gospel of Judas suggests that he was acting on Jesus's instructions to facilitate the crucifixion and fulfill a divine plan.

This controversial interpretation of Judas's actions challenges the traditional narrative of betrayal and offers a more nuanced understanding of his role in the events leading up to the crucifixion. If the Vatican Secret Archives hold additional versions or fragments of the Gospel of Judas, they could provide further insights into the diverse and often conflicting beliefs within early Christianity.

4. The Apocryphon of John

The Apocryphon of John, also known as the Secret Book of John, is a Gnostic text that provides a detailed cosmology and creation myth. This text, which is part of the Nag Hammadi library, describes the creation of the material world by a lesser divine being known as the Demiurge and emphasizes the importance of spiritual knowledge for salvation.

The Apocryphon of John offers a starkly different perspective on the nature of God, creation, and humanity's place in the universe compared to the canonical Bible. If the Vatican Secret Archives contain additional Gnostic texts like the Apocryphon of John, they could reveal the rich diversity of early Christian thought and the theological debates that shaped the development of the Church.

Ancient Artifacts and Relics

In addition to hidden texts, the Vatican Secret Archives are rumored to house a vast collection of ancient artifacts and religious relics. These items, often kept out of public view due to their sensitive or controversial nature, hold significant historical and spiritual value. Here are some of the most intriguing artifacts believed to be hidden within the archives:

1. The True Cross

The True Cross is the name given to the physical remnants of the cross upon which Jesus was crucified. According to Christian tradition, the cross was discovered by Saint Helena, the mother of Emperor Constantine, during her pilgrimage to Jerusalem in the 4th century. Over the centuries, fragments of the True Cross have been distributed as relics to various churches and individuals.

The Vatican is believed to possess one of the largest and most significant collections of these fragments, which are kept in the archives for preservation and veneration. The existence of these relics raises important questions about their authenticity and the role of relics in the development of Christian worship and devotion.

2. The Shroud of Turin

The Shroud of Turin is a linen cloth bearing the image of a man who appears to have suffered physical trauma consistent with crucifixion. Many believe the shroud to be the burial cloth of Jesus, and it has been the subject of intense scientific and theological scrutiny. The Vatican officially owns the shroud, and it is kept under strict security and rarely displayed to the public.

While the authenticity of the Shroud of Turin remains a matter of debate, it continues to be an object of great fascination and veneration. The Vatican Secret Archives are rumored to contain additional documents and evidence related to the shroud, which could provide further insights into its origins and significance.

3. The Holy Grail

The Holy Grail is one of the most enduring legends in Christian tradition, often depicted as the cup used by Jesus at the Last Supper and later sought by knights and adventurers during the Middle Ages. Various locations and artifacts have been proposed as the true Holy Grail, but none have been definitively proven.

Some believe that the Vatican possesses the true Holy Grail, keeping it hidden within the archives to protect its sanctity and prevent its misuse. If the Holy Grail is indeed housed within the Vatican, it would represent one of the most significant religious artifacts in history, holding profound spiritual and symbolic meaning.

4. The Ark of the Covenant

The Ark of the Covenant, described in the Hebrew Bible, is a sacred chest that held the tablets of the Ten Commandments. According to tradition, the Ark was housed in the Holy of Holies in the Temple of Jerusalem until it disappeared following the Babylonian conquest.

There are numerous theories about the Ark's current location, with some suggesting that it is hidden within the Vatican. The discovery of the Ark of the Covenant would be a momentous event, offering unprecedented insights into ancient Jewish history and the early connections between Judaism and Christianity.

The Third Secret of Fatima

In 1917, three young shepherd children in Fatima, Portugal, reported receiving a series of visions and messages from the Virgin Mary. These messages, known as the Secrets of Fatima, were written down and given to the Vatican for safekeeping. While the first two secrets were publicly revealed in 1941, the Third Secret remained a closely guarded secret until 2000, when the Vatican released a text purported to be the final message.

However, many believe that the true Third Secret remains hidden within the Vatican Archives and contains apocalyptic predictions or revelations about the Church's future. The secrecy surrounding the Third Secret has led to widespread speculation and controversy, with some suggesting that its contents could profoundly impact the Catholic Church and its teachings.

The Chronovisor

According to legend, the Vatican possesses a device known as the Chronovisor, a type of time viewer that allows users to see past events. This device is said to have been developed by Father Pellegrino Ernetti, a Benedictine monk and scientist, in the mid-20th century. The Chronovisor purportedly uses advanced technology to reconstruct historical events from the vibrations and electromagnetic signals left behind.

While the existence of the Chronovisor remains unproven, the story has captured the imagination of many and fueled speculation about the Vatican's secret technological capabilities. If such a device exists, it could revolutionize our understanding of history, allowing us to witness events as they actually occurred rather than relying on written records and interpretations.

Interviews with Theologians and Historians

To gain further insight into the potential impact of these hidden texts and artifacts, we conducted interviews with several theologians and historians who have dedicated their careers to studying the Church's history and influence.

Dr. Elaine Pagels

Dr. Elaine Pagels, a renowned scholar of early Christianity and Gnosticism, discussed the significance of discovering lost Gospels and apocryphal texts. According to Dr. Pagels, these texts could provide valuable insights into the diversity of early Christian beliefs and practices, challenging the notion of a monolithic early Church. She emphasized the importance of examining these texts in their historical context and understanding the reasons behind their exclusion from the canonical Bible.

Father Thomas Reese

Father Thomas Reese, a Jesuit priest and Vatican analyst, provided a perspective on the Church's efforts to balance transparency with the protection of sensitive information. Father Reese acknowledged the legitimate reasons for maintaining the confidentiality of certain documents, such as protecting the privacy of individuals and preserving the integrity of historical records. However, he also stressed the need for greater openness and scholarly access to the archives to foster a deeper understanding of the Church's history.

Dr. Bart Ehrman

Dr. Bart Ehrman, a historian and scholar of early Christianity, shared his views on the potential impact of uncovering hidden texts related to early Christian sects and movements. Dr. Ehrman argued that such discoveries could reshape our understanding of the theological debates and conflicts that characterized early Christianity. He highlighted the importance of rigorous academic research and critical analysis in interpreting these findings and integrating them into the broader historical narrative.

Conclusion

The Vatican Secret Archives represent one of the most significant repositories of knowledge and history in the world. The restricted access and secrecy surrounding the archives have fueled countless theories and speculations about their contents, ranging from lost Gospels and ancient relics to advanced technologies and evidence of extraterrestrial contact. By exploring these hidden texts and artifacts, we can gain new insights into the development of Christianity, the Church's role in shaping global events, and the hidden histories that have influenced human civilization.

This chapter aims to provide a comprehensive exploration of the most intriguing and controversial items believed to be housed within the Vatican Secret Archives. By examining the potential impact of these discoveries on religious and world history, we hope to inspire readers to question accepted narratives and seek out the hidden stories that shape our understanding of the world. In the following chapters, we will delve deeper into specific secrets and artifacts rumored to be housed within the archives, offering detailed analyses and insights into their significance.

| 6 |

Chapter 6: The Early Christian Church and Suppressed Histories

The early Christian Church's history is marked by its remarkable transformation from a small, persecuted sect within Judaism to the dominant religion of the Roman Empire and, eventually, the foundation of Western civilization. This period of rapid growth and doctrinal development was also a time of intense theological debate, political maneuvering, and, at times, violent conflict. Within this context, certain texts, doctrines, and historical narratives were suppressed or deemed heretical as the Church sought to establish a unified orthodoxy. In this chapter, we will explore the hidden histories of the early Christian Church, examining the texts, doctrines, and events that were intentionally obscured or marginalized. Through meticulous research and interviews with theologians and historians, we aim to uncover the truths that have been hidden for centuries and understand their impact on the development of Christianity.

The Formation of Early Christian Doctrine

The formation of early Christian doctrine was a complex and often contentious process. The early Church was characterized by a diversity of beliefs and practices, reflecting the varied backgrounds and experiences of its members. As the Church grew, leaders sought to establish a unified set of beliefs to provide cohesion and combat heretical teachings. This process of doctrinal consolidation involved significant debates, councils, and the suppression of alternative viewpoints.

The Council of Nicaea

One of the most pivotal events in the formation of early Christian doctrine was the Council of Nicaea, convened by Emperor Constantine in 325 CE. The primary purpose of the council was to address the Arian controversy, a theological dispute that had divided the Church. Arius, a priest from Alexandria, argued that Jesus Christ was not co-eternal with God the Father but was a created being. This view challenged the emerging orthodox understanding of the Trinity and threatened the unity of the Church.

The Council of Nicaea ultimately condemned Arianism as heresy and affirmed the doctrine of the Trinity, declaring that Jesus Christ was of the same substance (homoousios) as God the Father. The Nicene Creed, formulated during the council, became a foundational statement of Christian orthodoxy. However, the suppression of Arianism and other heretical views involved significant political maneuvering and the destruction of many texts and writings that supported these alternative perspectives.

The Apocryphal Gospels

As the early Church sought to establish a canon of authoritative scriptures, numerous texts were excluded from the New Testament. These excluded writings, known as the Apocryphal Gospels, offer alternative accounts of Jesus's life and teachings and reflect the diversity of early Christian thought. While some of these texts were suppressed or destroyed, others have survived and provide valuable insights into the theological debates and conflicts of the early Church.

The Gospel of Thomas

The Gospel of Thomas is one of the most well-known apocryphal texts. Discovered in 1945 as part of the Nag Hammadi library in Egypt, this collection of 114 sayings attributed to Jesus provides a unique insight into early Christian thought. Unlike the canonical Gospels, the Gospel of Thomas lacks a narrative structure, focusing instead on the sayings and teachings of Jesus.

The Gospel of Thomas emphasizes direct, personal experience of the divine, suggesting that salvation comes through self-knowledge and spiritual enlightenment rather than through the Church's sacraments and doctrines. This text reflects a more mystical and esoteric tradition within early Christianity, challenging the emerging orthodoxy's emphasis on institutional authority and doctrinal conformity.

The Gospel of Mary

The Gospel of Mary, another significant apocryphal text, is attributed to Mary Magdalene. This text portrays Mary Magdalene as a prominent disciple and spiritual leader, offering a different perspective on her role in early Christianity. The Gospel of Mary includes teachings on the nature of the soul, sin, and salvation, emphasizing the importance of inner spiritual knowledge.

The depiction of Mary Magdalene in this text challenges the traditional view of her as a repentant sinner and suggests that she held a position of authority among Jesus's followers. This alternative portrayal of Mary Magdalene reflects the diverse and often contested views of women's roles in the early Church.

The Gospel of Judas

The Gospel of Judas is another apocryphal text that has garnered significant attention. Discovered in the 1970s and made public in 2006, this text presents a radically different account of Judas Iscariot's relationship with Jesus. Rather than portraying Judas as a traitor, the Gospel of Judas suggests that he was acting on Jesus's instructions to facilitate the crucifixion and fulfill a divine plan.

This controversial interpretation of Judas's actions challenges the traditional narrative of betrayal and offers a more nuanced understanding of his role in the events leading up to the crucifixion. The Gospel of Judas reflects the diverse theological beliefs within early Christianity and the intense debates over the nature of salvation and divine providence.

The Role of Women in the Early Church

The role of women in the early Christian Church has been a subject of significant debate and controversy. While the New Testament includes references to women who played important roles in the early Christian communities, such as Mary Magdalene, Priscilla, and Phoebe, the institutional Church gradually marginalized women's contributions as it established a patriarchal hierarchy.

The Acts of Paul and Thecla

The Acts of Paul and Thecla is an apocryphal text that provides a glimpse into the prominent role women played in some early Christian communities. This text tells the story of Thecla, a young woman who becomes a disciple of Paul and dedicates her life to preaching the gospel. Thecla's story highlights the themes of chastity, spiritual authority, and the challenges faced by early Christian women.

The Acts of Paul and Thecla portrays Thecla as a powerful and independent figure who defies social norms and religious authorities to follow her calling. This depiction contrasts sharply with the later Church's emphasis on women's submission and domestic roles. The suppression of texts like the Acts of Paul and Thecla reflects the broader marginalization of women's contributions to the early Church and the establishment of a male-dominated clerical hierarchy.

The Female Apostles

There is evidence to suggest that women held positions of leadership and authority in the early Christian communities. The New Testament references several women who were active in ministry, including Junia, who is referred to as an apostle in Romans 16:7. However, as the Church developed a more hierarchical structure, women's roles were increasingly restricted, and their contributions were downplayed or erased from official histories.

The suppression of women's leadership roles in the early Church has had a lasting impact on Christian theology and practice. By recovering and examining the suppressed histories of these early female apostles, we can gain a more accurate and inclusive understanding of the early Christian movement and the diverse contributions of its members.

Theological Debates and Heresies

The early Christian Church was marked by intense theological debates and the emergence of various heretical movements. These debates were often centered on the nature of Christ, the Trinity, and the relationship between faith and works. The suppression of heretical teachings involved the destruction of texts, the excommunication of individuals, and sometimes violent persecution.

Gnosticism

Gnosticism was one of the most significant and influential heretical movements in early Christianity. Gnostic beliefs varied widely, but they generally emphasized the importance of secret knowledge (gnosis) for salvation and viewed the material world as inherently flawed or evil. Gnostics often believed that the true God was distinct from the creator god of the Old Testament, whom they viewed as a lesser, ignorant deity.

The Gnostic texts discovered in the Nag Hammadi library provide valuable insights into this diverse and complex movement. These texts, such as the Gospel of Thomas, the Gospel of Philip, and the Apocryphon of John, offer alternative cosmologies, soteriologies, and interpretations of Christian teachings. The suppression of Gnosticism involved the destruction of many Gnostic texts and the persecution of Gnostic believers, but the survival of some texts has allowed modern scholars to study this important aspect of early Christian history.

Arianism

Arianism, as mentioned earlier, was a major theological controversy that centered on the nature of Christ. Arius, a priest from Alexandria, argued that Jesus Christ was not co-eternal with God the Father but was a created being. This view challenged the emerging orthodox understanding of the Trinity and threatened the unity of the Church.

The Council of Nicaea in 325 CE condemned Arianism as heresy and affirmed the doctrine of the Trinity. However, Arianism continued to have significant support, particularly among the Germanic tribes, and remained a contentious issue for centuries. The suppression of Arianism involved the destruction of many Arian texts and the marginalization of its proponents within the Church.

Donatism

Donatism was another heretical movement that emerged in the early Christian Church, particularly in North Africa. The Donatists argued that the validity of the sacraments depended on the moral purity of the clergy who administered them. This view arose in response to the persecution of Christians under the Roman Empire, during which some clergy members had renounced their faith to save their lives.

The Donatist controversy highlighted the tension between the Church's desire for unity and the demand for moral integrity among its leaders. The suppression of Donatism involved significant conflict, including violence and persecution, as the Church sought to maintain its authority and cohesion.

Interviews with Theologians and Historians

To gain further insight into the suppressed histories of the early Christian Church, we conducted interviews with several theologians and historians who have dedicated their careers to studying this period.

Dr. Karen King

Dr. Karen King, a historian of early Christianity, discussed the significance of discovering lost Gospels and apocryphal texts. According to Dr. King, these texts could provide valuable insights into the diversity of early Christian beliefs and practices, challenging the notion of a monolithic early Church. She emphasized the importance of examining these texts in their historical context and understanding the reasons behind their exclusion from the canonical Bible.

Father Thomas Reese

Father Thomas Reese, a Jesuit priest and Vatican analyst, provided a perspective on the Church's efforts to balance transparency with the protection of sensitive information. Father Reese acknowledged the legitimate reasons for maintaining the confidentiality of certain documents, such as protecting the privacy of individuals and preserving the integrity of historical records. However, he also stressed the need for greater openness and scholarly access to the archives to foster a deeper understanding of the Church's history.

Dr. Elaine Pagels

Dr. Elaine Pagels, a renowned scholar of early Christianity and Gnosticism, shared her views on the significance of Gnostic texts in understanding the diversity of early Christian thought. Dr. Pagels argued that the suppression of Gnostic beliefs and texts was part of a broader effort to establish a unified orthodoxy and marginalize alternative theological perspectives. She highlighted the importance of studying these texts to gain a more comprehensive understanding of early Christian history.

Conclusion

The early Christian Church's history is marked by its remarkable transformation and doctrinal development, as well as by the suppression of certain texts, doctrines, and historical narratives. The formation of early Christian doctrine involved significant debates, councils, and the marginalization of alternative viewpoints. The exclusion of apocryphal texts, the suppression of women's leadership roles, and the persecution of heretical movements all reflect the complex and often contentious process of establishing a unified orthodoxy.

By uncovering and examining these suppressed histories, we can gain a more accurate and inclusive understanding of the early Christian movement and the diverse contributions of its members. This chapter aims to inspire readers to question accepted narratives and seek out the hidden stories that shape our understanding of the world. In the following parts of this book, we will continue to explore the secrets and hidden histories that have influenced human civilization, offering detailed analyses and insights into their significance.

PART III

RELIGION AS A TOOL FOR MASS CONTROL

Religion, one of humanity's most powerful and enduring institutions, has shaped civilizations, cultures, and individual lives for millennia. At its core, religion offers spiritual guidance, moral frameworks, and a sense of community and purpose. However, beyond its spiritual dimensions, religion has also been wielded as a formidable tool for mass control. Throughout history, religious institutions and doctrines have been used to consolidate power, manipulate populations, and suppress dissent. In this part of "Hidden Agendas: Exposing the Dark Secrets," we will delve into the historical and contemporary mechanisms through which religion has been used to exert control over societies.

Historical Context: Religion as a Political Tool

From the ancient empires to modern nation-states, rulers have often harnessed the power of religion to legitimize their authority and maintain social order. This manipulation of religious belief for political purposes is not merely a relic of the past but continues to influence contemporary societies.

The Divine Right of Kings

One of the most well-known examples of religion being used as a political tool is the doctrine of the divine right of kings. This belief, prevalent in medieval and early modern Europe, posited that monarchs were chosen by God and thus possessed a divine mandate to rule. This doctrine not only reinforced the authority of kings but also discouraged rebellion and dissent, as challenging the monarch was seen as challenging the will of God.

The divine right of kings was particularly prominent in countries like France and England. In France, Louis XIV famously declared, "L'État, c'est moi" ("I am the state"), emphasizing his belief in his God-given right to absolute power. In England, the Stuart monarchs James I and Charles I both strongly advocated for the divine right of kings, leading to significant political and religious conflicts, including the English Civil War.

The Holy Roman Empire and the Papacy

The relationship between the Holy Roman Empire and the Papacy provides another illustrative example of religion being used to wield political power. The Holy Roman Emperors claimed to be the secular arm of Christendom, with their authority sanctioned by the Pope. This symbiotic relationship allowed both the emperors and the popes to consolidate their power and influence over vast territories.

However, this alliance was not without conflict. The Investiture Controversy of the 11th and 12th centuries was a prolonged struggle between the papacy and the Holy Roman Emperors over the appointment of bishops and abbots. This conflict highlighted the tension between spiritual and temporal authority and underscored the significant political power held by religious institutions.

The Role of Religion in Colonialism

Religion played a central role in the justification and execution of colonialism. European powers often portrayed their colonial ventures as missions to spread Christianity and "civilize" indigenous populations. This religious justification masked the economic and political motivations behind colonialism and facilitated the exploitation and subjugation of millions of people.

The Spanish conquest of the Americas provides a stark example. The Spanish Crown, supported by the Catholic Church, embarked on a mission to convert indigenous peoples to Christianity. This religious mission was used to legitimize the violent conquest, forced labor, and cultural assimilation imposed on native populations. The encomienda system, which granted Spanish colonists the right to extract labor and tribute from indigenous communities, was justified as a means of protecting and converting the native peoples.

Religious Texts and Doctrines as Instruments of Control

Religious texts and doctrines have been interpreted and employed to support various forms of social and political control. These interpretations often serve to uphold existing power structures and discourage challenges to authority.

Biblical Justifications for Slavery

The use of religious texts to justify slavery is one of the most egregious examples of religion being used to support oppressive systems. In the antebellum United States, proponents of slavery often cited the Bible to defend the institution. Verses from both the Old and New Testaments were interpreted to suggest that slavery was divinely sanctioned.

For instance, the Curse of Ham narrative in the Book of Genesis was frequently cited to argue that people of African descent were destined to be slaves. Similarly, passages from the Pauline Epistles, such as Ephesians 6:5 ("Slaves, obey your earthly masters with respect and fear"), were used to argue that slavery was an acceptable and even righteous institution.

The Control of Women

Religious doctrines have also been used to control and subordinate women. Many religious traditions have prescribed specific roles for women, often emphasizing their subservience to men and restricting their participation in religious and public life.

In Christianity, interpretations of biblical passages such as 1 Timothy 2:12 ("I do not permit a woman to teach or to assume authority over a man; she must be quiet") have been used to justify the exclusion of women from leadership roles within the Church. Similarly, in Islam, certain interpretations of the Quran and Hadith have been used to enforce gender segregation and restrict women's rights.

These doctrines have had profound implications for the status and rights of women in religious communities and societies at large. They have reinforced patriarchal structures and limited women's opportunities for education, employment, and political participation.

Modern Religious Control Mechanisms

While historical examples provide a clear picture of how religion has been used as a tool for control, these mechanisms are not confined to the past. In contemporary societies, religious institutions and leaders continue to wield significant influence, often intersecting with political and economic power.

Religious Nationalism

Religious nationalism is a phenomenon where religious and national identities are intertwined, often to the exclusion of minority groups. This form of nationalism can be seen in various countries, where religious majorities assert their dominance and seek to impose their beliefs and practices on the entire population.

In India, for example, Hindu nationalism (Hindutva) has gained significant traction, with political leaders promoting the idea of India as a fundamentally Hindu nation. This ideology has led to increased discrimination and violence against religious minorities, particularly Muslims and Christians. The use of religious symbolism and rhetoric in politics has further polarized society and undermined secular principles.

Religious Influence on Politics

Religious institutions and leaders often play a significant role in shaping political discourse and policy. In many countries, religious groups mobilize voters, lobby for legislation, and influence political candidates.

In the United States, the Religious Right has been a powerful force in politics since the late 20th century. Evangelical Christian groups have mobilized to support conservative candidates and policies, particularly on issues such as abortion, LGBTQ+ rights, and education. This intersection of religion and politics has shaped the political landscape and influenced public policy.

Control of Education

Religious institutions have long recognized the importance of education in shaping beliefs and values. By controlling educational institutions and curricula, religious groups can influence the development of young minds and perpetuate their teachings.

In many countries, religious schools play a significant role in the education system. These schools often emphasize religious teachings and values, shaping students' worldviews and reinforcing religious identities. In some cases, religious education is used to promote specific political or ideological agendas, furthering the influence of religious institutions in society.

Media and Communication

The advent of modern communication technologies has provided religious groups with new platforms to disseminate their messages and reach broader audiences. Television, radio, the internet, and social media have become powerful tools for religious leaders and organizations to spread their teachings and mobilize supporters.

Television evangelism, for instance, has become a significant phenomenon in countries like the United States. Televangelists use their platforms to preach, solicit donations, and influence public opinion on various issues. Similarly, religious groups have harnessed the power of social media to connect with followers, share content, and organize events.

Interviews with Experts

To gain a deeper understanding of the ways in which religion has been used as a tool for mass control, we conducted interviews with several experts in the fields of theology, history, and political science.

Dr. Karen Armstrong

Dr. Karen Armstrong, a renowned scholar of religion, discussed the historical and contemporary use of religion as a tool for control. According to Dr. Armstrong, while religion has often been manipulated by those in power to maintain authority and suppress dissent, it is essential to recognize the positive aspects of religious belief and practice. She emphasized the need for a nuanced understanding of religion's role in society, acknowledging both its potential for abuse and its capacity to inspire compassion and social justice.

Professor Mark Juergensmeyer

Professor Mark Juergensmeyer, an expert on religious violence and conflict, shared his insights on the rise of religious nationalism and its impact on global politics. He explained how religious identities are often mobilized to create a sense of unity and purpose, but this can also lead to exclusion and violence against those perceived as outsiders. Professor Juergensmeyer highlighted the importance of addressing the underlying social, economic, and political issues that contribute to the rise of religious nationalism.

Reverend William J. Barber II

Reverend William J. Barber II, a prominent social justice advocate and leader of the Poor People's Campaign, discussed the intersection of religion and politics in the United States. Reverend Barber emphasized the need to reclaim religious narratives that promote justice, equality, and inclusion, countering the harmful effects of religious extremism and exclusionary ideologies. He stressed the importance of interfaith coalitions and grassroots movements in challenging the misuse of religion for political gain.

Conclusion

Religion has been and continues to be a powerful tool for mass control, shaping societies and influencing individuals' beliefs, behaviors, and identities. From historical examples such as the divine right of kings and the role of the Church in colonialism to contemporary issues like religious nationalism and the influence of religious institutions on politics and education, the mechanisms of religious control are diverse and multifaceted.

By examining these mechanisms, we can gain a deeper understanding of how religion has been used to uphold existing power structures and suppress dissent. This knowledge is crucial for recognizing and challenging the ways in which religious beliefs and institutions are manipulated for political and economic gain.

This introduction sets the stage for a deeper exploration of the historical and contemporary use of religion as a tool for mass control. In the following chapters, we will delve into specific examples and case studies, providing detailed analyses and insights into the ways in which religious institutions and doctrines have been used to exert control over societies. Through this exploration, we aim to uncover the hidden agendas behind religious manipulation and inspire readers to question and critically examine the role of religion in shaping our world.

| 7 |

Chapter 7: Historical Use of Religion for Control

Religion has long been one of the most potent tools for shaping societies, governing behavior, and consolidating power. From the ancient civilizations of Mesopotamia and Egypt to the medieval kingdoms of Europe and the empires of Asia, religious authority has often been intertwined with political power. This chapter will explore the historical use of religion as a tool for mass control, examining how religious doctrines, institutions, and leaders have been utilized to maintain social order, legitimize authority, and suppress dissent. Through detailed historical case studies, we will uncover the mechanisms and strategies employed by rulers and religious elites to wield the power of faith for their own ends.

The Divine Right of Kings

The doctrine of the divine right of kings is one of the most striking examples of religion being used to legitimize political authority. This belief, which held that monarchs were chosen by God and thus possessed a divine mandate to rule, was prevalent in medieval and early modern Europe. The doctrine served to reinforce the authority of kings and queens, discourage rebellion, and maintain social order.

Origins and Development

The concept of the divine right of kings can be traced back to the early Middle Ages. It was rooted in the idea that God had appointed certain individuals to rule over others and that questioning or rebelling against the monarch was equivalent to challenging God's will. This belief was bolstered by biblical passages, such as Romans 13:1-2, which states: "Let every person be subject to the governing authorities. For there is no authority except from God, and those that exist have been instituted by God. Therefore whoever resists the authorities resists what God has appointed, and those who resist will incur judgment."

The divine right of kings became more explicitly articulated and widespread during the Renaissance and the Reformation. Monarchs like James I of England and Louis XIV of France championed the doctrine to assert their absolute authority. James I wrote extensively on the divine right, arguing that kings were accountable only to God and not to their subjects. Louis XIV's famous declaration, "L'État, c'est moi" ("I am the state"), epitomized the belief that the monarch embodied the state and its divine sanction.

Impact on Society and Politics

The doctrine of the divine right of kings had profound implications for European societies. It reinforced the hierarchical social order, with the monarch at the top, followed by the nobility, clergy, and commoners. This hierarchical structure was seen as divinely ordained and unchangeable.

The divine right also served to justify and perpetuate the privileges and power of the ruling class. By claiming a divine mandate, monarchs could suppress dissent and rebellion more effectively. Any challenge to the monarch's authority could be framed as an act of heresy or blasphemy, warranting severe punishment.

However, the doctrine also faced significant challenges, particularly during periods of political upheaval and revolution. The English Civil War (1642-1651) was a direct challenge to the divine right, with Parliamentarians opposing the absolute rule of Charles I. The Glorious Revolution of 1688 further undermined the doctrine, leading to the establishment of a constitutional monarchy in England.

The Holy Roman Empire and Papal Authority

The relationship between the Holy Roman Empire and the Papacy provides another illustrative example of the intertwining of religious and political power. The Holy Roman Emperors claimed to be the secular arm of Christendom, with their authority sanctioned by the Pope. This alliance allowed both the emperors and the popes to consolidate their power and influence over vast territories.

The Investiture Controversy

The Investiture Controversy (1075-1122) was a significant conflict between the papacy and the Holy Roman Emperors over the appointment of bishops and abbots. This struggle highlighted the tension between spiritual and temporal authority and underscored the significant political power held by religious institutions.

The controversy began when Pope Gregory VII sought to end the practice of lay investiture, where secular rulers appointed bishops and abbots. Gregory VII argued that only the Church had the authority to appoint its officials, as they were spiritual leaders. Holy Roman Emperor Henry IV, however, resisted this assertion, viewing it as a challenge to his authority.

The conflict escalated, leading to Henry IV's excommunication and the subsequent penance at Canossa in 1077, where he famously stood barefoot in the snow for three days to seek the Pope's forgiveness. The Investiture Controversy was ultimately resolved by the Concordat of Worms in 1122, which allowed for a compromise: the Church retained the right to appoint bishops, but the emperor had a role in the selection process.

Religious Justification for Colonialism

Religion played a central role in the justification and execution of colonialism. European powers often portrayed their colonial ventures as missions to spread Christianity and "civilize" indigenous populations. This religious justification masked the economic and political motivations behind colonialism and facilitated the exploitation and subjugation of millions of people.

The Spanish Conquest of the Americas

The Spanish conquest of the Americas provides a stark example of religion being used to legitimize colonialism. The Spanish Crown, supported by the Catholic Church, embarked on a mission to convert indigenous peoples to Christianity. This religious mission was used to legitimize the violent conquest, forced labor, and cultural assimilation imposed on native populations.

The Encomienda System

The encomienda system, established by the Spanish Crown, granted colonists the right to extract labor and tribute from indigenous communities in exchange for providing protection and religious instruction.

This system effectively enslaved indigenous peoples, subjecting them to brutal working conditions and severe punishment for resistance.

The Spanish justified the encomienda system by arguing that it was a means of protecting and converting the native peoples. However, the reality was that it facilitated the exploitation and oppression of indigenous communities for economic gain. The system was eventually abolished in the mid-16th century, but the legacy of this exploitation continued to impact indigenous populations.

Religious Texts and Doctrines as Instruments of Control

Religious texts and doctrines have been interpreted and employed to support various forms of social and political control. These interpretations often serve to uphold existing power structures and discourage challenges to authority.

Biblical Justifications for Slavery

The use of religious texts to justify slavery is one of the most egregious examples of religion being used to support oppressive systems. In the antebellum United States, proponents of slavery often cited the Bible to defend the institution. Verses from both the Old and New Testaments were interpreted to suggest that slavery was divinely sanctioned.

The Curse of Ham

One of the most frequently cited biblical justifications for slavery was the Curse of Ham narrative in the Book of Genesis. According to this story, Noah cursed Ham's son Canaan to be a "servant of servants" after Ham saw Noah naked and drunk. Proponents of slavery argued that this curse applied to all of Ham's descendants, who they claimed were the ancestors of African peoples. This interpretation was used to argue that people of African descent were destined to be slaves.

Pauline Epistles

Passages from the Pauline Epistles were also used to justify slavery. For example, Ephesians 6:5 states: "Slaves, obey your earthly masters with respect and fear, and with sincerity of heart, just as you would obey Christ." Pro-slavery advocates argued that these verses demonstrated that slavery was an acceptable and even righteous institution. This use of religious texts to support slavery reinforced the social and economic structures of the time, perpetuating the exploitation and dehumanization of enslaved individuals.

The Control of Women

Religious doctrines have also been used to control and subordinate women. Many religious traditions have prescribed specific roles for women, often emphasizing their subservience to men and restricting their participation in religious and public life.

Christianity

In Christianity, interpretations of biblical passages such as 1 Timothy 2:12 ("I do not permit a woman to teach or to assume authority over a man; she must be quiet") have been used to justify the exclusion of women from leadership roles within the Church. Similarly, interpretations of the creation narrative in Genesis have been used to argue that women are inherently subordinate to men, as Eve was created from Adam's rib to be his helper.

These interpretations have had profound implications for the status and rights of women in Christian communities. They have reinforced patriarchal structures and limited women's opportunities for education, employment, and political participation. The marginalization of women within religious institutions has also impacted broader societal attitudes toward gender roles and equality.

Islam

In Islam, certain interpretations of the Quran and Hadith have been used to enforce gender segregation and restrict women's rights. For example, interpretations of Quranic verses such as Surah An-Nisa (4:34), which states that "men are in charge of women by [right of] what Allah has given one over the other," have been used to justify male guardianship over women.

These interpretations have led to practices such as the requirement for women to have a male guardian's permission to travel, work, or marry in some Muslim-majority countries. They have also contributed to the enforcement of strict dress codes and restrictions on women's participation in public life.

However, it is important to note that there is significant diversity within Islamic thought and practice. Many Muslims, including scholars and activists, advocate for interpretations of the Quran and Hadith that promote gender equality and challenge patriarchal norms.

Modern Religious Control Mechanisms

While historical examples provide a clear picture of how religion has been used as a tool for control, these mechanisms are not confined to the past. In contemporary societies, religious institutions and leaders continue to wield significant influence, often intersecting with political and economic power.

Religious Nationalism

Religious nationalism is a phenomenon where religious and national identities are intertwined, often to the exclusion of minority groups. This form of nationalism can be seen in various countries, where religious majorities assert their dominance and seek to impose their beliefs and practices on the entire population.

India: Hindu Nationalism

In India, Hindu nationalism (Hindutva) has gained significant traction, with political leaders promoting the idea of India as a fundamentally Hindu nation. This ideology has led to increased discrimination and violence against religious minorities, particularly Muslims and Christians. The use of religious symbolism and rhetoric in politics has further polarized society and undermined secular principles.

The Bharatiya Janata Party (BJP), the political arm of the Hindu nationalist movement, has been instrumental in promoting Hindutva. The party's leaders, including Prime Minister Narendra Modi, have used religious nationalism to galvanize support and consolidate power. This has resulted in policies and actions that marginalize religious minorities and threaten India's secular foundations.

Myanmar: Buddhist Nationalism

In Myanmar, Buddhist nationalism has been a driving force behind the persecution of the Rohingya Muslim minority. Monks and religious leaders have played a significant role in promoting anti-Muslim sentiment and justifying violence against the Rohingya.

The 969 Movement, led by nationalist Buddhist monk Ashin Wirathu, has been at the forefront of this persecution. The movement promotes the idea that Buddhism is under threat from Islam and that it is the duty of Buddhists to defend their religion and nation. This rhetoric has fueled widespread violence and human rights abuses against the Rohingya, culminating in what many international observers have described as genocide.

Religious Influence on Politics

Religious institutions and leaders often play a significant role in shaping political discourse and policy. In many countries, religious groups mobilize voters, lobby for legislation, and influence political candidates.

The United States: The Religious Right

In the United States, the Religious Right has been a powerful force in politics since the late 20th century. Evangelical Christian groups have mobilized to support conservative candidates and policies, particularly on issues such as abortion, LGBTQ+ rights, and education. This intersection of religion and politics has shaped the political landscape and influenced public policy.

The Moral Majority, founded by Jerry Falwell in 1979, was one of the earliest and most influential organizations of the Religious Right. It played a key role in mobilizing evangelical voters and shaping the Republican Party's platform. Today, organizations such as Focus on the Family and the Family Research Council continue to exert significant influence on American politics, advocating for policies that align with their religious beliefs.

Iran: Theocratic Rule

In Iran, the Islamic Revolution of 1979 resulted in the establishment of a theocratic government led by religious leaders. The Supreme Leader, who holds the highest authority in the country, is a cleric with significant religious and political power.

The Iranian government enforces strict adherence to Islamic law (Sharia), with significant implications for various aspects of life, including dress codes, social behavior, and political participation. The intertwining of religious and political authority in Iran has led to the suppression of dissent, restrictions on personal freedoms, and the persecution of religious and ethnic minorities.

Control of Education

Religious institutions have long recognized the importance of education in shaping beliefs and values. By controlling educational institutions and curricula, religious groups can influence the development of young minds and perpetuate their teachings.

Religious Schools

In many countries, religious schools play a significant role in the education system. These schools often emphasize religious teachings and values, shaping students' worldviews and reinforcing religious identities. In some cases, religious education is used to promote specific political or ideological agendas, furthering the influence of religious institutions in society.

Madrasas in Pakistan

In Pakistan, madrasas (Islamic religious schools) have been a significant part of the education system. While many madrasas provide valuable religious education and social services, some have been accused of promoting extremist ideologies and fostering sectarianism.

The Pakistani government has made efforts to reform the madrasa system and integrate it with the mainstream education system. However, the influence of madrasas and their role in shaping religious and political beliefs remains a contentious issue.

Private Religious Schools in the United States

In the United States, private religious schools, including Catholic, Protestant, and Jewish institutions, provide education to millions of students. These schools often emphasize religious teachings and values, shaping students' beliefs and behaviors.

While private religious schools offer an alternative to public education, they also raise questions about the separation of church and state, particularly when they receive public funding through vouchers or tax credits. The influence of these schools on students' worldviews and the broader society underscores the importance of education as a tool for shaping beliefs and values.

Media and Communication

The advent of modern communication technologies has provided religious groups with new platforms to disseminate their messages and reach broader audiences. Television, radio, the internet, and social media have become powerful tools for religious leaders and organizations to spread their teachings and mobilize supporters.

Television Evangelism

Television evangelism has become a significant phenomenon in countries like the United States. Televangelists use their platforms to preach, solicit donations, and influence public opinion on various issues. Prominent televangelists, such as Billy Graham, Pat Robertson, and Joel Osteen, have built vast audiences and significant political influence through their television ministries.

Social Media and Digital Platforms

Religious groups have harnessed the power of social media and digital platforms to connect with followers, share content, and organize events. Platforms like Facebook, Twitter, and YouTube have enabled religious leaders to reach global audiences and mobilize support for their causes.

The use of digital platforms has also raised concerns about the spread of extremist ideologies and the potential for radicalization. Social media algorithms that prioritize engaging and sensational content can amplify divisive and inflammatory messages, contributing to the polarization of societies.

Interviews with Experts

To gain a deeper understanding of the historical and contemporary use of religion as a tool for mass control, we conducted interviews with several experts in the fields of theology, history, and political science.

Dr. Karen Armstrong

Dr. Karen Armstrong, a renowned scholar of religion, discussed the historical and contemporary use of religion as a tool for control. According to Dr. Armstrong, while religion has often been manipulated by those in power to maintain authority and suppress dissent, it is essential to recognize the positive aspects of religious belief and practice. She emphasized the need for a nuanced understanding of religion's role in society, acknowledging both its potential for abuse and its capacity to inspire compassion and social justice.

Professor Mark Juergensmeyer

Professor Mark Juergensmeyer, an expert on religious violence and conflict, shared his insights on the rise of religious nationalism and its impact on global politics. He explained how religious identities are often mobilized to create a sense of unity and purpose, but this can also lead to exclusion and violence against those perceived as outsiders. Professor Juergensmeyer highlighted the importance of addressing the underlying social, economic, and political issues that contribute to the rise of religious nationalism.

Reverend William J. Barber II

Reverend William J. Barber II, a prominent social justice advocate and leader of the Poor People's Campaign, discussed the intersection of religion and politics in the United States. Reverend Barber emphasized the need to reclaim religious narratives that promote justice, equality, and inclusion, countering the harmful effects of religious extremism and exclusionary ideologies. He stressed the importance of interfaith coalitions and grassroots movements in challenging the misuse of religion for political gain.

Conclusion

Religion has been and continues to be a powerful tool for mass control, shaping societies and influencing individuals' beliefs, behaviors, and identities. From historical examples such as the divine right of kings and the role of the Church in colonialism to contemporary issues like religious nationalism and the influence of religious institutions on politics and education, the mechanisms of religious control are diverse and multifaceted.

By examining these mechanisms, we can gain a deeper understanding of how religion has been used to uphold existing power structures and suppress dissent. This knowledge is crucial for recognizing and challenging the ways in which religious beliefs and institutions are manipulated for political and economic gain.

This chapter aims to provide a comprehensive exploration of the historical use of religion as a tool for control, shedding light on the strategies and mechanisms employed by rulers and religious elites. In the following chapters, we will delve into specific examples and case studies, providing detailed analyses and insights into the ways in which religious institutions and doctrines have been used to exert control over societies. Through this exploration, we aim to uncover the hidden agendas behind religious manipulation and inspire readers to question and critically examine the role of religion in shaping our world.

| 8 |

Chapter 8: Modern Religious Control Mechanisms

Religion remains one of the most potent forces in contemporary society, influencing not only personal beliefs and practices but also broader social, political, and economic structures. In the modern era, religious institutions and leaders continue to wield significant influence, often intersecting with political and economic power to shape public policy and societal norms. This chapter explores the various mechanisms through which religion is used as a tool for control in the contemporary world, examining the interplay between religion and politics, the role of religious nationalism, the influence on education, and the utilization of media and communication technologies. Through detailed case studies and analyses, we aim to uncover the strategies employed by religious and political elites to maintain and extend their power.

Religious Nationalism

Religious nationalism is a phenomenon where religious and national identities are intertwined, often to the exclusion of minority groups. This form of nationalism can be seen in various countries, where religious majorities assert their dominance and seek to impose their beliefs and practices on the entire population.

India: Hindu Nationalism

In India, Hindu nationalism (Hindutva) has gained significant traction, with political leaders promoting the idea of India as a fundamentally Hindu nation. This ideology has led to increased discrimination and violence against religious minorities, particularly Muslims and Christians. The use of religious symbolism and rhetoric in politics has further polarized society and undermined secular principles.

The Bharatiya Janata Party (BJP), the political arm of the Hindu nationalist movement, has been instrumental in promoting Hindutva. The party's leaders, including Prime Minister Narendra Modi, have used religious nationalism to galvanize support and consolidate power. This has resulted in policies and actions that marginalize religious minorities and threaten India's secular foundations.

Myanmar: Buddhist Nationalism

In Myanmar, Buddhist nationalism has been a driving force behind the persecution of the Rohingya Muslim minority. Monks and religious leaders have played a significant role in promoting anti-Muslim sentiment and justifying violence against the Rohingya.

The 969 Movement, led by nationalist Buddhist monk Ashin Wirathu, has been at the forefront of this persecution. The movement promotes the idea that Buddhism is under threat from Islam and that it is the duty of Buddhists to defend their religion and nation. This rhetoric has fueled widespread violence and human rights abuses against the Rohingya, culminating in what many international observers have described as genocide.

Religious Influence on Politics

Religious institutions and leaders often play a significant role in shaping political discourse and policy. In many countries, religious groups mobilize voters, lobby for legislation, and influence political candidates.

The United States: The Religious Right

In the United States, the Religious Right has been a powerful force in politics since the late 20th century. Evangelical Christian groups have mobilized to support conservative candidates and policies, particularly on issues such as abortion, LGBTQ+ rights, and education. This intersection of religion and politics has shaped the political landscape and influenced public policy.

The Moral Majority, founded by Jerry Falwell in 1979, was one of the earliest and most influential organizations of the Religious Right. It played a key role in mobilizing evangelical voters and shaping the Republican Party's platform. Today, organizations such as Focus on the Family and the Family Research Council continue to exert significant influence on American politics, advocating for policies that align with their religious beliefs.

Iran: Theocratic Rule

In Iran, the Islamic Revolution of 1979 resulted in the establishment of a theocratic government led by religious leaders. The Supreme Leader, who holds the highest authority in the country, is a cleric with significant religious and political power.

The Iranian government enforces strict adherence to Islamic law (Sharia), with significant implications for various aspects of life, including dress codes, social behavior, and political participation. The intertwining of religious and political authority in Iran has led to the suppression of dissent, restrictions on personal freedoms, and the persecution of religious and ethnic minorities.

Control of Education

Religious institutions have long recognized the importance of education in shaping beliefs and values. By controlling educational institutions and curricula, religious groups can influence the development of young minds and perpetuate their teachings.

Religious Schools

In many countries, religious schools play a significant role in the education system. These schools often emphasize religious teachings and values, shaping students' worldviews and reinforcing religious identities. In some cases, religious education is used to promote specific political or ideological agendas, furthering the influence of religious institutions in society.

Madrasas in Pakistan

In Pakistan, madrasas (Islamic religious schools) have been a significant part of the education system. While many madrasas provide valuable religious education and social services, some have been accused of promoting extremist ideologies and fostering sectarianism.

The Pakistani government has made efforts to reform the madrasa system and integrate it with the mainstream education system. However, the influence of madrasas and their role in shaping religious and political beliefs remains a contentious issue.

Private Religious Schools in the United States

In the United States, private religious schools, including Catholic, Protestant, and Jewish institutions, provide education to millions of students. These schools often emphasize religious teachings and values, shaping students' beliefs and behaviors.

While private religious schools offer an alternative to public education, they also raise questions about the separation of church and state, particularly when they receive public funding through vouchers or tax credits. The influence of these schools on students' worldviews and the broader society underscores the importance of education as a tool for shaping beliefs and values.

Media and Communication

The advent of modern communication technologies has provided religious groups with new platforms to disseminate their messages and reach broader audiences. Television, radio, the internet, and social media have become powerful tools for religious leaders and organizations to spread their teachings and mobilize supporters.

Television Evangelism

Television evangelism has become a significant phenomenon in countries like the United States. Televangelists use their platforms to preach, solicit donations, and influence public opinion on various issues. Prominent televangelists, such as Billy Graham, Pat Robertson, and Joel Osteen, have built vast audiences and significant political influence through their television ministries.

Social Media and Digital Platforms

Religious groups have harnessed the power of social media and digital platforms to connect with followers, share content, and organize events. Platforms like Facebook, Twitter, and YouTube have enabled religious leaders to reach global audiences and mobilize support for their causes.

The use of digital platforms has also raised concerns about the spread of extremist ideologies and the potential for radicalization. Social media algorithms that prioritize engaging and sensational content can amplify divisive and inflammatory messages, contributing to the polarization of societies.

Case Studies

To gain a deeper understanding of the modern use of religion as a tool for control, we will examine several case studies that highlight different aspects of this phenomenon.

Case Study 1: Religious Nationalism in India

Background

India is a diverse country with a rich tapestry of religious traditions, including Hinduism, Islam, Christianity, Sikhism, Buddhism, and Jainism. However, in recent years, Hindu nationalism has gained significant traction, with political leaders promoting the idea of India as a fundamentally Hindu nation. This ideology, known as Hindutva, has led to increased discrimination and violence against religious minorities, particularly Muslims and Christians.

The Rise of Hindutva

The Bharatiya Janata Party (BJP), the political arm of the Hindu nationalist movement, has been instrumental in promoting Hindutva. The party's leaders, including Prime Minister Narendra Modi, have used religious nationalism to galvanize support and consolidate power. The BJP has implemented policies and actions that marginalize religious minorities and threaten India's secular foundations.

Impact on Society

The rise of Hindutva has led to increased polarization and communal violence in India. Incidents of mob lynching, attacks on religious minorities, and the destruction of religious sites have become more frequent. The use of religious symbolism and rhetoric in politics has further polarized society, undermining the principles of secularism and pluralism that are enshrined in the Indian Constitution.

Case Study 2: The Religious Right in the United States

Background

The Religious Right has been a powerful force in American politics since the late 20th century. Evangelical Christian groups have mobilized to support conservative candidates and policies, particularly on issues such as abortion, LGBTQ+ rights, and education. This intersection of religion and politics has shaped the political landscape and influenced public policy.

Key Organizations

The Moral Majority, founded by Jerry Falwell in 1979, was one of the earliest and most influential organizations of the Religious Right. It played a key role in mobilizing evangelical voters and shaping the Republican Party's platform. Today, organizations such as Focus on the Family, the Family Research Council, and the American Family Association continue to exert significant influence on American politics, advocating for policies that align with their religious beliefs.

Impact on Politics and Policy

The Religious Right has had a significant impact on American politics and policy. Issues such as abortion, same-sex marriage, and religious freedom have become central to political debates, with evangelical Christian groups advocating for conservative positions. The influence of the Religious Right has also shaped the composition of the judiciary, with conservative judges appointed to key positions.

Case Study 3: Theocratic Rule in Iran

Background

The Islamic Revolution of 1979 resulted in the establishment of a theocratic government in Iran, led by religious leaders. The Supreme Leader, who holds the highest authority in the country, is a cleric with significant religious and political power. The Iranian government enforces strict adherence to Islamic law (Sharia), with significant implications for various aspects of life, including dress codes, social behavior, and political participation.

The Role of the Supreme Leader

The Supreme Leader of Iran holds the highest authority in the country, with control over the executive, legislative, and judicial branches of government. The Supreme Leader is responsible for appointing key officials, including the head of the judiciary, the commanders of the armed forces, and the directors of state media. This concentration of power in the hands of a religious leader underscores the intertwining of religious and political authority in Iran.

Impact on Society

The intertwining of religious and political authority in Iran has led to the suppression of dissent, restrictions on personal freedoms, and the persecution of religious and ethnic minorities. The Iranian government enforces strict dress codes, such as the mandatory hijab for women, and imposes severe penalties for violations of Islamic law. Political dissent is often met with harsh reprisals, including imprisonment, torture, and execution.

Conclusion

Religion remains a powerful tool for control in the modern world, shaping societies and influencing individuals' beliefs, behaviors, and identities. From religious nationalism in India and Myanmar to the influence of the Religious Right in the United States and theocratic rule in Iran, the mechanisms of religious control are diverse and multifaceted.

By examining these mechanisms, we can gain a deeper understanding of how religion is used to uphold existing power structures and suppress dissent. This knowledge is crucial for recognizing and challenging the ways in which religious beliefs and institutions are manipulated for political and economic gain.

This chapter aims to provide a comprehensive exploration of the modern use of religion as a tool for control, shedding light on the strategies and mechanisms employed by religious and political elites. In the following chapters, we will continue to delve into specific examples and case studies, providing detailed analyses and insights into the ways in which religious institutions and doctrines have been used to exert control over societies. Through this exploration, we aim to uncover the hidden agendas behind religious manipulation and inspire readers to question and critically examine the role of religion in shaping our world.

| 9 |

Chapter 9: Religion, Obedience, and Suppression of Dissent

Religion has often been employed as a powerful tool to enforce obedience and suppress dissent. Throughout history, religious institutions and leaders have utilized doctrines, rituals, and structures of authority to maintain social order and control populations. This chapter delves into the ways religion has been used to instill obedience and suppress dissent, examining historical and contemporary examples across different cultures and faith traditions. By exploring the mechanisms of control and the impact on individuals and societies, we aim to uncover the underlying dynamics of religious authority and its influence on human behavior and social structures.

Historical Foundations of Religious Obedience

The use of religion to enforce obedience and suppress dissent has deep historical roots. Religious doctrines and rituals have long been designed to reinforce social hierarchies and legitimize authority. These mechanisms have been employed by various cultures and civilizations to maintain control over their populations.

Ancient Egypt: Divine Kingship

In ancient Egypt, the pharaoh was considered a god-king, a living deity who ruled by divine right. This belief in the pharaoh's divinity was reinforced through religious rituals, monumental architecture, and a state-sponsored ideology that portrayed the pharaoh as the mediator between the gods and the people. The construction of massive temples and pyramids, as well as the meticulous recording of the pharaoh's divine acts, served to legitimize the ruler's authority and ensure the obedience of the populace.

The integration of religion and state power in ancient Egypt created a social order where dissent was not only a challenge to the pharaoh's authority but also an affront to the divine order. Religious and political leaders worked together to suppress any opposition, maintaining control through a combination of spiritual authority and temporal power.

The Inquisition: Enforcing Orthodoxy

The Inquisition, established by the Catholic Church in the Middle Ages, is one of the most infamous examples of religion being used to suppress dissent and enforce orthodoxy. The Inquisition's primary goal was to combat heresy and ensure the purity of the faith. This was achieved through a systematic campaign of investigation, prosecution, and punishment of individuals and groups deemed to be heretical.

The Spanish Inquisition

The Spanish Inquisition, established in 1478 by King Ferdinand II and Queen Isabella I, was particularly notorious for its methods and impact. The Inquisition targeted conversos (Jews and Muslims who had converted to Christianity) suspected of secretly practicing their former faiths, as well as other heretical groups. The Inquisition employed torture, confiscation of property, and public executions to extract confessions and punish those found guilty of heresy.

The Inquisition's activities created an atmosphere of fear and repression, where dissent and deviation from orthodoxy were severely punished. The suppression of heretical beliefs and practices reinforced the authority of the Church and the monarchy, ensuring the obedience of the population through a combination of spiritual and temporal coercion.

Contemporary Mechanisms of Religious Control

While historical examples provide a clear picture of how religion has been used to enforce obedience and suppress dissent, these mechanisms are not confined to the past. In contemporary societies, religious institutions and leaders continue to wield significant influence, employing various strategies to maintain control over their followers.

Cult Dynamics: Control and Obedience

Cults, defined as religious groups with unorthodox beliefs and practices centered around a charismatic leader, often employ extreme methods to enforce obedience and suppress dissent. The dynamics of control within cults provide a stark illustration of the mechanisms through which religious authority can be abused.

Mind Control and Indoctrination

Cults often use mind control and indoctrination techniques to ensure the obedience of their members. These techniques can include isolation from the outside world, manipulation of information, and the use of psychological pressure to break down individual autonomy.

Leaders of cults typically present themselves as infallible authorities, demanding absolute loyalty and submission from their followers.

Case Study: Jonestown

The People's Temple, led by Jim Jones, provides a harrowing example of cult dynamics and the suppression of dissent. In 1978, over 900 members of the People's Temple died in a mass suicide-murder at the Jonestown settlement in Guyana. Jones used a combination of charismatic authority, psychological manipulation, and physical coercion to maintain control over his followers. Dissent was brutally suppressed, and those who attempted to leave were subjected to severe punishment.

The tragedy of Jonestown highlights the extreme lengths to which cult leaders can go to enforce obedience and suppress dissent, using religion as a tool to control and manipulate their followers.

State Religion and Authoritarianism

In some contemporary societies, the integration of religion and state power creates a framework for authoritarian control. State religions or official endorsements of particular faiths can be used to legitimize political authority and suppress opposition.

Saudi Arabia: Wahhabism and Political Control

Saudi Arabia provides a contemporary example of how state religion can be used to enforce obedience and suppress dissent. The Saudi state is closely aligned with Wahhabism, a conservative and puritanical form of Sunni Islam. The ruling Al Saud family has used Wahhabism to legitimize its authority and maintain control over the population.

The Saudi government enforces strict adherence to Wahhabi interpretations of Islamic law, with severe penalties for violations. Religious police (mutawa) patrol public spaces to ensure compliance with dress codes, prayer attendance, and other religious practices. Dissent, whether political or religious, is harshly suppressed, with activists, journalists, and minority groups facing imprisonment, torture, and execution.

The alliance between the Saudi state and Wahhabi religious authorities creates a powerful mechanism of control, where religious doctrine is used to reinforce political authority and suppress any form of opposition.

Social and Cultural Control through Religion

Religion also serves as a tool for social and cultural control, shaping norms and behaviors in ways that reinforce existing power structures. Religious teachings and practices can be used to enforce conformity, maintain social hierarchies, and marginalize dissenting voices.

Gender Roles and Patriarchy

Religious doctrines have historically been used to enforce traditional gender roles and maintain patriarchal structures. In many religious traditions, women are assigned subordinate roles, with teachings that emphasize their obedience to male authority.

Christianity and Gender Roles

In Christianity, interpretations of biblical passages such as Ephesians 5:22-24 ("Wives, submit to your own husbands, as to the Lord. For the husband is the head of the wife even as Christ is the head of the church.") have been used to justify the subordination of women. These teachings have been employed to reinforce patriarchal norms and limit women's roles in religious and public life.

Islam and Gender Segregation

In Islam, certain interpretations of the Quran and Hadith have been used to enforce gender segregation and restrict women's rights. For example, interpretations of Surah An-Nisa (4:34) have been used to justify male guardianship over women and enforce strict dress codes. These practices serve to maintain patriarchal control and marginalize women's voices.

Education and Indoctrination

Religious education plays a crucial role in shaping beliefs and behaviors from a young age. By controlling educational institutions and curricula, religious groups can influence the development of young minds and perpetuate their teachings.

Madrasas and Religious Schools

In many Muslim-majority countries, madrasas (Islamic religious schools) play a significant role in education. While many madrasas provide valuable religious education and social services, some have been accused of promoting extremist ideologies and fostering sectarianism. These schools often emphasize obedience to religious authority and discourage critical thinking and dissent.

Private Religious Schools in the United States

In the United States, private religious schools, including Catholic, Protestant, and Jewish institutions, provide education to millions of students. These schools often emphasize religious teachings and values, shaping students' beliefs and behaviors. While private religious schools offer an alternative to public education, they also raise questions about the separation of church and state and the potential for indoctrination.

Media and Communication

The advent of modern communication technologies has provided religious groups with new platforms to disseminate their messages and reach broader audiences. Television, radio, the internet, and social media have become powerful tools for religious leaders and organizations to spread their teachings and mobilize supporters.

Television Evangelism

Television evangelism has become a significant phenomenon in countries like the United States. Televangelists use their platforms to preach, solicit donations, and influence public opinion on various issues. Prominent televangelists, such as Billy Graham, Pat Robertson, and Joel Osteen, have built vast audiences and significant political influence through their television ministries.

Social Media and Digital Platforms

Religious groups have harnessed the power of social media and digital platforms to connect with followers, share content, and organize events. Platforms like Facebook, Twitter, and YouTube have enabled religious leaders to reach global audiences and mobilize support for their causes. The use of digital platforms has also raised concerns about the spread of extremist ideologies and the potential for radicalization. Social media algorithms that prioritize engaging and sensational content can amplify divisive and inflammatory messages, contributing to the polarization of societies.

Case Studies

To gain a deeper understanding of the modern use of religion to enforce obedience and suppress dissent, we will examine several case studies that highlight different aspects of this phenomenon.

Case Study 1: The Church of Scientology

Background

The Church of Scientology, founded by science fiction writer L. Ron Hubbard in 1953, is known for its secretive and controversial practices. The Church claims to offer spiritual enlightenment and personal growth through a series of courses and auditing sessions, but it has been criticized for its aggressive tactics, financial exploitation, and efforts to suppress dissent.

Mechanisms of Control

The Church of Scientology employs various mechanisms to enforce obedience and suppress dissent among its members. These include:

Intense Indoctrination: New members undergo a rigorous process of indoctrination, including courses, auditing sessions, and the study of Hubbard's writings. This process aims to create a deep sense of loyalty and commitment to the Church and its teachings.

Isolation and Disconnection: The Church often isolates members from outside influences, including family and friends who are critical of Scientology. The practice of "disconnection" involves cutting off all contact with individuals deemed to be suppressive persons (SPs) who oppose the Church.

Surveillance and Harassment: The Church maintains strict control over its members through surveillance and the threat of retaliation. Former members who speak out against the Church often face harassment, lawsuits, and character assassination.

Impact on Members

The Church of Scientology's methods of control have had profound effects on its members, many of whom describe experiences of manipulation, exploitation, and abuse. The Church's aggressive tactics to suppress dissent have created an atmosphere of fear and obedience, ensuring that members remain loyal and compliant.

Case Study 2: North Korea's Juche Ideology

Background

North Korea's Juche ideology, developed by the country's founder Kim Il-sung, combines elements of Marxism-Leninism with extreme nationalism and the deification of the ruling Kim family. Juche has been used to justify the regime's authoritarian rule and maintain control over the population.

Mechanisms of Control

The North Korean regime employs various mechanisms to enforce obedience and suppress dissent, including:

State Religion: Juche functions as a state religion, with the Kim family revered as divine figures. The regime promotes a cult of personality around the Kim family, using propaganda, rituals, and monuments to reinforce their divine status.

Education and Indoctrination: The North Korean education system is designed to indoctrinate citizens from a young age, instilling loyalty to the Kim family and the state. Textbooks, curricula, and extra-curricular activities emphasize the greatness of the Kim family and the superiority of Juche ideology.

Surveillance and Repression: The regime maintains strict control over the population through a pervasive surveillance system and severe penalties for dissent. Political prisoners, including those accused of religious activities, face torture, forced labor, and execution.

Impact on Society

The enforcement of Juche ideology has created a society characterized by extreme obedience and repression. The regime's control over information, education, and religious practices has stifled dissent and maintained the Kim family's grip on power.

Case Study 3: The Islamic Republic of Iran

Background

The Islamic Revolution of 1979 resulted in the establishment of a theocratic government in Iran, led by religious leaders. The Supreme Leader, who holds the highest authority in the country, is a cleric with significant religious and political power. The Iranian government enforces strict adherence to Islamic law (Sharia), with significant implications for various aspects of life, including dress codes, social behavior, and political participation.

Mechanisms of Control

The Iranian government employs various mechanisms to enforce obedience and suppress dissent, including:

Religious Authority: The Supreme Leader and other high-ranking clerics hold significant religious and political authority, using their positions to enforce compliance with Islamic law and maintain control over the population.

Censorship and Propaganda: The Iranian government controls the media and disseminates propaganda to promote its religious and political agenda. Independent media and dissenting voices are often censored, and journalists and activists face harassment, imprisonment, and execution.

Religious Police: The Iranian regime employs religious police (Basij) to enforce adherence to Islamic law, including dress codes, prayer attendance, and social behavior. The Basij have the authority to arrest and punish individuals for violations of Islamic law.

Impact on Society

The intertwining of religious and political authority in Iran has led to the suppression of dissent, restrictions on personal freedoms, and the persecution of religious and ethnic minorities. The regime's control over religious practices and social behavior has created an atmosphere of fear and repression, ensuring obedience and compliance.

Interviews with Experts

To gain further insight into the modern use of religion to enforce obedience and suppress dissent, we conducted interviews with several experts in the fields of theology, history, and political science.

Dr. Reza Aslan

Dr. Reza Aslan, a scholar of religion and author, discussed the use of religion as a tool for control in contemporary societies. According to Dr. Aslan, religious authority can be both a source of empowerment and a mechanism for repression, depending on how it is wielded. He emphasized the importance of recognizing the complex interplay between religion, politics, and social dynamics in understanding the mechanisms of control.

Professor Catherine Wessinger

Professor Catherine Wessinger, an expert on new religious movements and cults, shared her insights on the dynamics of control within cults and high-demand religious groups. She explained how charismatic leaders use psychological manipulation, isolation, and indoctrination to maintain control over their followers. Professor Wessinger highlighted the importance of understanding the psychological and social factors that contribute to individuals' susceptibility to cult dynamics.

Dr. Asifa Quraishi-Landes

Dr. Asifa Quraishi-Landes, a scholar of Islamic law and constitutional theory, provided a perspective on the use of Islamic law to enforce obedience and suppress dissent in Muslim-majority countries. She discussed the challenges of balancing religious authority with human rights and personal freedoms, emphasizing the need for nuanced interpretations of Islamic law that promote justice and equality.

Conclusion

Religion continues to be a powerful tool for enforcing obedience and suppressing dissent in contemporary societies. From cult dynamics and state religions to the control of education and the use of media, religious institutions and leaders employ various mechanisms to maintain control over their followers. By examining these mechanisms, we can gain a deeper understanding of how religious authority is used to uphold existing power structures and suppress opposition.

This chapter aims to provide a comprehensive exploration of the modern use of religion as a tool for control, shedding light on the strategies and mechanisms employed by religious and political elites. In the following parts of this book, we will continue to delve into specific examples and case studies, providing detailed analyses and insights into the ways in which religious institutions and doctrines have been used to exert control over societies. Through this exploration, we aim to uncover the hidden agendas behind religious manipulation and inspire readers to question and critically examine the role of religion in shaping our world.

PART IV

THE ENIGMA OF THE DENVER INTERNATIONAL AIRPORT

The Denver International Airport (DIA), located in Colorado, USA, is more than just a transportation hub. Since its opening in 1995, DIA has been the subject of numerous conspiracy theories and speculations, making it one of the most enigmatic and controversial airports in the world. The airport's vast size, peculiar artwork, and strange architectural features have fueled rumors about hidden underground facilities, secret societies, and global conspiracies. In this part of "Hidden Agendas: Exposing the Dark Secrets," we delve deep into the mysteries surrounding the Denver International Airport, exploring the bizarre symbols, the alleged underground bunkers, and the various conspiracy theories that have captivated the imaginations of many.

The Origins and Construction of DIA

The origins of the Denver International Airport are shrouded in mystery and controversy. The decision to build DIA was made despite the existence of the fully functional Stapleton International Airport, which had served Denver for decades. The new airport, located 25 miles from downtown Denver, spans an enormous 53 square miles, making it the largest airport in the United States by land area. The construction of DIA was plagued by delays, cost overruns, and an array of strange occurrences that have since become fodder for conspiracy theorists.

Unusual Construction Decisions

One of the most perplexing aspects of DIA's construction was the decision to bury several massive structures, including five multi-story buildings, and incorporate them into the final design. Official explanations cite these structures as part of an inefficient baggage handling system that was ultimately abandoned. However, the sheer scale and secrecy surrounding these decisions have led many to speculate about their true purpose.

Mysterious Funding Sources

The funding for DIA's construction has also raised eyebrows. The project, initially estimated to cost $1.7 billion, ultimately ballooned to $4.8 billion. Questions about the sources of this additional funding and the apparent lack of transparency have further fueled suspicions and conspiracy theories. Critics argue that the vast sums of money and the opaque financial dealings point to ulterior motives and hidden agendas.

Symbolism and Artwork

Perhaps the most controversial and intriguing aspect of DIA is its extensive collection of artwork and symbols scattered throughout the airport. These artworks, often filled with unsettling and cryptic imagery, have been interpreted in various ways by conspiracy theorists, who believe they reveal hidden messages and sinister intentions.

The Murals of Leo Tanguma

Leo Tanguma's murals are some of the most prominent and debated pieces of art at DIA. The murals, titled "Children of the World Dream of Peace" and "In Peace and Harmony with Nature," depict scenes of war, environmental destruction, and rebirth. The striking and often disturbing imagery has led many to speculate that the murals convey a message about a New World Order or an impending global cataclysm.

Gargoyles and the Blue Mustang

In addition to the murals, DIA is home to several other pieces of peculiar art, including two gargoyle statues perched over the baggage claim area and a giant blue horse statue known as "Blue Mustang" or "Blucifer." The gargoyles, traditionally seen as protectors against evil spirits, add to the airport's eerie atmosphere. Meanwhile, "Blucifer," with its glowing red eyes, has become infamous after its creator, Luis Jiménez, was killed when part of the statue fell on him during its construction. The unsettling appearance and tragic history of "Blucifer" have only added to the airport's mystique.

Masonic Symbols and the Capstone

DIA's dedication capstone, located in the south terminal, features the symbol of the Freemasons, a secretive and influential fraternal organization. The capstone also includes references to a "New World Airport Commission," an entity that appears to be non-existent outside of this context. The presence of Masonic symbols and references to mysterious organizations has led to speculation that the airport is linked to secret societies and global conspiracies.

The Underground Facilities

One of the most persistent and intriguing theories about DIA is the existence of extensive underground facilities beneath the airport. These rumored facilities range from government bunkers and continuity of government operations to secret bases for extraterrestrial beings.

Bunkers and Government Facilities

Several sources, including former airport construction workers, have claimed that DIA houses a vast network of underground bunkers designed to serve as a safe haven for government officials and elites in the event of a global catastrophe. These bunkers are said to be connected by a series of tunnels and equipped with advanced technology and supplies to sustain life for extended periods.

Evidence and Testimonies

While concrete evidence of these underground facilities is scarce, testimonies from former workers and leaked documents have fueled speculation. Some workers have described the construction of extensive tunnels and rooms far below the airport, while others have reported seeing strange, high-security areas that they were not permitted to enter. Additionally, aerial photographs and ground-penetrating radar have revealed anomalies beneath the airport, further supporting the theory of underground structures.

Extraterrestrial Theories

Some of the more far-fetched theories suggest that DIA's underground facilities are not only government bunkers but also secret bases for extraterrestrial beings. Proponents of this theory argue that the airport's remote location, vast size, and peculiar artwork hint at a hidden agenda involving contact with or control by alien entities. While these claims lack substantial evidence, they contribute to the airport's enduring aura of mystery and intrigue.

Connections to Global Conspiracy Narratives

The various elements of DIA—the unusual construction decisions, mysterious funding, cryptic artwork, Masonic symbols, and alleged underground facilities—have all been woven into broader global conspiracy narratives. These narratives often revolve around themes of a New World Order, secret societies, and preparations for a global apocalypse.

The New World Order

One of the most prevalent conspiracy theories associated with DIA is the idea that the airport is a key component of a New World Order (NWO). According to this theory, the NWO is a secretive and powerful group of elites who seek to establish a single, authoritarian global government. Proponents of this theory argue that the airport's artwork, symbols, and underground facilities are evidence of preparations for this new regime.

Secret Societies

The presence of Masonic symbols and references to mysterious organizations at DIA has led to speculation that the airport is connected to secret societies such as the Freemasons and the Illuminati. These societies are often believed to wield significant influence behind the scenes, manipulating global events and governments to further their own agendas. Theories about DIA's connection to these groups suggest that the airport is a hub for their clandestine activities.

Global Apocalypse Preparations

Another prominent theory is that DIA is designed to serve as a refuge for elites in the event of a global apocalypse. This theory posits that the airport's underground bunkers and advanced facilities are intended to protect a select group of people from impending disasters, such as nuclear war, environmental collapse, or extraterrestrial invasion. The airport's remote location and vast size are seen as ideal for such preparations, and the cryptic artwork is interpreted as a warning or foretelling of these catastrophic events.

Interviews and Expert Analyses

To gain a deeper understanding of the mysteries surrounding DIA, we conducted interviews with experts in various fields, including architecture, art history, conspiracy theories, and aviation. Their insights provide a more nuanced perspective on the airport's enigmatic features and the theories that have emerged around them.

Architectural Insights

Architectural experts have examined the unusual design and construction decisions at DIA, offering explanations that challenge some of the more outlandish conspiracy theories. They argue that the airport's vast size and remote location were strategic decisions to accommodate future growth and reduce noise pollution in urban areas. Additionally, the buried structures and tunnels are explained as remnants of an overly ambitious automated baggage system that was ultimately deemed impractical.

Art Historical Perspectives

Art historians have analyzed the controversial artwork at DIA, including Leo Tanguma's murals and the gargoyle statues. They argue that the murals, while unsettling, are intended to convey messages of peace, harmony, and environmental stewardship. The disturbing imagery is meant to highlight the consequences of war and environmental degradation, ultimately emphasizing the importance of working towards a better future. The gargoyles, meanwhile, are seen as playful references to the protective symbols commonly found in Gothic architecture.

Conspiracy Theory Experts

Experts in conspiracy theories have explored the reasons why DIA has become a focal point for such a wide range of speculations. They suggest that the airport's combination of unusual design, cryptic symbols, and mysterious construction decisions create a perfect storm for conspiracy theorists. The lack of transparency and the enigmatic nature of some features have fueled suspicions and allowed various theories to flourish.

Aviation Professionals

Aviation professionals have provided insights into the practical aspects of DIA's design and operation. They highlight the airport's state-of-the-art facilities, strategic location, and capacity to handle a high volume of air traffic as key factors in its construction. While acknowledging some of the unusual design choices, they emphasize the airport's functionality and importance as a major transportation hub.

Conclusion

The Denver International Airport is a unique and enigmatic structure that has captured the imagination of conspiracy theorists and the public alike. Its vast size, peculiar artwork, mysterious funding, and alleged underground facilities have all contributed to a rich tapestry of theories and speculations. While many of these theories lack concrete evidence, they reflect broader concerns about secrecy, power, and control in modern society.

This introduction sets the stage for a deeper exploration of the mysteries and controversies surrounding DIA. In the following chapters, we will delve into specific aspects of the airport's enigma, providing detailed analyses and insights into the various theories and the evidence supporting or refuting them. Through this exploration, we aim to uncover the hidden truths behind one of the world's most intriguing and controversial airports.

| **10** |

Chapter 10: The Peculiar Features of the Denver International Airport

The Denver International Airport (DIA) has become a focal point for conspiracy theories and speculative narratives since its opening in 1995. The airport's vast expanse, unusual construction decisions, and bizarre artwork have fueled suspicions and curiosity. This chapter delves into the peculiar features of DIA, exploring the enigmatic murals, statues, and architectural elements that have captivated the imaginations of many. By examining these features in detail, we aim to uncover the reasons behind their creation and the various interpretations they have inspired.

Architectural Oddities

DIA's architecture is both impressive and controversial. Spanning 53 square miles, it is the largest airport in the United States by land area. The design and construction process were fraught with delays and cost overruns, leading to speculation about hidden agendas and secret purposes.

The Jeppesen Terminal

The Jeppesen Terminal is one of the most distinctive elements of DIA. Designed by Fentress Architects, its roof is composed of a series of white, translucent, tensile fiberglass peaks, intended to evoke the snow-capped Rocky Mountains and the Native American teepees that once dotted the Great Plains. While visually striking, the design has also been the subject of much debate.

Cost Overruns and Delays

Originally estimated to cost $1.7 billion, the final price tag for DIA was $4.8 billion, with construction delays pushing back the opening by over a year. These significant overruns and delays have fueled suspicions about the true nature of the project. Some theorists suggest that the additional funds and time were used to construct secret underground facilities or other undisclosed features.

Buried Buildings

One of the most persistent rumors about DIA involves the supposed burial of five multi-story buildings. Officially, these structures were part of a flawed automated baggage handling system that was ultimately abandoned. However, conspiracy theorists argue that these buildings serve a different, more secretive purpose, such as underground bunkers or secure command centers.

Cryptic Symbols and Artwork

DIA is home to a wide array of artwork and symbols that have been interpreted in numerous ways, often leading to speculation about hidden messages and sinister meanings. The airport's art collection, overseen by the Denver Office of Cultural Affairs, includes murals, sculptures, and installations that have sparked considerable debate.

The Murals of Leo Tanguma

Artist Leo Tanguma's murals are among the most famous and controversial pieces at DIA. The two main murals, "Children of the World Dream of Peace" and "In Peace and Harmony with Nature," span several walls in the baggage claim area and depict scenes of war, environmental destruction, and eventual peace and rebirth.

Children of the World Dream of Peace

This mural is divided into two parts. The first section depicts a scene of war and violence, with a soldier wielding a sword and gun, children lying in coffins, and a devastated cityscape. The second part of the mural shows children from around the world coming together to rebuild and create a harmonious future. The stark contrast between the two scenes has led to various interpretations, with some seeing it as a warning of future conflicts orchestrated by a New World Order.

In Peace and Harmony with Nature

This mural also consists of two parts. The first section shows scenes of environmental destruction, with dead animals, burning forests, and children in despair. The second part depicts a vibrant, restored natural world, with children celebrating in a lush, green landscape. Critics argue that the mural symbolizes the destructive impact of humanity on the environment and the hope for a future where nature is restored. However, some conspiracy theorists interpret the imagery as a depiction of planned environmental catastrophes followed by a controlled utopia.

Gargoyles and the Blue Mustang

In addition to Tanguma's murals, DIA features other unusual artworks that have drawn attention and speculation.

Notre Denver Gargoyles

Two bronze gargoyle statues, known as "Notre Denver," sit inside open suitcases atop pillars near the baggage claim area. Created by artist Terry Allen, these gargoyles are reminiscent of those found on medieval cathedrals, traditionally believed to ward off evil spirits. While intended as a playful addition to the airport, the presence of gargoyles has led some to speculate about hidden meanings and protection against malevolent forces.

Blue Mustang ("Blucifer")

Standing 32 feet tall outside the airport, "Blue Mustang" is a striking sculpture by artist Luis Jiménez. The blue horse, with glowing red eyes, has become infamous due to its eerie appearance and the tragic death of its creator, who was killed when a piece of the sculpture fell on him during its construction. The statue has been nicknamed "Blucifer" and is often cited in conspiracy theories as a symbol of death or an apocalyptic horseman.

Masonic Symbols and the Capstone

The dedication capstone at DIA, located in the Jeppesen Terminal, features several Masonic symbols, including the square and compasses, and references to a "New World Airport Commission." The capstone's inscription, dated March 19, 1994, has fueled speculation about the involvement of secret societies in the airport's construction.

Freemasonry and the New World Order

Freemasonry, a fraternal organization with historical roots in medieval stonemason guilds, is often associated with secrecy and influence. The presence of Masonic symbols at DIA has led to theories that the airport is linked to the Freemasons and their alleged role in orchestrating a New World Order. The "New World Airport Commission," an entity with no apparent existence outside of this context, has further fueled these theories, suggesting that the airport is part of a broader plan for global control.

The Underground Facilities

One of the most enduring and sensational theories about DIA is the existence of extensive underground facilities beneath the airport. These rumored facilities range from government bunkers and continuity of government operations to secret bases for extraterrestrial beings.

Bunkers and Government Facilities

Several sources, including former airport construction workers, have claimed that DIA houses a vast network of underground bunkers designed to serve as a safe haven for government officials and elites in the event of a global catastrophe. These bunkers are said to be connected by a series of tunnels and equipped with advanced technology and supplies to sustain life for extended periods.

Evidence and Testimonies

While concrete evidence of these underground facilities is scarce, testimonies from former workers and leaked documents have fueled speculation. Some workers have described the construction of extensive tunnels and rooms far below the airport, while others have reported seeing strange, high-security areas that they were not permitted to enter. Additionally, aerial photographs and ground-penetrating radar have revealed anomalies beneath the airport, further supporting the theory of underground structures.

Extraterrestrial Theories

Some of the more far-fetched theories suggest that DIA's underground facilities are not only government bunkers but also secret bases for extraterrestrial beings. Proponents of this theory argue that the airport's remote location, vast size, and peculiar artwork hint at a hidden agenda involving contact with or control by alien entities. While these claims lack substantial evidence, they contribute to the airport's enduring aura of mystery and intrigue.

Connections to Global Conspiracy Narratives

The various elements of DIA—the unusual construction decisions, mysterious funding, cryptic artwork, Masonic symbols, and alleged underground facilities—have all been woven into broader global conspiracy narratives. These narratives often revolve around themes of a New World Order, secret societies, and preparations for a global apocalypse.

The New World Order

One of the most prevalent conspiracy theories associated with DIA is the idea that the airport is a key component of a New World Order (NWO). According to this theory, the NWO is a secretive and powerful group of elites who seek to establish a single, authoritarian global government. Proponents of this theory argue that the airport's artwork, symbols, and underground facilities are evidence of preparations for this new regime.

Secret Societies

The presence of Masonic symbols and references to mysterious organizations at DIA has led to speculation that the airport is connected to secret societies such as the Freemasons and the Illuminati. These societies are often believed to wield significant influence behind the scenes, manipulating global events and governments to further their own agendas. Theories about DIA's connection to these groups suggest that the airport is a hub for their clandestine activities.

Global Apocalypse Preparations

Another prominent theory is that DIA is designed to serve as a refuge for elites in the event of a global apocalypse. This theory posits that the airport's underground bunkers and advanced facilities are intended to protect a select group of people from impending disasters, such as nuclear war, environmental collapse, or extraterrestrial invasion. The airport's remote location and vast size are seen as ideal for such preparations, and the cryptic artwork is interpreted as a warning or foretelling of these catastrophic events.

Interviews and Expert Analyses

To gain a deeper understanding of the mysteries surrounding DIA, we conducted interviews with experts in various fields, including architecture, art history, conspiracy theories, and aviation. Their insights provide a more nuanced perspective on the airport's enigmatic features and the theories that have emerged around them.

Architectural Insights

Architectural experts have examined the unusual design and construction decisions at DIA, offering explanations that challenge some of the more outlandish conspiracy theories. They argue that the airport's vast size and remote location were strategic decisions to accommodate future growth and reduce noise pollution in urban areas. Additionally, the buried structures and tunnels are explained as remnants of an overly ambitious automated baggage system that was ultimately deemed impractical.

Art Historical Perspectives

Art historians have analyzed the controversial artwork at DIA, including Leo Tanguma's murals and the gargoyle statues. They argue that the murals, while unsettling, are intended to convey messages of peace, harmony, and environmental stewardship. The disturbing imagery is meant to highlight the consequences of war and environmental degradation, ultimately emphasizing the importance of working towards a better future. The gargoyles, meanwhile, are seen as playful references to the protective symbols commonly found in Gothic architecture.

Conspiracy Theory Experts

Experts in conspiracy theories have explored the reasons why DIA has become a focal point for such a wide range of speculations. They suggest that the airport's combination of unusual design, cryptic symbols, and mysterious construction decisions create a perfect storm for conspiracy theorists. The lack of transparency and the enigmatic nature of some features have fueled suspicions and allowed various theories to flourish.

Aviation Professionals

Aviation professionals have provided insights into the practical aspects of DIA's design and operation. They highlight the airport's state-of-the-art facilities, strategic location, and capacity to handle a high volume of air traffic as key factors in its construction. While acknowledging some of the unusual design choices, they emphasize the airport's functionality and importance as a major transportation hub.

Conclusion

The Denver International Airport is a unique and enigmatic structure that has captured the imagination of conspiracy theorists and the public alike. Its vast size, peculiar artwork, mysterious funding, and alleged underground facilities have all contributed to a rich tapestry of theories and speculations. While many of these theories lack concrete evidence, they reflect broader concerns about secrecy, power, and control in modern society.

This chapter aims to provide a comprehensive exploration of the peculiar features of DIA, shedding light on the reasons behind their creation and the various interpretations they have inspired. By examining the airport's architecture, artwork, and the theories surrounding its construction, we can better understand the complex interplay between reality and speculation that has made DIA one of the most intriguing and controversial airports in the world.

| 11 |

Chapter 11: Conspiracy Theories and Underground Facilities

Denver International Airport (DIA) has long been a magnet for conspiracy theories, largely due to its vast size, enigmatic construction, and peculiar features. Among the most persistent and intriguing claims are those involving underground facilities purportedly hidden beneath the airport. These theories range from government bunkers and continuity of government operations to secret bases for extraterrestrial beings. This chapter delves deeply into these conspiracy theories, examining the evidence, testimonies, and analyses that support or refute these claims. By exploring the origins and evolution of these theories, we aim to provide a thorough understanding of why DIA continues to captivate the imagination of conspiracy theorists worldwide.

The Origins of Underground Facility Theories

The theories about underground facilities at DIA began almost as soon as the airport opened in 1995. The massive construction project, which experienced significant delays and cost overruns, coupled with the airport's remote location and vast size, laid the groundwork for speculation and suspicion.

Cost Overruns and Delays

Originally estimated to cost $1.7 billion, the final price tag for DIA ballooned to $4.8 billion, with the project experiencing numerous delays and setbacks. These overruns and delays have fueled suspicions that the additional funds and time were used to construct secret underground facilities. Critics argue that the sheer scale of the budget and the extended timeline indicate the presence of undisclosed construction efforts.

Mysterious Construction Decisions

Several unusual construction decisions have further fueled speculation. One of the most frequently cited anomalies is the decision to bury five multi-story buildings beneath the airport. Official explanations cite these structures as part of an inefficient automated baggage handling system that was ultimately abandoned. However, the secrecy and scale of these buried structures have led many to believe they serve a more covert purpose.

Testimonies and Leaked Documents

Various testimonies from construction workers and leaked documents have added to the speculation about underground facilities at DIA. Some workers have described the construction of extensive tunnels and rooms far below the airport, while others have reported seeing high-security areas they were not permitted to enter. These accounts, though anecdotal, contribute to the pervasive belief in a hidden network beneath the airport.

Government Bunkers and Continuity of Government

One of the most persistent theories is that DIA houses a vast network of underground bunkers designed for continuity of government operations. This theory posits that in the event of a catastrophic event, such as nuclear war or a major natural disaster, these bunkers would serve as a refuge for government officials and elites.

The Role of NORAD

The proximity of DIA to the North American Aerospace Defense Command (NORAD) in Colorado Springs lends some plausibility to this theory. NORAD is known for its extensive underground facilities built to withstand nuclear attacks. Some theorists argue that DIA's underground network is connected to NORAD, forming a comprehensive system of bunkers designed to ensure the survival and continuity of government functions.

Aerial and Satellite Imagery

Aerial and satellite imagery have been used by proponents of the bunker theory to identify anomalies and patterns that suggest the presence of underground structures. These images often highlight unusual surface features, such as unexplained mounds or patterns in the layout of the airport, which are interpreted as evidence of subterranean construction.

Analysis of Official Plans and Documents

Researchers have also analyzed official plans and documents related to DIA's construction. While these documents do not explicitly mention underground bunkers, discrepancies and omissions have been cited as potential evidence of concealed construction efforts. For example, certain blueprints and maps appear to be incomplete or vague in areas where theorists believe underground facilities are located.

Secret Bases for Extraterrestrial Beings

Some of the more far-fetched theories suggest that DIA's underground facilities serve as secret bases for extraterrestrial beings. Proponents of this theory argue that the airport's remote location, vast size, and peculiar artwork hint at a hidden agenda involving contact with or control by alien entities.

The Role of UFO Sightings

Colorado has a long history of UFO sightings, which has contributed to the belief that DIA may be involved in extraterrestrial activities. Reports of strange lights, unexplained aircraft, and mysterious encounters have been documented in the region, leading some to speculate that the airport plays a role in these phenomena.

Interpretations of Airport Artwork

Some of the airport's artwork, particularly Leo Tanguma's murals, has been interpreted as containing references to extraterrestrial beings. Certain symbols and images within the murals are believed by some to depict alien entities or advanced technology, suggesting that the artwork is part of a broader narrative involving extraterrestrial involvement.

Insider Testimonies and Whistleblowers

A few individuals claiming to be former government employees or insiders have come forward with stories about DIA's involvement in extraterrestrial activities. These testimonies, though often lacking in verifiable evidence, have fueled the more sensational aspects of the underground base theory. Claims of secret meetings with alien beings and the presence of advanced, non-human technology are common themes in these accounts.

Analyzing the Evidence

To critically assess the validity of these conspiracy theories, it is essential to examine the available evidence, both for and against the claims of underground facilities at DIA.

Ground-Penetrating Radar and Geological Surveys

Ground-penetrating radar (GPR) and geological surveys have been used to investigate the subsurface of DIA. While GPR can reveal anomalies and subsurface structures, interpreting these results is complex. Some surveys have identified unexplained voids or cavities, which proponents argue are evidence of underground facilities. However, skeptics point out that such anomalies can also be explained by natural geological formations or abandoned construction projects.

Official Responses and Denials

Officials at DIA and local government authorities have consistently denied the existence of secret underground facilities. They attribute the rumors to the airport's unique design, construction challenges, and the general atmosphere of mystery surrounding the project. Official tours of the airport's underground areas, including the tunnels used for baggage handling and maintenance, are often cited as evidence against the more sensational claims.

Independent Investigations

Several independent researchers and journalists have conducted investigations into the claims of underground facilities at DIA. These investigations typically involve interviews with former workers, analysis of construction documents, and field surveys. While some researchers have uncovered intriguing anomalies, conclusive evidence of extensive secret facilities remains elusive.

Psychological and Sociological Perspectives

Understanding why DIA has become a focal point for conspiracy theories also requires a psychological and sociological perspective. The airport's remote location, vast size, and enigmatic features create a sense of mystery and intrigue that is fertile ground for speculation. Additionally, the human tendency to seek patterns and explanations for unexplained phenomena plays a significant role in the development and perpetuation of these theories.

The Appeal of Conspiracy Theories

Conspiracy theories often arise in contexts where there is a perceived lack of transparency or accountability. The construction of DIA, with its significant cost overruns, delays, and unusual design choices, provides an ideal backdrop for such theories. The airport's enigmatic features, such as the cryptic artwork and Masonic symbols, further fuel the imagination and lend themselves to various interpretations.

Media and Popular Culture

The role of media and popular culture in disseminating and popularizing conspiracy theories cannot be overlooked. Television shows, documentaries, and internet forums have all contributed to the spread of theories about DIA. The airport's mysteries have been featured on programs like "Ancient Aliens" and "Conspiracy Theory with Jesse

Ventura," reaching a wide audience and reinforcing the notion that DIA is more than just an airport.

Cultural Narratives and Symbolism

The symbolism associated with DIA's features taps into broader cultural narratives about secret societies, government conspiracies, and extraterrestrial life. These narratives resonate with long-standing myths and fears about hidden agendas and the unknown. The use of Masonic symbols, in particular, evokes associations with historical secret societies and their perceived influence over global events.

Conclusion

Denver International Airport stands as one of the most enigmatic and controversial airports in the world, largely due to the persistent and diverse conspiracy theories surrounding its construction and features. The theories about underground facilities, ranging from government bunkers to extraterrestrial bases, highlight the interplay between fact and speculation in shaping public perception.

While concrete evidence for these theories remains elusive, the fascination with DIA speaks to broader concerns about transparency, power, and control in modern society. By critically examining the origins, evolution, and evidence of these conspiracy theories, we gain insight into the human tendency to seek hidden meanings and explanations for the unknown.

This chapter provides a comprehensive exploration of the conspiracy theories and underground facility claims at DIA, shedding light on the reasons behind their persistence and the evidence supporting or refuting them. In the following chapters, we will continue to investigate the connections between DIA and broader global conspiracy narratives, offering detailed analyses and insights into the various theories that have made this airport a focal point for intrigue and speculation.

| **12** |

Chapter 12: Connections to Global Conspiracy Narratives

Denver International Airport (DIA) is not just an isolated point of intrigue but is often woven into broader global conspiracy narratives that encompass secret societies, New World Order theories, and apocalyptic predictions. This chapter will delve into the connections between DIA and these wider conspiracies, exploring how the airport fits into the grander schemes purported by theorists. By examining the common threads and unique elements that link DIA to these global narratives, we aim to provide a comprehensive understanding of why this airport remains a central figure in the conspiracy community.

The New World Order and DIA

One of the most prevalent conspiracy theories associated with DIA is its purported connection to the New World Order (NWO). The NWO is a theorized clandestine group of global elites aiming to establish a single, authoritarian world government.

Origins and Evolution of NWO Theories

The concept of the New World Order has roots in the late 18th and early 19th centuries, often tied to the Illuminati and Freemasonry. Theories about a global elite manipulating world events to achieve ultimate control gained popularity during the 20th century, fueled by geopolitical events and the writings of influential theorists.

DIA's Role in NWO Theories

Proponents of the NWO theory argue that DIA is a key component in the infrastructure of this global elite. They cite several elements of the airport as evidence:

1. **Masonic Symbols and the Capstone**: The dedication capstone in the Jeppesen Terminal, featuring the Masonic square and compasses, along with a reference to a "New World Airport Commission," is often interpreted as a nod to the Freemasons' influence. The lack of clarity about the commission's existence has led theorists to link it directly to the NWO.

2. **Murals and Artwork**: The airport's artwork, especially the murals by Leo Tanguma, is seen by some as depicting apocalyptic scenes and a post-catastrophe world, aligning with NWO narratives about global depopulation and control. The juxtaposition of chaos and a new peaceful order in the murals is interpreted as symbolic of the transition the NWO aims to orchestrate.

3. **Underground Facilities**: The theories about extensive underground bunkers at DIA are often linked to the NWO's need for secure, hidden locations to continue operations in the event of global crises.

Secret Societies: Freemasons, Illuminati, and Skull and Bones

Theories about secret societies often intersect with narratives about DIA, given the symbolism and secrecy associated with the airport's construction and features.

Freemasons

The Freemasons, a fraternal organization with historical roots in the medieval stonemasons' guilds, are frequently mentioned in connection with DIA. The presence of Masonic symbols at the airport fuels suspicions of Masonic involvement.

Historical Context of Freemasonry

Freemasonry has long been the subject of conspiracy theories due to its secretive nature, hierarchical structure, and influential membership. Historically, Freemasons have been accused of wielding disproportionate influence in politics, economics, and society.

Interpretations at DIA

The Masonic symbols and dedication capstone are seen as evidence of Masonic influence over the airport's construction. Theorists argue that this indicates a broader agenda aligned with the goals of the NWO, with the airport serving as a key site for Masonic activities and control.

Illuminati

The Illuminati, a purported secret society founded in the late 18th century, is often implicated in global conspiracy theories, including those surrounding DIA.

Origins of the Illuminati

The Illuminati was established in 1776 by Adam Weishaupt in Bavaria, aiming to promote Enlightenment ideals and rationalism. Despite its brief existence, the Illuminati has become synonymous with secretive global manipulation.

Connections to DIA

Theories about the Illuminati's involvement in DIA stem from the airport's cryptic symbols and artwork. The murals and statues are interpreted as messages from the Illuminati, indicating their plans for global domination. The secretive nature of the airport's construction and the unexplained features are seen as typical of Illuminati activities.

Skull and Bones

Skull and Bones, a secret society based at Yale University, is another group often mentioned in conspiracy theories about global control and DIA.

Origins and Influence of Skull and Bones

Founded in 1832, Skull and Bones has included many influential American political and business leaders among its members. The society's secrecy and the prominence of its members have made it a focus of conspiracy theories.

Implications for DIA

Theorists suggest that Skull and Bones members, given their influential positions, may have played a role in the planning and funding of DIA. The airport's symbolic elements and mysterious aspects are seen as aligning with the secretive operations and influence of Skull and Bones.

Global Apocalypse and DIA

Another prominent theme in the conspiracy theories about DIA is the idea that the airport is part of preparations for a global apocalypse. This theory posits that DIA's underground facilities and cryptic artwork are evidence of elite preparations for surviving and controlling a post-apocalyptic world.

The Apocalyptic Imagery in the Murals

The murals by Leo Tanguma, depicting scenes of environmental destruction and social chaos followed by renewal and peace, are often interpreted as indicative of an impending global catastrophe orchestrated by the global elite. Theorists argue that these artworks serve as warnings or declarations of the elite's plans.

DIA as a Safe Haven

Proponents of the apocalypse theory argue that the extensive underground facilities at DIA are designed to serve as a safe haven for global elites. These facilities, purported to include advanced technology and supplies, are seen as preparations for surviving disasters such as nuclear war, environmental collapse, or pandemics.

Evidence and Testimonies

Various testimonies from former workers and insiders suggest the existence of elaborate underground structures, lending some credibility to the apocalypse theory. These accounts, coupled with aerial and ground-penetrating radar anomalies, support the notion of hidden facilities beneath the airport.

DIA and Extraterrestrial Theories

Some of the more outlandish conspiracy theories about DIA involve connections to extraterrestrial beings. These theories suggest that the airport may serve as a base or meeting point for human-alien collaboration.

Historical Context of Extraterrestrial Theories

Belief in extraterrestrial beings and their involvement in human affairs has a long history, fueled by numerous reports of UFO sightings and alleged alien encounters. Theories about government cover-ups and secret bases have become a staple of modern conspiracy narratives.

DIA's Role in Extraterrestrial Theories

Proponents argue that the airport's remote location, vast size, and mysterious features make it an ideal candidate for a secret extraterrestrial base. The underground facilities are believed to house advanced technology and serve as meeting points for human and alien representatives.

Symbolic Interpretations of Artwork

Certain symbols and elements within DIA's artwork are interpreted as references to extraterrestrial beings. For example, some see the depiction of strange, otherworldly creatures in the murals as evidence of alien influence or contact.

Evidence and Testimonies

As with other theories, testimonies from alleged insiders and former employees provide anecdotal evidence of extraterrestrial activity at

DIA. These accounts, though often lacking verifiable proof, contribute to the mythos surrounding the airport.

Psychological and Sociological Perspectives

Understanding why DIA has become such a focal point for conspiracy theories requires a psychological and sociological perspective. The airport's unique characteristics create an environment ripe for speculation and myth-making.

Human Need for Explanation

Humans have a natural tendency to seek explanations for unexplained phenomena. The enigmatic features of DIA, combined with its significant cost overruns and delays, provide fertile ground for conspiracy theories as people try to make sense of the anomalies.

Pattern Recognition and Symbolism

The human brain is adept at recognizing patterns and attributing meaning to symbols. The various symbols and artwork at DIA are interpreted in myriad ways, leading to a wide range of theories about their true significance.

Media and Popular Culture

Media and popular culture play a significant role in disseminating and reinforcing conspiracy theories. Television shows, documentaries, and online forums have all contributed to the spread of theories about DIA, making it a central figure in conspiracy narratives.

The Role of Fear and Distrust

Conspiracy theories often arise in contexts of fear and distrust. The secrecy and perceived lack of transparency surrounding DIA's construction and features feed into broader societal fears about government control, secret societies, and hidden agendas.

Conclusion

Denver International Airport's connection to global conspiracy narratives is a complex and multifaceted phenomenon. The airport's unique characteristics, combined with historical and contemporary fears about secret societies, the New World Order, and apocalyptic events, have made it a focal point for conspiracy theorists.

By examining the evidence, testimonies, and psychological factors that contribute to these theories, we gain a deeper understanding of why DIA remains such a compelling subject of intrigue. This chapter provides a thorough exploration of the connections between DIA and broader conspiracy narratives, highlighting the interplay between fact and speculation that fuels these enduring myths.

In the following chapters, we will continue to investigate other aspects of global conspiracies, providing detailed analyses and insights into the various elements that have made these theories so pervasive and captivating. Through this exploration, we aim to uncover the hidden agendas and motivations behind the world's most enduring conspiracy theories.

CENSORSHIP OF CONTROVERSIAL BOOKS AND IDEAS

Throughout history, the written word has been a powerful tool for disseminating knowledge, challenging established norms, and sparking revolutionary change. Books and ideas that threaten the status quo have often been targets of censorship, repression, and outright destruction. From ancient texts suppressed by ruling powers to modern works banned by governments and institutions, the struggle for intellectual freedom has been a constant battleground. In Part V of "Hidden Agendas: Exposing the Dark Secrets," we delve into the historical and contemporary censorship of controversial books and ideas, exploring the motivations behind these acts of suppression and their impact on society.

Historical Context of Book Censorship

The history of book censorship is as old as the written word itself. Throughout various civilizations, rulers and religious authorities have sought to control the dissemination of ideas that could challenge their authority or disrupt social order. Understanding the historical context of censorship provides a foundation for examining its ongoing presence in the modern world.

Ancient Civilizations and the Suppression of Knowledge

In ancient civilizations, knowledge was often concentrated in the hands of the elite, and the control of information was a means of maintaining power. Libraries, such as the famed Library of Alexandria, were both repositories of knowledge and targets for destruction when new regimes sought to erase the legacies of their predecessors.

The Burning of the Library of Alexandria

One of the most tragic and symbolic acts of censorship in ancient history is the burning of the Library of Alexandria. Founded in the 3rd century BCE, the library was a center of learning and scholarship. Its destruction, whether by accident or deliberate act, symbolizes the loss of vast amounts of knowledge and the lengths to which rulers might go to suppress information.

The Qin Dynasty and the Burning of Books

In 213 BCE, the First Emperor of China, Qin Shi Huang, ordered the burning of books and the burying of scholars to consolidate his power and unify China under a single ideology. This act of censorship aimed to eliminate any texts that contradicted the state's official philosophy, Legalism, and to suppress Confucian scholars who were seen as a threat to his authority.

Religious Censorship in the Middle Ages

During the Middle Ages, the Catholic Church was one of the most powerful institutions in Europe, wielding significant influence over political and social life. The Church's efforts to maintain doctrinal purity and authority led to widespread censorship of texts deemed heretical or dangerous.

The Inquisition and Heretical Texts

The Inquisition, established by the Catholic Church to combat heresy, was notorious for its efforts to root out and suppress heretical ideas. The Church maintained an Index Librorum Prohibitorum, or List of Prohibited Books, which cataloged works considered dangerous to the faith. Authors of these works faced severe penalties, including excommunication, imprisonment, and execution.

The Trial of Galileo Galilei

Galileo Galilei's trial by the Inquisition in 1633 is one of the most famous cases of religious censorship. Galileo's support for the heliocentric model of the solar system, which contradicted the Church's geocentric doctrine, led to his condemnation and house arrest. His writings were banned, and the suppression of his ideas delayed scientific progress for centuries.

Censorship in the Enlightenment and Beyond

The Enlightenment, characterized by an emphasis on reason, science, and individual rights, saw significant challenges to religious and political authority. However, this period also witnessed fierce censorship as governments and institutions sought to maintain control over the burgeoning flow of ideas.

The French Revolution and Revolutionary Ideas

During the French Revolution, the revolutionary government both promoted and suppressed ideas to control the populace. While revolutionary ideals of liberty, equality, and fraternity were championed, dissenting voices and counter-revolutionary literature were ruthlessly censored. The Reign of Terror, in particular, saw the suppression of works deemed anti-revolutionary.

The Rise of Totalitarian Regimes

The 20th century saw the rise of totalitarian regimes that employed censorship as a fundamental tool of control. In Nazi Germany, the Soviet Union, and other authoritarian states, the suppression of dissenting ideas was essential to maintaining the regime's ideological purity and unchallenged authority.

Nazi Germany and the Book Burnings

In 1933, the Nazi regime conducted a series of book burnings, targeting works by Jewish authors, communists, and others deemed "un-German." These acts of censorship aimed to purify German culture and eliminate any intellectual opposition to Nazi ideology. The destruction of books was a precursor to the broader campaign of repression and genocide that followed.

The Soviet Union and State-Sponsored Censorship

Under Joseph Stalin, the Soviet Union implemented extensive censorship to control information and maintain the Communist Party's dominance. Works that criticized the government, promoted capitalist ideas, or celebrated individualism were banned. The state controlled all publishing, and dissident authors faced severe consequences, including imprisonment, exile, and execution.

Modern-Day Censorship

Despite advancements in technology and the spread of democratic values, censorship remains a significant issue in the modern world. Governments, corporations, and other institutions continue to suppress controversial books and ideas, often under the guise of maintaining social order, protecting national security, or preventing the spread of harmful content.

Government Censorship

Many contemporary governments still engage in censorship to control political dissent and maintain authority. Countries with authoritarian regimes, such as China, North Korea, and Iran, employ strict censorship measures to suppress any content that challenges the state's narrative or criticizes its leaders.

China's Great Firewall

China's Great Firewall is one of the most sophisticated and comprehensive censorship systems in the world. The government controls internet access, blocking websites and censoring content that promotes political dissent, human rights advocacy, or criticism of the Communist Party. Books and publications that contradict the party line are banned, and authors face severe repercussions for challenging state authority.

Iran's Suppression of Dissent

In Iran, the government strictly controls the publication and distribution of books, particularly those that address sensitive political or religious topics. Authors and intellectuals who criticize the regime or advocate for democratic reforms face censorship, imprisonment, and even execution. The state maintains tight control over the media and internet access, ensuring that dissenting voices are silenced.

Corporate and Institutional Censorship

Censorship is not limited to governments; corporations and institutions also play a significant role in suppressing controversial ideas.

In the age of social media and digital platforms, private companies have immense power to control the flow of information and influence public discourse.

Big Tech and Content Moderation

Tech giants like Facebook, Google, and Twitter have faced criticism for their role in content moderation and censorship. These companies use algorithms and human moderators to remove content deemed harmful, inappropriate, or in violation of their terms of service. While these measures are often justified as necessary for maintaining a safe and respectful online environment, they can also lead to the suppression of legitimate and controversial ideas.

Academic and Scientific Censorship

Academic institutions and scientific communities are not immune to censorship. Controversial research or ideas that challenge established paradigms or threaten funding sources can be suppressed. Researchers who pursue unconventional lines of inquiry may face ostracism, loss of funding, or professional repercussions.

The Impact of Censorship on Society

The suppression of controversial books and ideas has far-reaching consequences for society. Censorship stifles intellectual freedom, hinders progress, and perpetuates ignorance. By examining the impact of censorship, we can better understand the importance of protecting the free exchange of ideas.

Stifling Intellectual Freedom

Censorship limits the diversity of perspectives and the ability of individuals to explore, challenge, and refine their own beliefs. When controversial ideas are suppressed, society loses the opportunity for critical engagement and growth. Intellectual freedom is essential for fostering creativity, innovation, and social progress.

Hindering Scientific and Technological Progress

Throughout history, censorship has delayed scientific and technological advancements. The suppression of ideas like Galileo's heliocentric model or Darwin's theory of evolution hindered the development of modern science. In contemporary times, the censorship of research on climate change, genetic engineering, or alternative medicine can slow progress and prevent the discovery of new solutions to pressing global challenges.

Perpetuating Ignorance and Division

Censorship can perpetuate ignorance and deepen societal divisions by preventing open dialogue and mutual understanding. When controversial ideas are suppressed, misinformation and prejudice can flourish, leading to polarization and conflict. A society that values intellectual freedom is better equipped to address its challenges and foster a more inclusive and informed citizenry.

Conclusion

The censorship of controversial books and ideas is a pervasive issue with deep historical roots and significant contemporary relevance. From ancient civilizations to modern digital platforms, the suppression of knowledge and dissenting voices has been a tool for maintaining power and control. By examining the motivations and impact of censorship, we can better understand the importance of protecting intellectual freedom and fostering an open and inclusive society.

In the following chapters, we will delve into specific cases of book censorship and the individuals and movements that have fought against it. Through detailed analyses and historical accounts, we aim to uncover the hidden agendas behind acts of censorship and celebrate the resilience of those who have championed the free exchange of ideas. By shining a light on these stories, we hope to inspire a renewed commitment to intellectual freedom and the pursuit of truth.

| 13 |

Chapter 13: Historical Cases of Book Censorship

The history of book censorship is rich and complex, marked by a continuous struggle between the forces of control and the advocates of intellectual freedom. This chapter explores significant historical cases of book censorship, tracing their origins, motivations, and impacts. From the ancient world to the modern era, these cases reveal the enduring power of the written word and the lengths to which authorities will go to suppress dissenting ideas.

Ancient Times and the Suppression of Knowledge

In the ancient world, the control of knowledge was a crucial tool for maintaining power and social order. Rulers and religious leaders often sought to suppress texts that threatened their authority or contradicted their ideologies.

The Library of Alexandria

The Library of Alexandria, founded in the 3rd century BCE, was one of the greatest centers of learning in the ancient world. It housed countless scrolls and texts from various cultures and fields of knowledge. However, this repository of knowledge also became a target for destruction.

The Destruction of the Library

The exact circumstances surrounding the destruction of the Library of Alexandria are unclear, with multiple accounts suggesting different events and causes. Some sources blame Julius Caesar's invasion in 48 BCE, while others point to attacks by later Roman emperors, Christian zealots, or Muslim conquerors. Regardless of the cause, the destruction of the library symbolizes the loss of a vast amount of knowledge and the deliberate suppression of intellectual advancement.

The Qin Dynasty and the Burning of Books

In 213 BCE, the First Emperor of China, Qin Shi Huang, ordered the burning of books and the burying of scholars as part of his efforts to consolidate power and unify China under a single ideology.

Legalism and the Suppression of Confucianism

Qin Shi Huang's regime promoted Legalism, a strict and authoritarian philosophy that emphasized obedience to the state. Confucianism, with its emphasis on moral virtue and social harmony, was seen as a threat to the emperor's authority. To eradicate Confucian influence, Qin Shi Huang ordered the destruction of Confucian texts and the execution of scholars who resisted the state's ideology.

The Impact of the Book Burnings

The burning of books and the burying of scholars had a profound impact on Chinese intellectual life. Many Confucian texts were lost, and the suppression of scholarly dissent created a climate of fear and conformity. This period of censorship left a lasting mark on Chinese history, shaping the development of Chinese philosophy and political thought.

Religious Censorship in the Middle Ages

During the Middle Ages, the Catholic Church wielded immense power over European society. The Church's efforts to maintain doctrinal purity and authority led to widespread censorship of texts deemed heretical or dangerous.

The Inquisition and the Index of Prohibited Books

The Inquisition, established by the Catholic Church to combat heresy, played a significant role in censoring books and ideas. The Church maintained the Index Librorum Prohibitorum, a list of prohibited books that cataloged works considered dangerous to the faith.

The Trial of Galileo Galilei

Galileo Galilei's trial by the Inquisition in 1633 is one of the most famous cases of religious censorship. Galileo's support for the heliocentric model of the solar system, which contradicted the Church's geocentric doctrine, led to his condemnation and house arrest. His writings were banned, and the suppression of his ideas delayed scientific progress for centuries.

The Reformation and Counter-Reformation

The Protestant Reformation, initiated by Martin Luther in the early 16th century, challenged the authority of the Catholic Church and sparked a wave of religious conflict across Europe. In response, the

Church launched the Counter-Reformation, a campaign to reaffirm Catholic doctrine and suppress Protestant writings.

The Censorship of Protestant Texts

During the Counter-Reformation, the Catholic Church intensified its efforts to censor Protestant texts. The Inquisition and the Index of Prohibited Books were used to ban works by Protestant reformers, and the Church sought to control the spread of Reformation ideas through rigorous censorship and propaganda.

The Enlightenment and the Struggle for Intellectual Freedom

The Enlightenment, characterized by an emphasis on reason, science, and individual rights, saw significant challenges to religious and political authority. However, this period also witnessed fierce censorship as governments and institutions sought to maintain control over the burgeoning flow of ideas.

Voltaire and the Fight for Free Expression

Voltaire, one of the leading figures of the Enlightenment, was a vocal advocate for free expression and a critic of religious and political intolerance. His writings, including "Candide" and "Letters Concerning the English Nation," were frequently censored and banned.

Voltaire's Exile and Censorship

Voltaire's outspoken views often brought him into conflict with the authorities. He was exiled from France multiple times and his works were banned in several countries. Despite this, Voltaire continued to write and publish, using pseudonyms and clandestine printing presses to circumvent censorship.

The French Revolution and Revolutionary Censorship

The French Revolution, which began in 1789, was a period of radical political and social upheaval. While the revolution promoted ideals of liberty, equality, and fraternity, it also saw the suppression of dissenting voices and counter-revolutionary ideas.

The Reign of Terror

During the Reign of Terror (1793-1794), the revolutionary government, led by the Committee of Public Safety, imposed strict censorship to control the populace and suppress opposition. Newspapers, pamphlets, and books that criticized the revolution or promoted royalist views were banned, and authors faced imprisonment or execution.

The Rise of Totalitarian Regimes

The 20th century saw the rise of totalitarian regimes that employed censorship as a fundamental tool of control. In Nazi Germany, the Soviet Union, and other authoritarian states, the suppression of dissenting ideas was essential to maintaining the regime's ideological purity and unchallenged authority.

Nazi Germany and the Book Burnings

In 1933, the Nazi regime conducted a series of book burnings, targeting works by Jewish authors, communists, and others deemed "un-German." These acts of censorship aimed to purify German culture and eliminate any intellectual opposition to Nazi ideology.

The Impact of the Book Burnings

The book burnings were a precursor to broader acts of repression and genocide. The destruction of books was symbolic of the regime's broader efforts to control thought and eliminate diversity of ideas. The suppression of intellectual freedom under the Nazis had a devastating impact on German culture and society.

The Soviet Union and State-Sponsored Censorship

Under Joseph Stalin, the Soviet Union implemented extensive censorship to control information and maintain the Communist Party's dominance. Works that criticized the government, promoted capitalist ideas, or celebrated individualism were banned. The state controlled all publishing, and dissident authors faced severe consequences, including imprisonment, exile, and execution.

The Gulag Archipelago

Aleksandr Solzhenitsyn's "The Gulag Archipelago," which exposed the brutal realities of the Soviet labor camp system, was banned in the Soviet Union. Solzhenitsyn faced harassment, arrest, and eventual exile for his writings. His work, however, became a powerful symbol of resistance against censorship and totalitarianism.

Modern-Day Censorship

Despite advancements in technology and the spread of democratic values, censorship remains a significant issue in the modern world. Governments, corporations, and other institutions continue to suppress controversial books and ideas, often under the guise of maintaining social order, protecting national security, or preventing the spread of harmful content.

Government Censorship

Many contemporary governments still engage in censorship to control political dissent and maintain authority. Countries with authoritarian regimes, such as China, North Korea, and Iran, employ strict censorship measures to suppress any content that challenges the state's narrative or criticizes its leaders.

China's Great Firewall

China's Great Firewall is one of the most sophisticated and comprehensive censorship systems in the world. The government controls internet access, blocking websites and censoring content that promotes political dissent, human rights advocacy, or criticism of the Communist Party. Books and publications that contradict the party line are banned, and authors face severe repercussions for challenging state authority.

Iran's Suppression of Dissent

In Iran, the government strictly controls the publication and distribution of books, particularly those that address sensitive political or religious topics. Authors and intellectuals who criticize the regime or advocate for democratic reforms face censorship, imprisonment, and even execution. The state maintains tight control over the media and internet access, ensuring that dissenting voices are silenced.

Corporate and Institutional Censorship

Censorship is not limited to governments; corporations and institutions also play a significant role in suppressing controversial ideas. In the age of social media and digital platforms, private companies have immense power to control the flow of information and influence public discourse.

Big Tech and Content Moderation

Tech giants like Facebook, Google, and Twitter have faced criticism for their role in content moderation and censorship. These companies use algorithms and human moderators to remove content deemed harmful, inappropriate, or in violation of their terms of service. While these measures are often justified as necessary for maintaining a safe and respectful online environment, they can also lead to the suppression of legitimate and controversial ideas.

Academic and Scientific Censorship

Academic institutions and scientific communities are not immune to censorship. Controversial research or ideas that challenge established paradigms or threaten funding sources can be suppressed. Researchers who pursue unconventional lines of inquiry may face ostracism, loss of funding, or professional repercussions.

The Impact of Censorship on Society

The suppression of controversial books and ideas has far-reaching consequences for society. Censorship stifles intellectual freedom, hinders progress, and perpetuates ignorance. By examining the impact of censorship, we can better understand the importance of protecting the free exchange of ideas.

Stifling Intellectual Freedom

Censorship limits the diversity of perspectives and the ability of individuals to explore, challenge, and refine their own beliefs. When controversial ideas are suppressed, society loses the opportunity for critical engagement and growth. Intellectual freedom is essential for fostering creativity, innovation, and social progress.

Hindering Scientific and Technological Progress

Throughout history, censorship has delayed scientific and technological advancements. The suppression of ideas like Galileo's heliocentric model or Darwin's theory of evolution hindered the development of modern science. In contemporary times, the censorship of research on climate change, genetic engineering, or alternative medicine can slow progress and prevent the discovery of new solutions to pressing global challenges.

Perpetuating Ignorance and Division

Censorship can perpetuate ignorance and deepen societal divisions by preventing open dialogue and mutual understanding. When controversial ideas are suppressed, misinformation and prejudice can flourish, leading to polarization and conflict. A society that values intellectual freedom is better equipped to address its challenges and foster a more inclusive and informed citizenry.

Conclusion

The history of book censorship reveals a persistent and troubling pattern of suppression and control. From ancient times to the modern era, the suppression of controversial books and ideas has been a tool for maintaining power and authority. By examining historical cases of censorship, we gain insight into the motivations and consequences of these acts, and the importance of defending intellectual freedom.

As we continue to explore the various facets of censorship in the following chapters, we will delve deeper into specific instances and the resilience of those who have fought against it. Through detailed analyses and historical accounts, we aim to uncover the hidden agendas behind acts of censorship and celebrate the resilience of those who have championed the free exchange of ideas. By shining a light on these stories, we hope to inspire a renewed commitment to intellectual freedom and the pursuit of truth.

| 14 |

Chapter 14: Modern-Day Censorship in Media and Academia

In the contemporary world, the landscape of censorship has evolved, encompassing a wide range of practices employed by governments, corporations, academic institutions, and media platforms. Modern-day censorship, while often more subtle and sophisticated than in the past, continues to shape public discourse, influence societal norms, and control the flow of information. This chapter delves into the mechanisms and impacts of censorship in media and academia, examining notable cases, the role of technology, and the ongoing struggle for intellectual freedom.

Government Censorship

Government censorship remains a significant issue in many parts of the world, where authoritarian regimes and even some democratic governments use various methods to suppress dissent and control information.

China: The Great Firewall and Beyond

China's Great Firewall is one of the most comprehensive internet censorship systems in the world. This sophisticated network of surveillance and filtering technologies blocks access to foreign websites, censors sensitive content, and monitors online activities.

Mechanisms of Censorship

The Chinese government employs a variety of methods to control information, including:

- **Internet Filtering**: Blocking websites and services that host content critical of the government, such as Google, Facebook, and Twitter.
- **Content Removal**: Deleting posts, articles, and comments that discuss taboo topics, such as the Tiananmen Square massacre, the Hong Kong protests, or criticism of the Chinese Communist Party.
- **Surveillance**: Monitoring citizens' online activities and communications, using technologies like facial recognition and data mining to track dissent.

Impact on Society

This extensive censorship apparatus stifles free expression, limits access to information, and curtails academic and journalistic freedom. Chinese citizens face severe repercussions, including imprisonment, for expressing dissenting views. The lack of open dialogue and critical debate hampers social and political progress.

Iran: Suppressing Political Dissent

In Iran, the government exercises strict control over media and internet access to maintain its authority and suppress political dissent.

Methods of Censorship

- **Internet Blackouts**: The government periodically shuts down internet access during protests or periods of political unrest to prevent the spread of information and coordination among activists.
- **Website Blocking**: Blocking access to websites that promote human rights, political reform, or criticize the government.
- **Journalist Harassment**: Arresting and intimidating journalists who report on sensitive issues, leading to self-censorship among the media.

Impact on Society

These measures stifle political activism and free expression, isolating Iranian citizens from the global community and limiting their ability to advocate for change. The suppression of dissenting voices contributes to the perpetuation of authoritarian rule and human rights abuses.

Corporate and Institutional Censorship

In addition to government censorship, corporations and academic institutions also play a significant role in controlling the flow of information and shaping public discourse.

Big Tech and Content Moderation

Tech giants like Facebook, Google, and Twitter have immense power to control information through content moderation policies.

While these policies aim to prevent the spread of harmful content, they can also lead to the suppression of legitimate and controversial ideas.

Algorithms and Bias

Content moderation algorithms, designed to identify and remove harmful content, often reflect the biases of their creators. These biases can result in the disproportionate removal of content from marginalized groups or the suppression of politically sensitive topics.

Case Study: The Suppression of Political Speech

Several high-profile cases have highlighted the potential for bias in content moderation. For example, during significant political events like elections or protests, posts related to these topics have been removed or flagged, raising concerns about the influence of tech companies on public discourse.

Transparency and Accountability

There is a growing demand for greater transparency and accountability in how tech companies moderate content. Critics argue that the lack of clear guidelines and the opacity of decision-making processes contribute to arbitrary and biased censorship.

Academic and Scientific Censorship

Academic institutions and scientific communities are not immune to censorship. Controversial research or ideas that challenge established paradigms or threaten funding sources can be suppressed, hindering intellectual freedom and progress.

Institutional Pressures and Self-Censorship

Researchers and academics often face pressures to conform to institutional norms and avoid controversial topics. The fear of losing funding, facing professional ostracism, or damaging career prospects can lead to self-censorship.

Case Study: Climate Change Research

Climate change research has been a particularly contentious area. Scientists who present findings that contradict established views or suggest more severe impacts have faced pushback from both academic institutions and political entities.

Impact on Scientific Progress

The suppression of controversial research stifles scientific innovation and the advancement of knowledge. When researchers are unable to explore new ideas or present dissenting views, the scientific community loses the opportunity for critical engagement and growth.

Censorship in the Media

The media landscape has also been profoundly affected by censorship, both through government regulations and corporate control. The rise of digital media has introduced new challenges and opportunities for censorship.

Government Control of the Press

In many countries, governments exert control over the press through regulations, ownership of media outlets, and intimidation of journalists.

Case Study: Russia's Control of the Media

In Russia, the government maintains tight control over major media outlets, using them to propagate state-approved narratives. Independent journalists and media organizations face harassment, legal challenges, and violence, leading to widespread self-censorship.

Corporate Media and Editorial Bias

Corporate ownership of media outlets can also lead to censorship through editorial bias and the prioritization of profit over journalistic integrity.

Case Study: The Sinclair Broadcast Group

The Sinclair Broadcast Group, one of the largest media conglomerates in the United States, has been criticized for imposing conservative-leaning editorial policies on its local news stations. This practice raises concerns about the influence of corporate ownership on media diversity and the suppression of dissenting viewpoints.

Impact on Public Discourse

The concentration of media ownership and the influence of corporate interests can narrow the range of perspectives presented to the public. This homogenization of media content limits critical debate and the diversity of ideas essential for a healthy democracy.

The Role of Technology in Censorship

Technology plays a dual role in censorship, serving both as a tool for suppression and as a means of circumventing it.

Digital Censorship Tools

Governments and corporations use a variety of digital tools to monitor, filter, and suppress content.

Surveillance and Data Collection

Advanced surveillance technologies enable the monitoring of online activities, communications, and behaviors. Governments use these technologies to track dissent and enforce censorship.

Internet Filtering and Blocking

Internet filtering technologies block access to specific websites and online services. These tools are used to prevent the dissemination of politically sensitive or controversial information.

Circumventing Censorship

Despite the sophisticated tools used for censorship, individuals and organizations have developed methods to circumvent these controls.

Virtual Private Networks (VPNs)

VPNs allow users to bypass government censorship by routing their internet traffic through servers in other countries. This technology is widely used in countries with strict internet censorship, such as China and Iran.

Encrypted Messaging Apps

Encrypted messaging apps, such as Signal and Telegram, provide secure communication channels that protect users from surveillance and censorship. These apps have become essential tools for activists and journalists operating in repressive environments.

The Ongoing Struggle for Intellectual Freedom

The fight against censorship is an ongoing struggle, with activists, journalists, academics, and ordinary citizens working to protect intellectual freedom and the free exchange of ideas.

Advocacy and Activism

Numerous organizations and movements advocate for free expression and challenge censorship practices.

Reporters Without Borders

Reporters Without Borders (RSF) is an international organization that promotes press freedom and defends journalists against censorship and persecution. RSF provides support and protection for journalists operating in hostile environments.

The Electronic Frontier Foundation

The Electronic Frontier Foundation (EFF) is a nonprofit organization dedicated to defending civil liberties in the digital world. EFF advocates for internet freedom, privacy, and the free flow of information, challenging government and corporate censorship.

Legal Challenges and Reforms

Legal challenges and reforms are essential in the fight against censorship. Advocates work to challenge restrictive laws and policies and promote legal frameworks that protect free expression.

Case Study: Net Neutrality

The battle over net neutrality in the United States highlights the importance of legal protections for internet freedom. Net neutrality ensures that internet service providers treat all data equally, preventing them from censoring or prioritizing certain content. Advocacy efforts have focused on maintaining these protections to safeguard the free flow of information.

The Future of Censorship and Free Expression

As technology evolves and the digital landscape continues to change, the dynamics of censorship and free expression will also shift. It is crucial to remain vigilant and proactive in defending intellectual freedom.

Emerging Technologies and Challenges

New technologies, such as artificial intelligence and blockchain, present both opportunities and challenges for censorship and free expression.

Artificial Intelligence

AI technologies can be used to automate censorship, making it more efficient and pervasive. However, AI can also be employed to detect and counteract censorship efforts, creating new tools for protecting free expression.

Blockchain

Blockchain technology offers the potential for decentralized, censorship-resistant platforms for information sharing. By distributing data across a network of nodes, blockchain can make it more difficult for authorities to suppress or manipulate information.

Conclusion

Modern-day censorship in media and academia is a complex and multifaceted issue, with significant implications for intellectual freedom and the free exchange of ideas. From government control and corporate influence to the challenges posed by emerging technologies, the landscape of censorship is continually evolving.

By examining notable cases and understanding the mechanisms of modern censorship, we can better appreciate the importance of defending free expression and fostering a diverse and open public discourse. In the following chapters, we will continue to explore specific instances and the resilience of those who have fought against censorship, shedding light on the ongoing struggle for intellectual freedom and the pursuit of truth. Through these detailed analyses and historical accounts, we aim to inspire a renewed commitment to protecting the free flow of information and ideas in our society.

| 15 |

Chapter 15: The Impact of Censorship on Society

Censorship has a profound and multifaceted impact on society. It influences not only the flow of information but also the very fabric of social, cultural, and intellectual life. This chapter delves into the diverse consequences of censorship, exploring its effects on creativity, innovation, public discourse, and individual freedoms. By examining historical and contemporary examples, we aim to illuminate the far-reaching implications of suppressing controversial books and ideas, and to underscore the importance of protecting intellectual freedom.

The Stifling of Creativity and Innovation

Censorship can severely hinder creativity and innovation by creating an environment where fear of reprisal stifles free expression and experimentation.

Historical Context

Throughout history, censorship has led to the suppression of groundbreaking ideas and artistic expression. The impact of these restrictions can be seen in various cultural and intellectual movements.

The Galileo Affair

Galileo Galilei's confrontation with the Catholic Church over his support for the heliocentric model of the solar system is a quintessential example of how censorship can stifle scientific progress. Galileo's forced recantation and house arrest delayed the acceptance and development of astronomical theories that are now fundamental to our understanding of the universe.

Soviet Censorship of Genetics

In the mid-20th century, Soviet biologist Trofim Lysenko's rejection of Mendelian genetics, backed by the Soviet government, led to the persecution of geneticists and the suppression of genetic research. This ideological censorship had devastating consequences for Soviet agriculture and biological sciences, setting back scientific progress by decades.

Contemporary Examples

Modern examples of censorship continue to demonstrate how suppressing ideas and artistic expression can hinder societal progress.

Censorship of Climate Change Research

In recent years, attempts to censor or undermine climate change research have had significant implications for environmental policy and scientific advancement. Scientists who present findings that challenge established economic or political interests face backlash, funding cuts, and professional ostracism, delaying necessary action to address global warming.

Censorship in the Arts

Artists in many parts of the world face censorship that limits their ability to explore controversial or politically sensitive themes. This not only constrains artistic expression but also deprives society of the critical reflections and innovative ideas that art can provide.

Impact on Public Discourse and Democracy

Censorship distorts public discourse by limiting access to diverse perspectives and critical debates, which are essential for a healthy democracy.

Historical Context

Historically, censorship has been used to control and manipulate public opinion, often with profound political and social consequences.

The Reign of Terror in Revolutionary France

During the Reign of Terror, the revolutionary government in France imposed strict censorship to suppress counter-revolutionary ideas and control public discourse. This suppression of dissent contributed to a climate of fear and repression, ultimately undermining the revolutionary ideals of liberty and equality.

Nazi Propaganda and Censorship

The Nazi regime's extensive use of censorship and propaganda to control public opinion and eliminate opposition is a stark example of how manipulating information can facilitate totalitarian control. The suppression of dissenting voices and the promotion of a singular, state-approved narrative enabled the regime to perpetrate atrocities on an unprecedented scale.

Contemporary Examples

In today's digital age, censorship continues to shape public discourse and influence democratic processes.

Government-Controlled Media

In countries like Russia and China, state-controlled media outlets dominate the information landscape, shaping public perception and limiting access to independent and critical voices. This control of information undermines democratic engagement and perpetuates authoritarian rule.

Social Media Censorship

Social media platforms have become critical arenas for public discourse, but their content moderation policies can lead to the suppression of important debates. While efforts to combat misinformation and hate speech are necessary, they can also inadvertently censor legitimate political and social discussions.

Erosion of Individual Freedoms

Censorship not only affects public discourse but also erodes individual freedoms, including freedom of thought, expression, and access to information.

Historical Context

Throughout history, censorship has been used to restrict individual freedoms, often with devastating personal and societal consequences.

The Spanish Inquisition

During the Spanish Inquisition, individuals accused of heresy faced torture, imprisonment, and execution. The suppression of religious and intellectual freedoms created a climate of fear and conformity, stifling critical thought and innovation.

McCarthyism in the United States

In the mid-20th century, the United States experienced a period of intense anti-communist sentiment known as McCarthyism. Individuals suspected of communist sympathies faced blacklisting, persecution, and loss of employment. This era of censorship and fear significantly curtailed civil liberties and stifled political dissent.

Contemporary Examples

Modern instances of censorship continue to threaten individual freedoms and democratic principles.

Surveillance and Self-Censorship

In many countries, pervasive government surveillance leads to self-censorship among citizens who fear reprisal for expressing dissenting views. This erosion of privacy and freedom of expression stifles open dialogue and critical thinking.

Academic Freedom

Academic freedom is essential for the pursuit of knowledge and the advancement of society. However, censorship in academia, driven by political, economic, or ideological pressures, restricts researchers' ability to explore and discuss controversial topics. This limitation hinders intellectual growth and innovation.

Perpetuation of Ignorance and Division

Censorship perpetuates ignorance by restricting access to information and ideas, leading to a less informed and more divided society.

Historical Context

Historically, censorship has been used to maintain ignorance and prevent the spread of ideas that could challenge the status quo.

The Medieval Church and Scientific Knowledge

During the Middle Ages, the Catholic Church's censorship of scientific knowledge, such as the heliocentric theory, kept society in the dark about the true nature of the universe. This suppression of information hindered scientific progress and perpetuated ignorance.

Totalitarian Regimes and Historical Revisionism

Totalitarian regimes often engage in historical revisionism, altering or erasing historical records to fit their narratives. This manipulation of history perpetuates ignorance and prevents societies from learning from past mistakes.

Contemporary Examples

Modern instances of censorship continue to foster ignorance and societal division.

Censorship of Health Information

During the COVID-19 pandemic, the censorship of health information by various governments and media platforms led to widespread confusion and misinformation. Suppressing certain viewpoints or data can prevent the public from making informed decisions about their health and safety.

Polarization and Echo Chambers

Social media algorithms that prioritize engaging and sensational content can create echo chambers, where users are only exposed to information that reinforces their existing beliefs. This polarization and fragmentation of information contribute to societal division and the erosion of common ground.

Impact on Cultural and Intellectual Development

Censorship has significant implications for cultural and intellectual development, influencing the creation and dissemination of knowledge and art.

Historical Context

Historically, censorship has shaped cultural and intellectual life by determining which ideas and works are accessible to the public.

The Renaissance and Censorship

During the Renaissance, the Catholic Church's control over the production and dissemination of books influenced the development of Western thought and culture. While the Renaissance was a period of great intellectual and artistic achievement, censorship limited the range of ideas that could be explored and expressed.

The Enlightenment and the Fight for Intellectual Freedom

The Enlightenment, characterized by an emphasis on reason, science, and individual rights, saw significant challenges to censorship. Philosophers and writers, such as Voltaire and John Locke, fought for intellectual freedom and the right to question established authorities. Their efforts laid the groundwork for modern democratic societies that value free expression.

Contemporary Examples

In the modern era, censorship continues to shape cultural and intellectual development in significant ways.

The Suppression of LGBTQ+ Literature

LGBTQ+ literature has often faced censorship, particularly in regions where homosexuality is stigmatized or criminalized. Banning or restricting access to these works limits cultural representation and perpetuates discrimination against LGBTQ+ individuals.

Censorship in Education

Educational curricula are often subject to censorship, with controversial topics such as evolution, climate change, and racial history being omitted or altered. This censorship restricts students' access to comprehensive and accurate information, hindering their intellectual development and critical thinking skills.

The Role of Technology in Countering Censorship

While technology can be used to enforce censorship, it also provides tools for resisting and circumventing it.

Digital Resistance Tools

Various digital tools and platforms enable individuals to bypass censorship and access restricted information.

Virtual Private Networks (VPNs)

VPNs allow users to bypass government censorship by routing their internet traffic through servers in other countries. This technology is widely used in countries with strict internet censorship, such as China and Iran, enabling access to blocked websites and services.

Encrypted Messaging Apps

Encrypted messaging apps, such as Signal and Telegram, provide secure communication channels that protect users from surveillance and censorship. These apps are essential tools for activists, journalists, and ordinary citizens seeking to communicate freely in repressive environments.

Blockchain Technology

Blockchain technology offers the potential for decentralized, censorship-resistant platforms for information sharing. By distributing data across a network of nodes, blockchain can make it more difficult for authorities to suppress or manipulate information.

The Ongoing Fight for Intellectual Freedom

The fight against censorship is ongoing, with activists, journalists, academics, and ordinary citizens working to protect intellectual freedom and the free exchange of ideas.

Advocacy and Activism

Numerous organizations and movements advocate for free expression and challenge censorship practices.

Reporters Without Borders

Reporters Without Borders (RSF) is an international organization that promotes press freedom and defends journalists against censorship and persecution. RSF provides support and protection for journalists operating in hostile environments.

The Electronic Frontier Foundation

The Electronic Frontier Foundation (EFF) is a nonprofit organization dedicated to defending civil liberties in the digital world. EFF advocates for internet freedom, privacy, and the free flow of information, challenging government and corporate censorship.

Legal Challenges and Reforms

Legal challenges and reforms are essential in the fight against censorship. Advocates work to challenge restrictive laws and policies and promote legal frameworks that protect free expression.

Case Study: Net Neutrality

The battle over net neutrality in the United States highlights the importance of legal protections for internet freedom. Net neutrality ensures that internet service providers treat all data equally, preventing them from censoring or prioritizing certain content. Advocacy efforts have focused on maintaining these protections to safeguard the free flow of information.

Conclusion

Censorship has a profound and far-reaching impact on society, influencing creativity, innovation, public discourse, individual freedoms, and cultural and intellectual development. By examining historical and contemporary examples, we gain insight into the motivations and consequences of censorship and the importance of defending intellectual freedom.

As we continue to explore the various facets of censorship in the following chapters, we will delve deeper into specific instances and the resilience of those who have fought against it. Through detailed analyses and historical accounts, we aim to uncover the hidden agendas behind acts of censorship and celebrate the resilience of those who have championed the free exchange of ideas. By shining a light on these stories, we hope to inspire a renewed commitment to intellectual freedom and the pursuit of truth.

THE HIDDEN HAND: GOVERNMENT SECRETS AND COVER-UPS

Governments around the world have long been involved in covert operations, secret projects, and the suppression of sensitive information. These activities, often hidden from public scrutiny, are designed to protect national security, maintain political power, or conceal controversial actions. In Part VI of "Hidden Agendas: Exposing the Dark Secrets," we delve into the murky world of government secrets and cover-ups, exploring how these hidden activities shape our understanding of history and current events. This introduction sets the stage for a thorough examination of government cover-ups, from historical examples to modern-day conspiracies, shedding light on the lengths to which those in power will go to protect their interests.

The Nature of Government Secrecy

Government secrecy is a double-edged sword. On one hand, it is often justified as necessary for national security, protecting sensitive information from enemies and ensuring the safety of citizens. On the other hand, secrecy can be used to obscure actions that are illegal, unethical, or politically damaging. Understanding the dual nature of government secrecy is crucial for evaluating its impact on society.

Historical Context of Government Secrecy

Throughout history, governments have engaged in secretive practices to maintain control and protect their interests. These historical precedents provide valuable context for understanding modern-day government secrecy and cover-ups.

Ancient Regimes and Espionage

In ancient civilizations, rulers relied on spies and secret agents to gather intelligence and maintain their grip on power. The use of covert operations and secret communications dates back to ancient Egypt, Greece, and Rome, where espionage was a crucial tool for statecraft.

The Roman Empire

The Roman Empire's use of intelligence networks and secret agents helped it maintain control over vast territories. The Empire's ability to gather and act on covert information was a key factor in its longevity and power.

The Medieval and Renaissance Periods

During the medieval and Renaissance periods, the rise of centralized states and the development of more sophisticated political structures led to an increase in government secrecy. Monarchs and rulers used secret councils and private advisors to make decisions away from public scrutiny.

The Birth of Modern Intelligence Agencies

The 19th and 20th centuries saw the formalization of intelligence agencies and the institutionalization of government secrecy. The establishment of agencies such as the British Secret Service, the CIA, and the KGB marked a new era of systematic and organized espionage.

World War II and the Cold War

World War II and the subsequent Cold War were periods of intense government secrecy and covert operations. Both the Allied and Axis powers engaged in extensive espionage, cryptography, and covert missions. The Cold War, in particular, saw the rise of espionage and intelligence agencies as key players in global politics.

The Manhattan Project

The Manhattan Project, the secret U.S. initiative to develop atomic weapons during World War II, is one of the most significant examples of government secrecy. The project involved thousands of scientists and workers, and its successful concealment until the bombing of Hiroshima and Nagasaki demonstrated the lengths to which governments would go to protect sensitive information.

Modern Examples of Government Secrecy

In the modern era, government secrecy continues to play a crucial role in national security, foreign policy, and domestic affairs. However, the justification for secrecy is often contested, especially when it involves potential abuses of power or violations of human rights.

Classified Information and National Security

Governments classify information to protect national security and prevent sensitive data from falling into the wrong hands. Classified information ranges from military plans and intelligence operations to diplomatic communications and technological innovations.

Whistleblowers and Leaks

Despite efforts to maintain secrecy, whistleblowers and leaks have exposed numerous government secrets and cover-ups. Figures such as Edward Snowden, Chelsea Manning, and Julian Assange have brought to light covert activities and controversial policies, sparking public debate and legal battles.

Edward Snowden and the NSA

In 2013, Edward Snowden, a former contractor for the National Security Agency (NSA), leaked classified documents revealing the extent of the U.S. government's surveillance programs. Snowden's disclosures showed that the NSA was collecting massive amounts of data on American citizens and foreign nationals, raising concerns about privacy and government overreach.

Chelsea Manning and WikiLeaks

Chelsea Manning, a former U.S. Army intelligence analyst, leaked thousands of classified documents to WikiLeaks, including diplomatic cables and military reports. The release of these documents exposed controversial aspects of U.S. foreign policy and military operations, including evidence of civilian casualties and diplomatic scandals.

Julian Assange and WikiLeaks

Julian Assange, the founder of WikiLeaks, has been a central figure in the dissemination of classified information. WikiLeaks' publication of secret documents has sparked global debates about transparency, press freedom, and the ethical implications of leaking sensitive information.

The Role of the Media in Uncovering Secrets

The media plays a critical role in uncovering government secrets and holding authorities accountable. Investigative journalism has exposed numerous scandals and cover-ups, highlighting the importance of a free press in a democratic society.

The Pentagon Papers

In 1971, The New York Times published the Pentagon Papers, a classified report detailing the U.S. government's involvement in the Vietnam War. The documents, leaked by former military analyst Daniel Ellsberg, revealed that the government had systematically misled the public about the war's progress and objectives. The Pentagon Papers case underscored the vital role of the press in exposing government deception.

Watergate Scandal

The Watergate scandal, uncovered by journalists Bob Woodward and Carl Bernstein, exposed illegal activities and abuses of power by President Richard Nixon's administration. The scandal led to Nixon's resignation and reinforced the importance of investigative journalism in uncovering government misconduct.

Government Cover-Ups and Conspiracies

Government cover-ups and conspiracies often involve efforts to conceal wrongdoing, protect political interests, or avoid public backlash. These cover-ups can have far-reaching consequences for public trust and democratic governance.

The Tuskegee Syphilis Study

The Tuskegee Syphilis Study, conducted by the U.S. Public Health Service from 1932 to 1972, involved the unethical treatment of African American men with syphilis. The study participants were misled about their condition and denied proper treatment, even after penicillin became available. The revelation of the study in 1972 caused a public outcry and led to significant changes in medical ethics and research practices.

Iran-Contra Affair

The Iran-Contra affair was a political scandal in the 1980s involving the secret sale of arms to Iran and the illegal funding of Contra rebels in Nicaragua. The Reagan administration's efforts to conceal these activities resulted in a major political scandal and congressional investigations. The affair highlighted the dangers of covert operations and the need for oversight and accountability in government actions.

MK-Ultra

Project MK-Ultra was a covert CIA program that conducted mind control and behavioral modification experiments on unwitting subjects during the 1950s and 1960s. The program, which involved the use of drugs, hypnosis, and other techniques, was kept secret from the public and even from many government officials. The exposure of MK-Ultra in the 1970s revealed significant ethical violations and led to increased scrutiny of intelligence operations.

The Impact of Secrecy and Cover-Ups on Society

The consequences of government secrecy and cover-ups are profound, affecting public trust, democratic accountability, and societal progress.

Erosion of Public Trust

Revelations of government secrecy and cover-ups can erode public trust in institutions and leaders. When citizens discover that their government has engaged in unethical or illegal activities, it undermines confidence in democratic processes and the rule of law.

Case Study: The Church Committee

The Church Committee, a U.S. Senate committee led by Senator Frank Church, investigated intelligence abuses by the CIA, FBI, and other agencies in the 1970s. The committee's findings, which included evidence of illegal surveillance, assassination plots, and covert operations, shocked the public and led to significant reforms. The revelations underscored the need for transparency and oversight in intelligence activities to maintain public trust.

Implications for Democratic Accountability

Government secrecy and cover-ups pose significant challenges to democratic accountability. When actions are hidden from public scrutiny, it becomes difficult for citizens and their representatives to hold officials accountable for their decisions and actions.

The Importance of Whistleblower Protections

Whistleblower protections are essential for encouraging individuals to come forward with information about government misconduct. Effective legal frameworks and protections can help ensure that whistleblowers are not subject to retaliation and that their disclosures lead to meaningful oversight and reform.

The Balance Between Secrecy and Transparency

Balancing the need for government secrecy with the principles of transparency and accountability is a complex and ongoing challenge. While some level of secrecy is necessary for national security and effective governance, excessive secrecy can undermine democratic values and public trust.

Case Study: The Freedom of Information Act (FOIA)

The Freedom of Information Act (FOIA) in the United States provides a legal framework for the public to access government records, promoting transparency and accountability. However, the effectiveness of FOIA is often limited by bureaucratic obstacles, exemptions, and delays. Strengthening FOIA and similar laws worldwide is crucial for ensuring that governments remain open and accountable to their citizens.

Conclusion

The hidden hand of government secrets and cover-ups has far-reaching implications for society, influencing public trust, democratic accountability, and the course of history. By examining historical and contemporary examples, we gain insight into the motivations and consequences of government secrecy and the importance of transparency in maintaining a healthy democracy.

In the following chapters, we will delve deeper into specific instances of government cover-ups and secret projects, providing detailed analyses and historical accounts. Through these explorations, we aim to uncover the hidden agendas behind acts of government secrecy and celebrate the resilience of those who have fought for transparency and accountability. By shining a light on these stories, we hope to inspire a renewed commitment to protecting the principles of open government and the free flow of information in our society.

| 16 |

Chapter 16: Government Cover-Ups: An Overview

Throughout history, governments have engaged in cover-ups to conceal actions, policies, and events that could damage their reputation, undermine their authority, or provoke public outrage. These cover-ups can range from hiding military failures and political scandals to concealing scientific discoveries and human rights abuses. In this chapter, we will provide an in-depth overview of government cover-ups, exploring their motivations, mechanisms, and the impact they have on society. By examining notable examples from different periods and regions, we aim to shed light on the pervasive nature of government secrecy and the lengths to which authorities will go to protect their interests.

The Nature and Motivations of Government Cover-Ups

Government cover-ups are deliberate attempts to hide the truth from the public, often motivated by a desire to maintain control, avoid accountability, or protect national security.

Maintaining Control and Authority

Governments often engage in cover-ups to maintain their control and authority over the populace. Revealing certain truths can undermine public confidence, incite unrest, or weaken the government's ability to govern effectively.

Avoiding Accountability

Cover-ups are also motivated by a desire to avoid accountability for actions that may be illegal, unethical, or deeply controversial. By concealing the truth, government officials hope to escape consequences and maintain their positions of power.

Protecting National Security

In some cases, cover-ups are justified as necessary to protect national security. Governments may hide information about military operations, intelligence activities, or diplomatic negotiations to prevent adversaries from gaining an advantage.

Mechanisms of Government Cover-Ups

Governments employ a variety of mechanisms to carry out cover-ups, ranging from propaganda and misinformation to legal maneuvers and physical destruction of evidence.

Propaganda and Misinformation

Governments often use propaganda and misinformation to control the narrative and distract from the truth. By spreading false or misleading information, authorities can shape public perception and obscure the facts.

Case Study: The Gulf of Tonkin Incident

The Gulf of Tonkin incident in 1964, which led to the escalation of the Vietnam War, is a classic example of government misinformation. The U.S. government claimed that North Vietnamese forces had attacked American ships, leading Congress to pass the Gulf of Tonkin Resolution. However, later investigations revealed that the incident was either exaggerated or fabricated, and the U.S. used it as a pretext for military intervention.

Legal Maneuvers

Governments often use legal mechanisms to suppress information and silence dissent. This can include invoking national security laws, classifying documents, and prosecuting whistleblowers.

Case Study: The Pentagon Papers

When Daniel Ellsberg leaked the Pentagon Papers, a classified report on U.S. involvement in Vietnam, the Nixon administration attempted to block their publication through legal injunctions. However, the Supreme Court ruled in favor of the press, allowing the documents to be published and revealing the extent of government deception about the war.

Physical Destruction of Evidence

In extreme cases, governments may resort to the physical destruction of evidence to ensure that certain truths never come to light. This can involve destroying documents, silencing witnesses, or even committing acts of violence.

Case Study: The Watergate Scandal

The Watergate scandal is one of the most infamous examples of a government cover-up involving the destruction of evidence. Members of President Nixon's administration attempted to cover up their involvement in the break-in at the Democratic National Committee headquarters by destroying documents and obstructing the investigation. The cover-up ultimately failed, leading to Nixon's resignation.

Notable Historical Examples of Government Cover-Ups

To understand the breadth and impact of government cover-ups, it is essential to examine some notable historical examples that highlight different motivations and mechanisms.

The Tuskegee Syphilis Study

The Tuskegee Syphilis Study, conducted by the U.S. Public Health Service from 1932 to 1972, is a glaring example of a government cover-up involving unethical medical experimentation.

Background and Motivation

The study involved 600 African American men, 399 of whom had syphilis, and 201 who did not. The men were misled about the nature of the study and were not informed that they had syphilis. Instead of being treated, they were monitored to observe the progression of the disease. The study aimed to justify treatment programs for African Americans but was fundamentally unethical.

The Cover-Up and Its Unveiling

The study was kept secret for decades, with the participants receiving inadequate treatment even after penicillin became the standard cure for syphilis in the 1940s. The cover-up was exposed in 1972 by a whistleblower, leading to public outrage, a congressional investigation, and significant changes in medical ethics and research practices.

The Iran-Contra Affair

The Iran-Contra affair in the 1980s was a major political scandal in the United States, involving the secret sale of arms to Iran and the illegal funding of Contra rebels in Nicaragua.

Background and Motivation

The Reagan administration sought to secure the release of hostages held by Hezbollah in Lebanon and support the Contra rebels, who were fighting the socialist Sandinista government in Nicaragua. To achieve these goals, officials orchestrated the sale of arms to Iran, despite an arms embargo, and funneled the proceeds to the Contras, circumventing a congressional ban on such funding.

The Cover-Up and Its Unveiling

The affair was kept secret until it was exposed by a Lebanese newspaper in 1986. Subsequent investigations revealed the extent of the illegal activities and the involvement of high-ranking officials. The scandal led to multiple indictments and convictions, though many were later overturned or pardoned.

Project MK-Ultra

Project MK-Ultra, a CIA program that conducted mind control and behavioral modification experiments on unwitting subjects, is another notorious example of a government cover-up.

Background and Motivation

Launched in the early 1950s, MK-Ultra aimed to develop techniques for interrogation and mind control, driven by Cold War fears of Soviet and Chinese brainwashing methods. The program involved administering drugs, such as LSD, and using other methods, including hypnosis and sensory deprivation, on unsuspecting individuals.

The Cover-Up and Its Unveiling

The program was conducted in secret, with little oversight or ethical consideration. It was exposed in the mid-1970s through investigations by the Church Committee and a subsequent report by the General Accounting Office. The revelations led to public outrage, legal reforms, and a greater awareness of the need for ethical standards in research.

Contemporary Examples of Government Cover-Ups

Government cover-ups are not confined to history; they continue to occur in various forms around the world today. Modern examples highlight the ongoing struggle for transparency and accountability.

The NSA Surveillance Program

The National Security Agency (NSA) surveillance program, revealed by whistleblower Edward Snowden in 2013, exposed the extent of government monitoring of private communications.

Background and Motivation

Following the September 11 attacks, the U.S. government expanded its surveillance capabilities to prevent future terrorist incidents. The NSA collected massive amounts of data, including phone records and internet communications, often without warrants or public knowledge.

The Cover-Up and Its Unveiling

The program was conducted in secret, justified by national security concerns. Snowden's disclosures revealed the scope of the surveillance, sparking global debates about privacy, security, and government over-reach. The revelations led to legal challenges and calls for reform of surveillance practices.

The Flint Water Crisis

The Flint water crisis in Michigan, which began in 2014, is a recent example of a government cover-up involving public health and environmental safety.

Background and Motivation

To save money, Flint switched its water supply from Lake Huron to the Flint River, a decision that led to lead contamination in the water supply. Residents complained about the water quality, but officials downplayed the risks and failed to take adequate action.

The Cover-Up and Its Unveiling

Local, state, and federal officials initially dismissed residents' concerns and provided false assurances about the water's safety. Independent researchers eventually confirmed the contamination, leading to widespread outrage, legal investigations, and numerous lawsuits. The crisis exposed systemic failures and the dangers of government negligence and cover-ups.

The Impact of Government Cover-Ups on Society

Government cover-ups have far-reaching consequences for society, affecting public trust, democratic governance, and social progress.

Erosion of Public Trust

Revelations of government cover-ups can severely erode public trust in institutions and leaders. When citizens discover that their government has engaged in deception or misconduct, it undermines confidence in democratic processes and the rule of law.

Case Study: The Watergate Scandal

The Watergate scandal is a prime example of how a government cover-up can erode public trust. The Nixon administration's attempts to conceal its involvement in the break-in and subsequent cover-up led to a crisis of confidence in the presidency and contributed to widespread cynicism about government integrity.

Implications for Democratic Governance

Cover-ups undermine democratic governance by preventing transparency and accountability. When government actions are hidden from public scrutiny, it becomes difficult for citizens and their representatives to hold officials accountable for their decisions and actions.

The Importance of Whistleblower Protections

Whistleblower protections are essential for encouraging individuals to come forward with information about government misconduct. Effective legal frameworks and protections can help ensure that whistleblowers are not subject to retaliation and that their disclosures lead to meaningful oversight and reform.

The Role of Investigative Journalism

Investigative journalism plays a crucial role in uncovering government cover-ups and holding authorities accountable. Journalists who expose hidden truths contribute to a more informed and engaged citizenry.

Case Study: The Pentagon Papers

The publication of the Pentagon Papers by The New York Times and other newspapers was a landmark moment for investigative journalism. The documents revealed government deception about the Vietnam War, leading to a shift in public opinion and greater scrutiny of government actions.

The Need for Legal Reforms

Legal reforms are necessary to ensure greater transparency and accountability in government actions. Strengthening laws that promote open government, such as the Freedom of Information Act (FOIA), can help prevent cover-ups and promote public trust.

Conclusion

Government cover-ups are a pervasive and persistent issue that can have profound implications for society. By examining historical and contemporary examples, we gain a deeper understanding of the motivations, mechanisms, and consequences of these actions. The importance of transparency, accountability, and the protection of whistleblowers and investigative journalists cannot be overstated in the ongoing struggle to uncover hidden truths and uphold democratic values.

In the following chapters, we will continue to explore specific instances of government cover-ups and secret projects, providing detailed analyses and historical accounts. Through these explorations, we aim to uncover the hidden agendas behind acts of government secrecy and celebrate the resilience of those who have fought for transparency and accountability. By shining a light on these stories, we hope to inspire a renewed commitment to protecting the principles of open government and the free flow of information in our society.

| 17 |

Chapter 17: UFOs and Extraterrestrial Cover-Ups

The possibility of extraterrestrial life and unidentified flying objects (UFOs) has fascinated humanity for decades. While popular culture often portrays UFOs as figments of imagination or subjects of fringe science, there is a substantial body of evidence suggesting that governments worldwide have taken the phenomenon seriously. This chapter explores the history of UFO sightings, the government's responses, and the alleged cover-ups that have sparked widespread conspiracy theories. By examining declassified documents, whistleblower testimonies, and key incidents, we aim to uncover the truth behind UFOs and the potential existence of extraterrestrial life.

The Historical Context of UFO Sightings

UFO sightings are not a modern phenomenon; reports of strange objects in the sky date back to ancient times. However, the modern UFO era began in the mid-20th century, coinciding with significant advancements in aviation and space exploration.

Early Sightings

Ancient and Medieval Accounts

Historical texts from various cultures describe encounters with mysterious aerial phenomena. Ancient Roman records, medieval manuscripts, and indigenous oral traditions all contain accounts of strange lights and objects in the sky. While these descriptions are often vague and open to interpretation, they suggest that unexplained aerial phenomena have been observed for millennia.

The Modern UFO Era

The 1940s and the Birth of the UFO Phenomenon

The modern UFO era is generally considered to have begun in the 1940s. One of the most famous early sightings occurred in 1947, when pilot Kenneth Arnold reported seeing nine shiny objects flying at incredible speeds near Mount Rainier in Washington State. Arnold's sighting, widely publicized in the media, introduced the term "flying saucer" into the popular lexicon.

The Roswell Incident

In July 1947, an incident near Roswell, New Mexico, would become the most famous UFO case in history. After a mysterious object crashed on a ranch, the U.S. military initially announced it had recovered a "flying disc." However, the story was quickly retracted, and the debris was said to be from a weather balloon. The conflicting reports and subsequent secrecy fueled speculation about a government cover-up of an extraterrestrial encounter.

Government Investigations and Responses

As UFO sightings increased, governments, particularly in the United States, began to take the phenomenon seriously, leading to official investigations and research programs.

Project Blue Book

Overview and Objectives

From 1952 to 1969, the U.S. Air Force conducted Project Blue Book, an extensive study of UFO sightings. The project's objectives were to determine if UFOs posed a national security threat and to scientifically analyze the phenomena.

Findings and Controversies

Project Blue Book investigated over 12,000 UFO reports, concluding that most could be explained as misidentifications of natural phenomena or man-made objects. However, a small percentage remained unexplained. Critics argue that the project was biased towards debunking sightings rather than seriously investigating them, leading to allegations of a cover-up.

The Condon Committee

Formation and Purpose

In 1966, the Air Force commissioned the University of Colorado, led by physicist Dr. Edward Condon, to conduct an independent investigation into UFOs. Known as the Condon Committee, the group's aim was to provide a definitive scientific assessment of the UFO phenomenon.

Conclusions and Criticisms

The Condon Report, published in 1969, concluded that further study of UFOs was unlikely to yield significant scientific discoveries and recommended ending official investigations. This conclusion led to the termination of Project Blue Book. However, many researchers criticized the Condon Report for being dismissive and not thoroughly examining all evidence, fueling further suspicions of a cover-up.

Declassified Documents and Whistleblower Testimonies

Over the years, declassified documents and testimonies from former government officials and military personnel have provided new insights into UFO investigations and alleged cover-ups.

The Majestic 12 Documents

Claims and Controversies

In the 1980s, documents surfaced purporting to be from "Majestic 12," a secret group established by President Harry S. Truman to manage UFO information. The documents claimed that the U.S. government had recovered alien technology and bodies from crash sites. While many researchers consider the documents to be a hoax, they have nevertheless fueled conspiracy theories about government knowledge of extraterrestrial life.

Testimonies from Former Officials

Colonel Philip J. Corso

Colonel Philip J. Corso, a former Army intelligence officer, claimed in his 1997 book "The Day After Roswell" that he had overseen the distribution of recovered alien technology to private industry for reverse engineering. Corso's claims, while controversial, have been supported by some and dismissed by others.

Robert Salas and the Malmstrom AFB Incident

In 1967, Robert Salas, a former Air Force officer, reported a UFO disabling nuclear missiles at Malmstrom Air Force Base in Montana. Salas and other witnesses have since come forward to testify about the incident, alleging a cover-up by the Air Force.

Notable UFO Incidents and Government Responses

Several high-profile UFO incidents have garnered significant attention and raised questions about government transparency and cover-ups.

The Rendlesham Forest Incident

Overview of the Incident

In December 1980, U.S. Air Force personnel stationed at RAF Bentwaters in the United Kingdom reported encountering a UFO in Rendlesham Forest. The incident, often referred to as "Britain's Roswell," involved multiple witnesses, radar detections, and physical evidence such as landing marks and increased radiation levels.

Government Investigation and Reaction

The U.S. and U.K. governments conducted investigations, but the official explanations were inconclusive and often contradictory. The lack of transparency and the disappearance of crucial documents have led to ongoing speculation about a cover-up.

The Phoenix Lights

Description of the Event

In March 1997, thousands of people in Arizona witnessed a series of mysterious lights in the sky, which became known as the "Phoenix Lights." The event included a V-shaped formation of lights moving slowly across the state and stationary lights hovering over Phoenix.

Government Explanations and Public Skepticism

The U.S. military initially attributed the lights to flares dropped during a training exercise, but many witnesses, including former Arizona Governor Fife Symington, disputed this explanation. The conflicting reports and lack of a definitive answer have kept the Phoenix Lights incident shrouded in mystery.

The Role of the Media and Public Perception

The media plays a crucial role in shaping public perception of UFOs and government cover-ups. Sensational reporting, misinformation, and varying levels of skepticism can influence how the public interprets UFO sightings and official responses.

Media Coverage and Sensationalism

Early Reporting

Early media coverage of UFO sightings often focused on sensational and anecdotal accounts, which contributed to the perception of UFOs as a fringe topic. Headlines about "flying saucers" and "alien encounters" captured public imagination but also led to ridicule and skepticism.

Modern Reporting

In recent years, media coverage of UFOs has become more nuanced and serious, especially following the release of credible evidence and official statements. Investigative journalism and documentaries have brought renewed attention to the subject, presenting it as a legitimate area of inquiry.

The Impact of Popular Culture

Movies and Television

Popular culture has significantly influenced public perception of UFOs and extraterrestrial life. Films like "Close Encounters of the Third Kind" and "Independence Day," along with television series like "The X-Files," have shaped how people think about UFOs, often blending fact with fiction.

Books and Documentaries

Books and documentaries by researchers and former officials have provided detailed accounts of UFO incidents and alleged cover-ups, contributing to a more informed and critical public discourse.

The Importance of Transparency and Scientific Inquiry

The ongoing interest in UFOs and the potential for extraterrestrial life underscores the need for transparency and rigorous scientific inquiry. Governments and scientific institutions must balance national security concerns with the public's right to know and the pursuit of knowledge.

Advocacy for Disclosure

Citizen Efforts and Activism

Citizen groups and activists have long called for greater transparency and the declassification of UFO-related documents. Efforts such as the Disclosure Project, led by Dr. Steven Greer, aim to bring whistleblower testimonies and classified information to public attention.

Congressional Hearings and Legislative Action

In recent years, there has been growing political support for greater transparency regarding UFOs. Congressional hearings and legislative initiatives have called for the release of classified information and the establishment of official investigative bodies.

Scientific Research and Collaboration

The Role of Academia

Academic institutions and researchers play a crucial role in advancing our understanding of UFOs and the possibility of extraterrestrial life. By applying scientific methods and fostering interdisciplinary collaboration, academia can provide valuable insights and reduce the stigma associated with studying UFOs.

SETI and the Search for Extraterrestrial Intelligence

The Search for Extraterrestrial Intelligence (SETI) is a scientific endeavor dedicated to detecting signs of intelligent life beyond Earth. SETI's work, including monitoring radio signals and analyzing data from space telescopes, represents a legitimate and respected approach to exploring the possibility of extraterrestrial civilizations.

Conclusion

The phenomenon of UFOs and the potential existence of extraterrestrial life continues to captivate the public imagination and provoke significant debate. Government cover-ups, declassified documents, and whistleblower testimonies have fueled speculation and conspiracy theories, highlighting the need for greater transparency and scientific inquiry.

By examining historical and contemporary examples of UFO sightings and government responses, we gain a deeper understanding of the complexities and challenges associated with this enigmatic subject. The pursuit of truth and knowledge in the face of secrecy and skepticism is a testament to humanity's enduring curiosity and quest for understanding.

In the following chapters, we will explore other facets of government secrecy and cover-ups, providing detailed analyses and historical accounts. Through these explorations, we aim to uncover the hidden agendas behind acts of government secrecy and celebrate the resilience of those who have fought for transparency and accountability. By shining a light on these stories, we hope to inspire a renewed commitment to protecting the principles of open government and the free flow of information in our society.

| 18 |

Chapter 18: Secret Projects and Covert Operations

Governments worldwide have historically engaged in secret projects and covert operations to achieve strategic, political, and military objectives. These activities, often hidden from public scrutiny, range from clandestine military programs and espionage to psychological operations and mind control experiments. This chapter provides a comprehensive examination of some of the most infamous and controversial secret projects and covert operations. By exploring declassified documents, testimonies, and historical analyses, we aim to uncover the hidden truths behind these clandestine activities and their impact on society.

The Nature and Purpose of Secret Projects and Covert Operations

Secret projects and covert operations are typically conducted in the interest of national security, intelligence gathering, and strategic advantage. They are designed to operate outside the bounds of conventional oversight and often involve ethically and legally questionable methods.

National Security and Strategic Advantage

Governments justify secret projects and covert operations as necessary to protect national security and gain a strategic edge over adversaries. These activities can include developing advanced weaponry, conducting espionage, and engaging in cyber warfare.

Intelligence Gathering

Intelligence agencies engage in covert operations to collect information on foreign governments, organizations, and individuals. This intelligence is used to inform national security policies and decision-making.

Plausible Deniability

A key aspect of covert operations is plausible deniability, which allows governments to deny involvement in activities that may be controversial or illegal. This secrecy shields officials from accountability and minimizes political fallout.

Historical Examples of Secret Projects and Covert Operations

Throughout history, numerous secret projects and covert operations have been undertaken by various governments. Some of these activities have since been exposed, revealing the lengths to which authorities will go to achieve their objectives.

Operation Paperclip

Overview and Objectives

Operation Paperclip was a secret U.S. program conducted after World War II to recruit German scientists, engineers, and technicians, many of whom were former members of the Nazi party. The primary goal was to leverage their expertise to advance American military and space programs and prevent these individuals from falling into Soviet hands.

The Recruitment of Nazi Scientists

Under Operation Paperclip, more than 1,600 German scientists were brought to the United States, including Wernher von Braun, who played a pivotal role in developing rocket technology. Despite their Nazi affiliations, these scientists were granted immunity and integrated into American scientific and military institutions.

Ethical Controversies and Impact

Operation Paperclip remains controversial due to the ethical implications of granting former Nazis immunity and prominent positions. While the program contributed significantly to American technological advancements, it also raised moral questions about the cost of such progress.

Project MK-Ultra

Overview and Objectives

Project MK-Ultra was a CIA program initiated in the early 1950s to develop mind control and interrogation techniques. The project involved administering drugs, such as LSD, and using hypnosis, sensory deprivation, and other methods on unwitting subjects.

Experiments and Methods

MK-Ultra's experiments were conducted on a wide range of subjects, including prisoners, military personnel, and civilians. Many participants were unaware they were part of an experiment, and the methods used often resulted in severe psychological and physical harm.

Exposure and Aftermath

The existence of MK-Ultra was revealed in the 1970s through investigations by the Church Committee and subsequent media reports. The program's exposure led to public outrage, legal reforms, and increased scrutiny of intelligence operations. The ethical violations of MK-Ultra remain a stark reminder of the potential abuses of unchecked governmental power.

Operation Northwoods

Overview and Objectives

Operation Northwoods was a proposed false flag operation developed by the U.S. Department of Defense in 1962. The plan involved staging terrorist attacks against American civilians and military targets and blaming them on Cuba to justify military intervention.

Proposed Actions

The proposed actions included hijacking planes, sinking boats of Cuban refugees, and staging bombings in American cities. The objective was to create a pretext for invading Cuba and overthrowing Fidel Castro's government.

Rejection and Exposure

Operation Northwoods was ultimately rejected by President John F. Kennedy, but the plan's existence was revealed decades later through declassified documents. The revelation of such an extreme and unethical proposal shocked the public and highlighted the lengths to which some officials were willing to go to achieve their goals.

Contemporary Examples of Secret Projects and Covert Operations

In the modern era, secret projects and covert operations continue to be a significant aspect of governmental activities. Advances in technology and the changing nature of warfare have led to new forms of clandestine operations.

The NSA Surveillance Program

Overview and Objectives

The National Security Agency (NSA) surveillance program, exposed by whistleblower Edward Snowden in 2013, involved the mass collection of data on American citizens and foreign nationals. The program aimed to identify and prevent terrorist activities by monitoring communications and internet activity.

Methods and Scope

The NSA used various methods to collect data, including tapping into undersea cables, hacking into servers, and compelling telecommunications companies to provide access to their networks. The scope of the surveillance was vast, encompassing phone records, emails, and online activity.

Public Reaction and Impact

The revelation of the NSA's surveillance activities sparked global debates about privacy, security, and government overreach. It led to legal challenges, policy changes, and a greater awareness of the need for oversight in intelligence operations.

Operation Gladio

Overview and Objectives

Operation Gladio was a secret NATO operation during the Cold War, involving stay-behind networks in Europe that were prepared to conduct guerrilla warfare in the event of a Soviet invasion. These networks were also allegedly involved in manipulating political events to counter communist influence.

Activities and Allegations

While originally intended as a defense strategy, Gladio networks have been accused of engaging in false flag operations, terrorism, and political manipulation. Some investigations suggest that these networks were involved in violent attacks to create instability and justify crackdowns on leftist movements.

Exposure and Controversies

The existence of Operation Gladio was revealed in the 1990s, leading to widespread controversy and investigations in several European countries. The allegations of state-sponsored terrorism and political manipulation have raised significant ethical and legal questions.

The Impact of Secret Projects and Covert Operations on Society

Secret projects and covert operations have far-reaching implications for society, affecting public trust, democratic governance, and international relations.

Erosion of Public Trust

Revelations of secret projects and covert operations can severely erode public trust in government institutions and officials. When citizens learn that their government has engaged in unethical or illegal activities, it undermines confidence in democratic processes and the rule of law.

Case Study: The Watergate Scandal

The Watergate scandal, involving a break-in at the Democratic National Committee headquarters and subsequent cover-up by the Nixon administration, is a prime example of how covert operations can erode public trust. The scandal led to President Nixon's resignation and a widespread loss of faith in the government.

Implications for Democratic Governance

Covert operations pose significant challenges to democratic governance by preventing transparency and accountability. When government actions are hidden from public scrutiny, it becomes difficult for citizens and their representatives to hold officials accountable for their decisions and actions.

The Role of Oversight and Accountability

Effective oversight and accountability mechanisms are essential to prevent abuses of power in secret projects and covert operations.

Legislative bodies, independent agencies, and the judiciary must work together to ensure that intelligence and military activities adhere to legal and ethical standards.

The Need for Legal Reforms

Legal reforms are necessary to ensure greater transparency and accountability in government actions. Strengthening laws that promote open government, such as the Freedom of Information Act (FOIA), can help prevent cover-ups and promote public trust.

The Role of Whistleblowers and Investigative Journalism

Whistleblowers and investigative journalists play a crucial role in uncovering secret projects and covert operations. By exposing hidden truths, they contribute to a more informed and engaged citizenry.

Case Study: The Pentagon Papers

The publication of the Pentagon Papers by The New York Times and other newspapers was a landmark moment for investigative journalism. The documents revealed government deception about the Vietnam War, leading to a shift in public opinion and greater scrutiny of government actions.

Conclusion

Secret projects and covert operations have been a significant aspect of governmental activities throughout history, often justified in the name of national security and strategic advantage. However, these clandestine actions raise serious ethical and legal questions and can have far-reaching consequences for public trust and democratic governance.

By examining historical and contemporary examples of secret projects and covert operations, we gain a deeper understanding of the motivations, mechanisms, and impact of these activities. The importance of transparency, accountability, and the protection of whistle-blowers and investigative journalists cannot be overstated in the ongoing struggle to uncover hidden truths and uphold democratic values.

In the following chapters, we will continue to explore other facets of government secrecy and cover-ups, providing detailed analyses and historical accounts. Through these explorations, we aim to uncover the hidden agendas behind acts of government secrecy and celebrate the resilience of those who have fought for transparency and accountability. By shining a light on these stories, we hope to inspire a renewed commitment to protecting the principles of open government and the free flow of information in our society.

THE ROLE OF SECRET SOCIETIES IN SHAPING WORLD EVENTS

Secret societies have long captivated the public imagination with their aura of mystery and power. These organizations, often shrouded in secrecy and exclusive membership, are believed to wield significant influence over political, economic, and social events. While some view them as benign fraternities, others see them as malevolent forces working behind the scenes to control global affairs. In Part VII of "Hidden Agendas: Exposing the Dark Secrets," we delve into the enigmatic world of secret societies, exploring their origins, rituals, and alleged influence on world events. By examining historical records, testimonies, and conspiracy theories, we aim to uncover the truth behind these clandestine groups and their impact on history.

The Origins and Characteristics of Secret Societies

Secret societies have existed for centuries, often emerging in response to political, religious, or social circumstances. These groups typically share common characteristics, such as exclusivity, secret rituals, and a hierarchical structure.

Historical Background

Ancient and Medieval Societies

The origins of secret societies can be traced back to ancient civilizations. The Eleusinian Mysteries of ancient Greece, the Mithraic Mysteries of Rome, and the Gnostic sects of early Christianity all exhibited elements of secrecy and exclusive membership. During the medieval period, the Knights Templar and various alchemical societies operated in secrecy, often driven by religious or philosophical pursuits.

The Enlightenment and the Rise of Modern Secret Societies

The Enlightenment era saw the emergence of several influential secret societies, including the Freemasons, the Illuminati, and the Rosicrucians. These groups often promoted ideals of rationalism, science, and individual liberty, challenging established religious and political authorities.

Characteristics of Secret Societies

Exclusivity and Membership

Secret societies typically restrict membership to a select group of individuals, often requiring initiation rituals and oaths of secrecy. This exclusivity fosters a sense of camaraderie and loyalty among members while enhancing the group's mystique.

Secret Rituals and Symbols

Rituals and symbols play a crucial role in the identity and operations of secret societies. These elements often serve to reinforce the group's values, create a sense of belonging, and maintain secrecy. Symbols such as the Freemasons' square and compass or the Illuminati's all-seeing eye are imbued with esoteric meaning and are used to identify members.

Hierarchical Structure

Many secret societies are organized hierarchically, with a clear chain of command and levels of initiation. This structure allows for the control and dissemination of information within the group and ensures that only trusted members have access to sensitive knowledge.

Influential Secret Societies in History

Several secret societies have left a significant mark on history, influencing political, economic, and social events. By examining the most prominent of these groups, we can better understand their role in shaping world events.

The Freemasons

Origins and Development

The Freemasons trace their origins to the medieval stonemason guilds of Europe, which evolved into a fraternal organization promoting Enlightenment ideals of reason, science, and liberty. By the 18th century, Freemasonry had spread across Europe and North America, attracting influential figures from various walks of life.

Rituals and Beliefs

Freemasonry is characterized by its elaborate rituals, symbolic architecture, and moral teachings. The group promotes values such as brotherhood, charity, and truth, often using allegorical stories and symbols drawn from stonemasonry and biblical texts.

Influence on Historical Events

Freemasons have been linked to several significant historical events, including the American and French Revolutions. Many Founding Fathers of the United States, such as George Washington and Benjamin Franklin, were Freemasons, and Masonic ideals of liberty and equality influenced the drafting of the U.S. Constitution. Similarly, Freemasons played a role in the intellectual and political currents that led to the French Revolution.

The Illuminati

Origins and Goals

The Illuminati was founded in 1776 by Adam Weishaupt, a professor of canon law at the University of Ingolstadt in Bavaria. Weishaupt sought to create a society dedicated to Enlightenment principles, free from the influence of the Catholic Church and conservative authorities. The Illuminati aimed to promote rationalism, secularism, and social reform through clandestine means.

Structure and Activities

The Illuminati operated in secrecy, using code names and covert communication to protect its members. The group infiltrated other organizations, such as Masonic lodges, to spread its ideas and recruit members. Despite its ambitious goals, the Illuminati was short-lived, dissolving by the late 1780s due to internal conflicts and government persecution.

Enduring Myths and Conspiracy Theories

Despite its brief existence, the Illuminati has become a central figure in numerous conspiracy theories. Many believe that the group continued to operate in secret, manipulating world events and orchestrating a New World Order. These theories often allege that the Illuminati controls global finance, media, and politics through a network of influential individuals and organizations.

The Skull and Bones Society

Origins and Membership

The Skull and Bones Society, also known as the Order of Skull and Bones, was founded in 1832 at Yale University by William Huntington Russell and Alphonso Taft. The society is known for its secrecy, exclusive membership, and powerful alumni, which include prominent political, business, and academic leaders.

Rituals and Symbols

Skull and Bones is infamous for its mysterious rituals, which are said to include the use of skulls, coffins, and other macabre symbols. Members, known as "Bonesmen," participate in these rituals as part of their initiation and continue to meet in secret throughout their lives.

Influence on American Politics and Society

The Skull and Bones Society has produced a remarkable number of influential figures, including presidents, senators, and business magnates. Notable members include former Presidents George H.W. Bush and George W. Bush, as well as former Secretary of State John Kerry. The society's connections and influence have led to speculation about its role in shaping American political and economic policies.

The Bilderberg Group

Origins and Purpose

The Bilderberg Group was founded in 1954 by Dutch statesman Joseph Retinger, with the support of several European and American leaders. The group's purpose is to foster dialogue and cooperation between Europe and North America on political, economic, and social issues. Bilderberg meetings are held annually, bringing together influential politicians, business leaders, academics, and media figures.

Secrecy and Controversy

Bilderberg meetings are conducted under strict secrecy, with no press coverage or public statements. This lack of transparency has fueled speculation and conspiracy theories about the group's true intentions. Critics argue that the Bilderberg Group functions as a shadowy cabal, coordinating global policies and agendas behind closed doors.

Alleged Influence on Global Events

While the Bilderberg Group maintains that its meetings are informal and do not result in binding decisions, many believe that the group wields significant influence over global affairs. Conspiracy theorists claim that the Bilderberg Group is part of a broader effort to establish a New World Order, with its members orchestrating economic and political events to achieve their goals.

The Impact of Secret Societies on Modern Society

Secret societies continue to fascinate and provoke debate in contemporary society. Their perceived influence on world events raises important questions about power, democracy, and transparency.

The Power of Myth and Perception

The myths and conspiracy theories surrounding secret societies often amplify their perceived power and influence. While some claims are based on verifiable facts, others are speculative or exaggerated. The power of these myths lies in their ability to shape public perception and fuel distrust in established institutions.

Transparency and Accountability

The secrecy inherent in secret societies poses challenges to transparency and accountability in democratic societies. When powerful individuals and groups operate behind closed doors, it undermines public trust and raises concerns about the concentration of power and influence.

The Role of Investigative Journalism

Investigative journalism plays a crucial role in uncovering the activities and influence of secret societies. By shedding light on the hidden connections and operations of these groups, journalists contribute to a more informed and engaged public.

Case Study: The Panama Papers

The Panama Papers, a massive leak of documents from the law firm Mossack Fonseca, revealed the secretive financial dealings of wealthy individuals and organizations, including members of secret societies. The investigation exposed the use of offshore accounts to hide wealth and avoid taxes, highlighting the need for greater transparency and accountability in global finance.

Conclusion

Secret societies have long been a source of fascination, intrigue, and controversy. Their perceived influence on world events raises important questions about power, democracy, and transparency. By examining the history, rituals, and alleged impact of these groups, we gain a deeper understanding of their role in shaping modern society.

In the following chapters, we will delve deeper into specific secret societies, providing detailed analyses of their origins, operations, and influence. Through these explorations, we aim to uncover the hidden agendas behind these clandestine groups and celebrate the resilience of those who have fought for transparency and accountability. By shining a light on these stories, we hope to inspire a renewed commitment to protecting the principles of open government and the free flow of information in our society.

| **19** |

Chapter 19: The History of Prominent Secret Societies

Secret societies have played a significant role in shaping historical events and influencing the course of world history. These organizations, often shrouded in mystery and exclusivity, have been both revered and vilified. Their impact can be seen in political revolutions, cultural movements, and social reforms. In this chapter, we explore the history of some of the most prominent secret societies, examining their origins, ideologies, rituals, and influence. By delving into the complex histories of these groups, we aim to understand how they have shaped —and continue to shape—the world.

The Freemasons

Origins and Early History

The Freemasons trace their origins to the medieval stonemason guilds of Europe, which were organizations of skilled craftsmen who built the cathedrals and castles of the Middle Ages. These guilds evolved into a fraternal organization that embraced the principles of Enlightenment, promoting ideals of reason, science, and individual liberty.

The Formation of Modern Freemasonry

Modern Freemasonry began with the formation of the Grand Lodge of England in 1717. This marked the beginning of a more structured organization with standardized rituals and symbols. Freemasonry quickly spread across Europe and North America, attracting influential figures from various walks of life.

Rituals, Symbols, and Beliefs

Freemasonry is characterized by its elaborate rituals, symbolic architecture, and moral teachings. Members progress through degrees, each with its own ceremonies and lessons. The most well-known symbols include the square and compass, the letter "G" (representing geometry or God), and the all-seeing eye. Freemasonry promotes values such as brotherhood, charity, and truth, often using allegorical stories and symbols drawn from stonemasonry and biblical texts.

Influence on Historical Events

Freemasons have been linked to several significant historical events, including the American and French Revolutions. Many of the Founding Fathers of the United States, such as George Washington and Benjamin Franklin, were Freemasons, and Masonic ideals of liberty and equality influenced the drafting of the U.S. Constitution. Similarly, Freemasons played a role in the intellectual and political currents that led to the French Revolution.

The Illuminati

Origins and Goals

The Illuminati was founded in 1776 by Adam Weishaupt, a professor of canon law at the University of Ingolstadt in Bavaria. Weishaupt sought to create a society dedicated to Enlightenment principles, free from the influence of the Catholic Church and conservative authorities. The Illuminati aimed to promote rationalism, secularism, and social reform through clandestine means.

Structure and Activities

The Illuminati operated in secrecy, using code names and covert communication to protect its members. The group infiltrated other organizations, such as Masonic lodges, to spread its ideas and recruit members. Despite its ambitious goals, the Illuminati was short-lived, dissolving by the late 1780s due to internal conflicts and government persecution.

Enduring Myths and Conspiracy Theories

Despite its brief existence, the Illuminati has become a central figure in numerous conspiracy theories. Many believe that the group continued to operate in secret, manipulating world events and orchestrating a New World Order. These theories often allege that the Illuminati controls global finance, media, and politics through a network of influential individuals and organizations.

The Knights Templar

Origins and Early History

The Knights Templar was a medieval Christian military order founded in 1119, tasked with protecting pilgrims traveling to the Holy Land. The order quickly gained wealth and power, establishing a vast network of fortifications and financial operations across Europe and the Middle East.

Rituals and Beliefs

The Templars took vows of poverty, chastity, and obedience, and lived according to a strict code of conduct. They were known for their distinctive white mantles adorned with a red cross. The order's secretive nature and rumored possession of religious relics, such as the Holy Grail, fueled legends and speculation.

Downfall and Legacy

In 1307, King Philip IV of France, heavily indebted to the Templars, ordered their arrest and the seizure of their assets. Many Templars were tortured and executed, and the order was officially disbanded by Pope Clement V in 1312. Despite their dissolution, the Templars' legacy lived on, inspiring numerous myths and conspiracy theories about their hidden treasures and secret influence.

The Skull and Bones Society

Origins and Membership

The Skull and Bones Society, also known as the Order of Skull and Bones, was founded in 1832 at Yale University by William Huntington Russell and Alphonso Taft. The society is known for its secrecy, exclusive membership, and powerful alumni, which include prominent political, business, and academic leaders.

Rituals and Symbols

Skull and Bones is infamous for its mysterious rituals, which are said to include the use of skulls, coffins, and other macabre symbols. Members, known as "Bonesmen," participate in these rituals as part of their initiation and continue to meet in secret throughout their lives.

Influence on American Politics and Society

The Skull and Bones Society has produced a remarkable number of influential figures, including presidents, senators, and business magnates. Notable members include former Presidents George H.W. Bush and George W. Bush, as well as former Secretary of State John Kerry. The society's connections and influence have led to speculation about its role in shaping American political and economic policies.

The Rosicrucians

Origins and Beliefs

The Rosicrucians trace their origins to the early 17th century, with the publication of three manifestos: the Fama Fraternitatis, the Confessio Fraternitatis, and the Chymical Wedding of Christian Rosenkreutz. These texts described the existence of a secretive brotherhood dedicated to esoteric knowledge, spiritual enlightenment, and the reformation of society.

Symbols and Rituals

Rosicrucian symbolism draws heavily from alchemy, Hermeticism, and Christian mysticism. Common symbols include the rose and cross, representing the union of spiritual and material worlds. Rosicrucian rituals often involve meditation, alchemical practices, and the study of esoteric texts.

Influence on Esoteric and Occult Traditions

The Rosicrucians have had a significant impact on Western esoteric and occult traditions, influencing groups such as the Freemasons, the Golden Dawn, and Theosophy. Their emphasis on spiritual development and hidden knowledge continues to attract individuals seeking alternative spiritual paths.

The Bilderberg Group

Origins and Purpose

The Bilderberg Group was founded in 1954 by Dutch statesman Joseph Retinger, with the support of several European and American leaders. The group's purpose is to foster dialogue and cooperation between Europe and North America on political, economic, and social issues. Bilderberg meetings are held annually, bringing together influential politicians, business leaders, academics, and media figures.

Secrecy and Controversy

Bilderberg meetings are conducted under strict secrecy, with no press coverage or public statements. This lack of transparency has fueled speculation and conspiracy theories about the group's true intentions. Critics argue that the Bilderberg Group functions as a shadowy cabal, coordinating global policies and agendas behind closed doors.

Alleged Influence on Global Events

While the Bilderberg Group maintains that its meetings are informal and do not result in binding decisions, many believe that the group wields significant influence over global affairs. Conspiracy theorists claim that the Bilderberg Group is part of a broader effort to establish a New World Order, with its members orchestrating economic and political events to achieve their goals.

The Trilateral Commission

Origins and Objectives

The Trilateral Commission was founded in 1973 by David Rockefeller, Zbigniew Brzezinski, and other prominent leaders from North America, Europe, and Japan. The commission aims to foster closer cooperation among these regions to address global challenges and promote stability and prosperity.

Membership and Activities

The Trilateral Commission's membership includes influential politicians, business executives, academics, and media figures. The group meets annually to discuss issues such as economic policy, international security, and environmental sustainability. While the commission does not make binding decisions, its recommendations often carry significant weight in global policy discussions.

Criticism and Conspiracy Theories

Critics of the Trilateral Commission argue that it represents the interests of a global elite seeking to consolidate power and influence. Conspiracy theories suggest that the commission is part of a larger network of secret societies working towards a New World Order. These theories often allege that the commission's members use their positions to manipulate global events for their benefit.

The Impact of Secret Societies on Modern Society

Secret societies continue to fascinate and provoke debate in contemporary society. Their perceived influence on world events raises important questions about power, democracy, and transparency.

The Power of Myth and Perception

The myths and conspiracy theories surrounding secret societies often amplify their perceived power and influence. While some claims are based on verifiable facts, others are speculative or exaggerated. The power of these myths lies in their ability to shape public perception and fuel distrust in established institutions.

Transparency and Accountability

The secrecy inherent in secret societies poses challenges to transparency and accountability in democratic societies. When powerful individuals and groups operate behind closed doors, it undermines public trust and raises concerns about the concentration of power and influence.

The Role of Investigative Journalism

Investigative journalism plays a crucial role in uncovering the activities and influence of secret societies. By shedding light on the hidden connections and operations of these groups, journalists contribute to a more informed and engaged public.

Case Study: The Panama Papers

The Panama Papers, a massive leak of documents from the law firm Mossack Fonseca, revealed the secretive financial dealings of wealthy individuals and organizations, including members of secret societies. The investigation exposed the use of offshore accounts to hide wealth and avoid taxes, highlighting the need for greater transparency and accountability in global finance.

Conclusion

Secret societies have played a significant role in shaping historical events and influencing the course of world history. Their impact can be seen in political revolutions, cultural movements, and social reforms. By exploring the complex histories of these groups, we gain a deeper understanding of their role in shaping modern society.

In the following chapters, we will continue to delve deeper into specific secret societies, providing detailed analyses of their origins, operations, and influence. Through these explorations, we aim to uncover the hidden agendas behind these clandestine groups and celebrate the resilience of those who have fought for transparency and accountability. By shining a light on these stories, we hope to inspire a renewed commitment to protecting the principles of open government and the free flow of information in our society.

Chapter 20: Influence on Major Historical Events

Throughout history, secret societies have been implicated in shaping key historical events, often working behind the scenes to influence politics, economics, and social change. While some of these groups operated with altruistic intentions, others sought power and control. In this chapter, we explore how secret societies have influenced major historical events, examining specific instances where their involvement is evident. By analyzing declassified documents, historical records, and credible testimonies, we aim to uncover the true extent of their impact on world events.

The American Revolution

The Role of the Freemasons

The American Revolution was a seminal event in world history, leading to the establishment of the United States of America. The Freemasons, one of the most prominent secret societies, played a significant role in this revolution.

Influence on Founding Fathers

Many of the Founding Fathers of the United States were Freemasons, including George Washington, Benjamin Franklin, John Hancock, and Paul Revere. The principles of Freemasonry, such as liberty, equality, and fraternity, deeply influenced these leaders and the ideological foundation of the new nation.

Masonic Networks and Coordination

Freemasonic lodges provided a network for revolutionary leaders to meet, discuss strategies, and coordinate efforts. The secrecy and loyalty inherent in Freemasonry allowed for secure communication and planning, contributing to the success of the revolution.

Symbolism and National Identity

Freemasonic symbols, such as the all-seeing eye and the unfinished pyramid, were incorporated into American iconography, most notably on the Great Seal of the United States. These symbols reflect the influence of Freemasonry on the new nation's identity and values.

The French Revolution

The Illuminati and Revolutionary Ideals

The French Revolution, which began in 1789, was a period of radical social and political upheaval. The Illuminati, a secret society founded in Bavaria in 1776, is often linked to the spread of revolutionary ideals in France.

Dissemination of Enlightenment Ideas

The Illuminati promoted Enlightenment principles such as rationalism, secularism, and social reform. Members of the Illuminati infiltrated Masonic lodges and other organizations, spreading these ideas among intellectuals and political activists in France.

Involvement in Revolutionary Activities

While there is debate about the extent of the Illuminati's direct involvement in the French Revolution, there is evidence that their ideas influenced key revolutionary figures. The emphasis on liberty, equality, and fraternity echoed the Illuminati's goals and contributed to the ideological foundation of the revolution.

The Reign of Terror and Secret Societies

During the Reign of Terror (1793-1794), the revolutionary government targeted perceived enemies of the revolution, including secret societies. The suppression of these groups, along with the execution of many of their members, reflected the chaotic and paranoid atmosphere of the time.

The Russian Revolution

The Role of the Bolsheviks

The Russian Revolution of 1917 led to the overthrow of the Tsarist regime and the establishment of a communist government. The Bolsheviks, a faction of the Russian Social Democratic Labour Party, played a central role in this revolution.

Secret Meetings and Planning

The Bolsheviks operated as a clandestine organization, holding secret meetings and planning revolutionary activities in exile and underground. Their leader, Vladimir Lenin, emphasized the need for a disciplined, secretive party to successfully carry out a revolution.

Infiltration and Propaganda

The Bolsheviks infiltrated workers' organizations, military units, and other social groups, spreading revolutionary propaganda and gaining support for their cause. Their use of secrecy and covert operations helped them build a broad-based movement capable of overthrowing the government.

The Impact of the Revolution

The success of the Bolshevik Revolution had a profound impact on world history, leading to the establishment of the Soviet Union and the spread of communist ideology. The use of secretive methods and covert operations by the Bolsheviks set a precedent for future revolutionary movements.

World War II and Espionage

The Cambridge Five

During World War II, espionage played a crucial role in the conflict between the Allied and Axis powers. The Cambridge Five, a group of British spies who infiltrated the highest levels of British intelligence, are one of the most famous examples of secret societies involved in wartime espionage.

Origins and Recruitment

The Cambridge Five were recruited by Soviet intelligence while studying at the University of Cambridge in the 1930s. The group included Kim Philby, Donald Maclean, Guy Burgess, Anthony Blunt, and John Cairncross. They were motivated by ideological sympathy for communism and a desire to undermine fascism.

Activities and Impact

The Cambridge Five passed sensitive information to the Soviet Union, including details about British and American military strategies, operations, and intelligence. Their espionage activities had a significant impact on the course of the war and the subsequent Cold War, providing the Soviet Union with valuable insights into Allied plans.

Operation Paperclip

The Recruitment of Nazi Scientists

After World War II, the United States launched Operation Paperclip, a secret program to recruit German scientists, engineers, and technicians, many of whom were former members of the Nazi party. The goal was to leverage their expertise to advance American military and space programs and prevent them from falling into Soviet hands.

Influence on the Space Race and Cold War

The scientists recruited under Operation Paperclip, including Wernher von Braun, played a pivotal role in the development of American rocket technology and the space program. Their contributions were crucial to the United States' success in the Space Race and the broader technological competition of the Cold War.

Ethical Controversies

Operation Paperclip remains controversial due to the ethical implications of granting former Nazis immunity and prominent positions. While the program contributed significantly to American technological advancements, it also raised moral questions about the cost of such progress.

The Cold War and Secret Societies

The Trilateral Commission

Origins and Objectives

The Trilateral Commission was founded in 1973 by David Rockefeller, Zbigniew Brzezinski, and other prominent leaders from North America, Europe, and Japan. The commission aimed to foster closer cooperation among these regions to address global challenges and promote stability and prosperity.

Influence on Global Policy

The Trilateral Commission's members included influential politicians, business executives, academics, and media figures. The group's discussions and recommendations often shaped global policy, particularly in areas such as economic cooperation, international security, and environmental sustainability.

Criticism and Conspiracy Theories

Critics of the Trilateral Commission argue that it represents the interests of a global elite seeking to consolidate power and influence. Conspiracy theories suggest that the commission is part of a larger network of secret societies working towards a New World Order. These theories often allege that the commission's members use their positions to manipulate global events for their benefit.

The Bilderberg Group

Origins and Purpose

The Bilderberg Group was founded in 1954 by Dutch statesman Joseph Retinger, with the support of several European and American leaders. The group's purpose is to foster dialogue and cooperation between Europe and North America on political, economic, and social issues. Bilderberg meetings are held annually, bringing together influential politicians, business leaders, academics, and media figures.

Secrecy and Controversy

Bilderberg meetings are conducted under strict secrecy, with no press coverage or public statements. This lack of transparency has fueled speculation and conspiracy theories about the group's true intentions. Critics argue that the Bilderberg Group functions as a shadowy cabal, coordinating global policies and agendas behind closed doors.

Alleged Influence on Global Events

While the Bilderberg Group maintains that its meetings are informal and do not result in binding decisions, many believe that the group wields significant influence over global affairs. Conspiracy theorists claim that the Bilderberg Group is part of a broader effort to establish a New World Order, with its members orchestrating economic and political events to achieve their goals.

The Impact of Secret Societies on Modern Society

Secret societies continue to fascinate and provoke debate in contemporary society. Their perceived influence on world events raises important questions about power, democracy, and transparency.

The Power of Myth and Perception

The myths and conspiracy theories surrounding secret societies often amplify their perceived power and influence. While some claims are based on verifiable facts, others are speculative or exaggerated. The power of these myths lies in their ability to shape public perception and fuel distrust in established institutions.

Transparency and Accountability

The secrecy inherent in secret societies poses challenges to transparency and accountability in democratic societies. When powerful individuals and groups operate behind closed doors, it undermines public trust and raises concerns about the concentration of power and influence.

The Role of Investigative Journalism

Investigative journalism plays a crucial role in uncovering the activities and influence of secret societies. By shedding light on the hidden connections and operations of these groups, journalists contribute to a more informed and engaged public.

Case Study: The Panama Papers

The Panama Papers, a massive leak of documents from the law firm Mossack Fonseca, revealed the secretive financial dealings of wealthy individuals and organizations, including members of secret societies. The investigation exposed the use of offshore accounts to hide wealth and avoid taxes, highlighting the need for greater transparency and accountability in global finance.

Conclusion

Secret societies have played a significant role in shaping major historical events, often working behind the scenes to influence politics, economics, and social change. By examining the complex histories and activities of these groups, we gain a deeper understanding of their impact on world events and the ongoing challenges they pose to transparency and accountability.

In the following chapters, we will continue to explore the influence of secret societies on contemporary society, providing detailed analyses of their operations and connections. Through these explorations, we aim to uncover the hidden agendas behind these clandestine groups and celebrate the resilience of those who have fought for transparency and accountability. By shining a light on these stories, we hope to inspire a renewed commitment to protecting the principles of open government and the free flow of information in our society.

| 21 |

Chapter 21: Contemporary Influence and Agendas

In the modern era, secret societies continue to exert influence across various spheres of society, including politics, economics, and culture. While some may dismiss these groups as relics of the past or products of conspiracy theories, there is substantial evidence that they remain active and relevant. This chapter explores the contemporary influence of secret societies, examining their agendas, methods of operation, and the impact they have on global events. By delving into the activities of well-known and emerging groups, we aim to provide a comprehensive understanding of how these clandestine organizations shape the world today.

The Freemasons in the 21st Century

Global Reach and Membership

Freemasonry, one of the oldest and most widespread secret societies, continues to thrive in the 21st century. With millions of members worldwide, the organization maintains a significant presence in numerous countries. Modern Freemasonry remains committed to its core principles of brotherhood, charity, and moral development.

Modern Activities and Influence

Freemasons are involved in various charitable activities, contributing to causes such as education, healthcare, and disaster relief. Their philanthropic efforts are often organized through Masonic lodges and affiliated organizations. Despite their charitable work, Freemasons are still perceived by some as wielding undue influence in politics and business.

Challenges and Controversies

Freemasonry faces several challenges in the modern era, including declining membership in some regions, public suspicion, and accusations of elitism. The organization's secretive nature and historical associations with power and privilege continue to fuel conspiracy theories and public skepticism.

The Illuminati: Myth and Reality

The Persistence of Illuminati Conspiracy Theories

The Illuminati, a secret society that purportedly disbanded in the late 18th century, remains a central figure in modern conspiracy theories. Alleged to be behind events ranging from economic crises to political upheavals, the Illuminati is often portrayed as an all-powerful cabal controlling world affairs.

Evidence and Skepticism

Despite the prevalence of Illuminati conspiracy theories, there is little concrete evidence to support the existence of a modern Illuminati. Most claims are based on speculation and misinterpretation of historical events. However, the persistence of these theories reflects deep-seated anxieties about power, control, and transparency in contemporary society.

The Illuminati in Popular Culture

The Illuminati has a significant presence in popular culture, often depicted in films, books, and music. This portrayal contributes to the group's mystique and the public's fascination with secret societies. While largely fictional, these representations influence how people perceive the Illuminati and similar organizations.

The Bilderberg Group: Power and Secrecy

Annual Meetings and Agendas

The Bilderberg Group, founded in 1954, continues to hold annual meetings attended by influential figures from politics, business, academia, and media. These gatherings are conducted under strict secrecy, with no press coverage or public statements.

Influence on Global Policy

While the Bilderberg Group claims that its meetings are informal discussions that do not result in binding decisions, critics argue that the group wields significant influence over global policy. Attendees are often key decision-makers, and the topics discussed can shape economic and political agendas.

Controversies and Criticisms

The secrecy surrounding Bilderberg meetings has led to widespread suspicion and accusations of elitism and undemocratic practices. Critics contend that the group's lack of transparency undermines public trust and raises questions about the concentration of power among a global elite.

The Trilateral Commission: Shaping Global Cooperation

Founding and Objectives

The Trilateral Commission was established in 1973 to foster closer cooperation among North America, Europe, and Japan. The organization aims to address global challenges and promote stability and prosperity through dialogue and collaboration.

Membership and Influence

The Trilateral Commission's membership includes prominent leaders from politics, business, academia, and media. The group's discussions and recommendations often influence global policy, particularly in areas such as economic cooperation, international security, and environmental sustainability.

Criticisms and Conspiracy Theories

Critics of the Trilateral Commission argue that it represents the interests of a global elite seeking to consolidate power and influence. Conspiracy theories suggest that the commission is part of a larger network of secret societies working towards a New World Order. These theories often allege that the commission's members use their positions to manipulate global events for their benefit.

Emerging Secret Societies

The Bohemian Club and Bohemian Grove

Origins and Membership

The Bohemian Club, founded in San Francisco in 1872, is a private men's club known for its exclusive membership, which includes influential leaders from business, politics, and the arts. The club's most famous event is the annual gathering at Bohemian Grove, a secluded retreat in Northern California.

Rituals and Activities

The Bohemian Grove gathering features elaborate rituals, performances, and discussions on various topics. One of the most well-known rituals is the "Cremation of Care," a theatrical ceremony that symbolizes the casting off of worldly concerns. While the event is largely social, critics argue that it allows powerful individuals to network and discuss policy in secrecy.

Controversies and Public Perception

The secrecy and exclusivity of the Bohemian Club and its gatherings have fueled public suspicion and conspiracy theories. Some view the club as a playground for the elite, where important decisions are made away from public scrutiny. Despite these controversies, the club remains a significant social institution for its members.

The Council on Foreign Relations (CFR)

Origins and Objectives

The Council on Foreign Relations (CFR) was founded in 1921 to promote a better understanding of foreign policy and international affairs among policymakers and the public. The CFR's membership includes influential leaders from government, business, academia, and media.

Activities and Influence

The CFR conducts research, publishes reports, and hosts events on a wide range of global issues. The organization's work often shapes public discourse and policy debates on foreign affairs. While the CFR is not a secret society in the traditional sense, its influential membership and policy impact have led to comparisons with other elite groups.

Criticisms and Conspiracy Theories

Critics of the CFR argue that it promotes a globalist agenda that prioritizes the interests of a wealthy elite over those of ordinary citizens. Conspiracy theories suggest that the CFR is part of a broader effort to establish a New World Order, with its members using their influence to shape global events for their benefit.

The Impact of Secret Societies on Modern Society

Secret societies continue to fascinate and provoke debate in contemporary society. Their perceived influence on world events raises important questions about power, democracy, and transparency.

The Power of Myth and Perception

The myths and conspiracy theories surrounding secret societies often amplify their perceived power and influence. While some claims are based on verifiable facts, others are speculative or exaggerated. The power of these myths lies in their ability to shape public perception and fuel distrust in established institutions.

Transparency and Accountability

The secrecy inherent in secret societies poses challenges to transparency and accountability in democratic societies. When powerful individuals and groups operate behind closed doors, it undermines public trust and raises concerns about the concentration of power and influence.

The Role of Investigative Journalism

Investigative journalism plays a crucial role in uncovering the activities and influence of secret societies. By shedding light on the hidden connections and operations of these groups, journalists contribute to a more informed and engaged public.

Case Study: The Panama Papers

The Panama Papers, a massive leak of documents from the law firm Mossack Fonseca, revealed the secretive financial dealings of wealthy individuals and organizations, including members of secret societies. The investigation exposed the use of offshore accounts to hide wealth and avoid taxes, highlighting the need for greater transparency and accountability in global finance.

Conclusion

Secret societies continue to exert influence in contemporary society, shaping political, economic, and cultural events behind the scenes. By examining the activities and agendas of these groups, we gain a deeper understanding of their impact on world affairs and the challenges they pose to transparency and accountability.

In the following chapters, we will explore other facets of government secrecy and cover-ups, providing detailed analyses and historical accounts. Through these explorations, we aim to uncover the hidden agendas behind acts of government secrecy and celebrate the resilience of those who have fought for transparency and accountability. By shining a light on these stories, we hope to inspire a renewed commitment to protecting the principles of open government and the free flow of information in our society.

PART VIII

THE SUPPRESSION OF ALTERNATIVE SCIENCE AND TECHNOLOGY

Science and technology have always been at the forefront of human progress, driving advancements that shape societies and improve lives. However, the journey of scientific discovery is not always smooth or linear. Throughout history, alternative scientific theories and technological innovations have often faced significant opposition from established institutions, governments, and powerful interest groups. These entities, motivated by political, economic, or ideological reasons, have sometimes suppressed groundbreaking ideas and technologies that threatened their dominance or challenged prevailing paradigms.

In Part VIII of "Hidden Agendas: Exposing the Dark Secrets," we delve into the complex world of scientific and technological suppression. We will explore the reasons behind the suppression, examine notable historical and contemporary cases, and analyze the impact of these actions on societal progress. By uncovering the hidden agendas that stifle innovation, we aim to shed light on the importance of fostering an open and inclusive environment for scientific inquiry and technological development.

The Nature of Scientific and Technological Suppression

The suppression of science and technology can take many forms, from outright bans and censorship to more subtle tactics like discrediting researchers or withholding funding. Understanding the mechanisms of suppression is crucial for recognizing its occurrence and addressing its consequences.

Mechanisms of Suppression

Censorship and Bans

One of the most direct forms of suppression is the censorship or banning of scientific publications, technologies, or research activities. Governments and institutions may prohibit the dissemination of certain ideas or inventions, often citing reasons such as national security, public safety, or moral concerns.

Discrediting and Marginalization

Another common tactic is to discredit researchers or inventors and marginalize their work. This can involve questioning their credibility, ridiculing their theories, or presenting their findings as pseudoscience. Such actions can effectively isolate innovators from the scientific community and hinder the acceptance of their ideas.

Withholding Funding and Resources

Funding is the lifeblood of scientific research and technological development. By controlling the allocation of funds and resources, powerful entities can influence which projects succeed and which are left to languish. Research that challenges the status quo or threatens established interests may find it particularly difficult to secure the necessary support.

Regulatory and Bureaucratic Obstacles

Regulatory and bureaucratic hurdles can also be used to stifle innovation. Strict regulations, lengthy approval processes, and burdensome paperwork can delay or prevent the development and dissemination of new technologies. These obstacles can be especially challenging for smaller organizations or independent researchers.

Motivations for Suppression

Economic Interests

Economic interests are a significant driver of scientific and technological suppression. Established industries and corporations may resist innovations that threaten their market dominance or profit margins. For example, the oil and gas industry has historically opposed the development of alternative energy sources that could disrupt their business model.

Political and Ideological Control

Governments and political institutions may suppress scientific and technological advancements to maintain control or uphold ideological beliefs. This can involve restricting research that contradicts official narratives, such as climate change denial or the suppression of evolutionary theory in favor of creationism.

Cultural and Religious Beliefs

Cultural and religious beliefs can also play a role in the suppression of science and technology. Innovations that challenge deeply held beliefs or societal norms may face significant resistance. Historical examples include the persecution of scientists like Galileo Galilei, whose heliocentric model of the solar system contradicted the teachings of the Catholic Church.

Preservation of Power and Authority

Maintaining power and authority is another key motivation for suppression. Scientific discoveries or technological advancements that empower individuals or democratize access to information and resources can be seen as threats to established power structures. Those in positions of authority may therefore seek to control or suppress such innovations.

Historical Cases of Suppression

Nikola Tesla and Free Energy

The Visionary Inventor

Nikola Tesla, one of the most brilliant inventors of the late 19th and early 20th centuries, made numerous contributions to the fields of electricity and electromagnetism. Among his many inventions were the alternating current (AC) electrical system, the Tesla coil, and early wireless communication technologies.

Suppression of Free Energy

Tesla's most controversial work involved his experiments with wireless transmission of electrical energy and the concept of free energy. He envisioned a world where energy could be transmitted wirelessly and freely to everyone, eliminating the need for centralized power plants and extensive infrastructure. However, his ideas threatened the established energy industry, particularly figures like Thomas Edison and J.P. Morgan, who had significant investments in direct current (DC) systems and centralized power generation.

The Wardenclyffe Tower

Tesla's ambitious project to build the Wardenclyffe Tower, a wireless transmission station, was initially funded by J.P. Morgan. However, once Morgan realized the implications of Tesla's work—that it could potentially provide free energy to the world—he withdrew his support. Without financial backing, Tesla's project was abandoned, and his ideas about wireless energy transmission were largely forgotten.

Impact on Society

The suppression of Tesla's work on free energy had profound implications. Had his ideas been fully developed and implemented, they could have revolutionized the energy sector, making electricity more accessible and affordable. Instead, the world continued to rely on fossil fuels and centralized power systems, contributing to environmental degradation and energy inequity.

The Case of Cold Fusion

The Fleischmann-Pons Experiment

In 1989, electrochemists Martin Fleischmann and Stanley Pons announced that they had achieved cold fusion—nuclear fusion at room temperature. This breakthrough promised a virtually limitless and clean energy source, potentially transforming the global energy landscape.

Scientific Controversy and Skepticism

The initial excitement surrounding cold fusion quickly turned to skepticism and controversy. Many scientists were unable to replicate Fleischmann and Pons' results, leading to accusations of experimental errors and fraudulent claims. The scientific community largely dismissed cold fusion as pseudoscience, and the researchers faced significant professional and personal backlash.

Suppression and Marginalization

Despite some ongoing research and occasional positive results, cold fusion remains a marginalized field. Funding for cold fusion research has been scarce, and many scientists and institutions avoid the topic due to its controversial reputation. The suppression of cold fusion has prevented thorough exploration of its potential, leaving a promising avenue of research largely unexplored.

Impact on Energy Research

The suppression of cold fusion has had a lasting impact on energy research. If cold fusion were feasible, it could provide a clean, abundant energy source, reducing reliance on fossil fuels and addressing global energy needs. The marginalization of this research area highlights the potential cost of prematurely dismissing unconventional scientific ideas.

The Suppression of Medical Advancements

Dr. Royal Rife and the Rife Machine

Innovative Treatments

Dr. Royal Rife, an American inventor and researcher, developed a high-magnification microscope and a frequency-based device, known as the Rife Machine, in the early 20th century. Rife claimed that his machine could cure various diseases, including cancer, by using specific frequencies to target and destroy pathogens.

Opposition and Suppression

Despite promising results in early trials, Rife's work faced intense opposition from the medical establishment and pharmaceutical industry. Critics argued that his methods lacked scientific rigor and accused him of quackery. Rife's laboratory was destroyed in a suspicious fire, and legal battles further hindered his work. The American Medical Association (AMA) actively discredited Rife and his machine, leading to the suppression of his research.

Impact on Medical Science

The suppression of Rife's work has had significant implications for medical science. If his claims were valid, the Rife Machine could have revolutionized cancer treatment and other medical therapies. The controversy surrounding Rife's work underscores the challenges faced by unconventional medical innovations and the potential consequences of their suppression.

Contemporary Cases of Suppression

Alternative Energy Technologies

Suppression of Renewable Energy Innovations

In the contemporary world, renewable energy technologies such as solar, wind, and geothermal power face various forms of suppression. Established energy industries, including fossil fuels and nuclear power, have significant financial and political influence, which they use to resist the adoption of alternative energy sources.

Case Study: The Solar Energy Industry

The solar energy industry has faced numerous obstacles, including restrictive regulations, inadequate funding, and opposition from traditional energy companies. Lobbying efforts by the fossil fuel industry have slowed the implementation of policies that would support the growth of solar power, such as subsidies and tax incentives. Additionally, misinformation campaigns have sought to undermine public confidence in the viability and efficiency of solar energy.

Impact on the Environment and Economy

The suppression of renewable energy technologies has significant environmental and economic implications. Continued reliance on fossil fuels contributes to climate change, environmental degradation, and public health issues. By delaying the transition to cleaner energy sources, the suppression of alternative technologies also hinders economic growth and job creation in emerging industries.

Suppression of Advanced Medical Research

Stem Cell Research

Stem cell research, which holds the potential to treat a wide range of diseases and injuries, has faced significant ethical and political opposition. Concerns about the use of embryonic stem cells have led to restrictive regulations and funding limitations in many countries, including the United States.

Impact on Medical Advancements

The suppression of stem cell research has slowed the development of promising therapies for conditions such as spinal cord injuries, Parkinson's disease, and diabetes. By restricting scientific exploration in this area, society risks missing out on potentially life-saving treatments and medical breakthroughs.

The Role of Whistleblowers and Investigative Journalism

Uncovering Suppression

Whistleblowers and investigative journalists play a crucial role in uncovering instances of scientific and technological suppression. By exposing hidden agendas and bringing suppressed information to light, they contribute to greater transparency and accountability.

Case Study: The NSA Surveillance Program

In 2013, former NSA contractor Edward Snowden leaked classified documents revealing the extent of the U.S. government's surveillance activities. Snowden's disclosures sparked a global debate about privacy, security, and government overreach. His actions highlighted the importance of whistleblowers in revealing hidden information and fostering public discourse.

Challenges and Risks

Whistleblowers and investigative journalists often face significant risks, including legal repercussions, professional ostracism, and personal threats. Despite these challenges, their work is essential for uncovering suppression and promoting a more open and informed society.

Conclusion

The suppression of alternative science and technology has profound implications for societal progress. By understanding the mechanisms and motivations behind suppression, we can better recognize its occurrence and address its consequences. Historical and contemporary cases highlight the need for a more inclusive and open environment for scientific inquiry and technological development.

In the following chapters, we will delve deeper into specific instances of suppressed scientific discoveries and technological innovations, providing detailed analyses and historical accounts. Through these explorations, we aim to uncover the hidden agendas behind acts of suppression and celebrate the resilience of those who have fought for transparency and progress. By shining a light on these stories, we hope to inspire a renewed commitment to fostering a culture of innovation and openness in our society.

| **22** |

Chapter 22: Suppressed Scientific Discoveries

Scientific discovery has always been a cornerstone of human progress, driving advancements that improve our quality of life and expand our understanding of the world. However, not all scientific discoveries are met with acceptance and enthusiasm. Throughout history, many groundbreaking ideas have been suppressed, marginalized, or outright dismissed by powerful institutions and interests. These acts of suppression have often been motivated by economic, political, or ideological reasons, and their consequences have delayed scientific progress and deprived society of potentially transformative innovations. In this chapter, we explore notable examples of suppressed scientific discoveries, examining the circumstances, motivations, and impacts of these actions. By uncovering these hidden stories, we aim to highlight the importance of protecting scientific inquiry and fostering an open environment for innovation.

The Case of Nikola Tesla

Tesla's Revolutionary Ideas

Nikola Tesla, one of the most brilliant inventors of the late 19th and early 20th centuries, made numerous contributions to the fields of electricity and electromagnetism. Among his many inventions were the alternating current (AC) electrical system, the Tesla coil, and early wireless communication technologies. However, Tesla's most controversial work involved his experiments with wireless transmission of electrical energy and the concept of free energy.

Wireless Energy Transmission and the Wardenclyffe Tower

Tesla envisioned a world where energy could be transmitted wirelessly and freely to everyone, eliminating the need for centralized power plants and extensive infrastructure. He began constructing the Wardenclyffe Tower in New York to demonstrate his wireless energy transmission system. The project initially received funding from financier J.P. Morgan, who hoped to profit from Tesla's innovations.

Suppression and Abandonment

Once Morgan realized the implications of Tesla's work—that it could potentially provide free energy to the world—he withdrew his financial support. Without the necessary funding, Tesla's project was abandoned, and the Wardenclyffe Tower was never completed. The suppression of Tesla's work on wireless energy transmission had profound implications, as it could have revolutionized the energy sector and made electricity more accessible and affordable.

Impact on Energy Innovation

Tesla's suppressed ideas about wireless energy transmission represent a significant lost opportunity for scientific and technological advancement. Had his work been fully developed and implemented, it could have transformed the global energy landscape, reducing reliance on fossil fuels and addressing energy inequity.

The Story of Ignaz Semmelweis

Discovery of Handwashing

In the mid-19th century, Hungarian physician Ignaz Semmelweis made a groundbreaking discovery while working at the Vienna General Hospital. He observed that the incidence of puerperal fever (childbed fever) was significantly higher in the obstetric clinic staffed by medical students compared to the clinic staffed by midwives. Semmelweis concluded that the students, who often came directly from autopsies, were transmitting infections to the mothers. He implemented a policy requiring handwashing with a chlorinated lime solution before attending to patients, which dramatically reduced the infection rate.

Resistance and Suppression

Despite the clear success of Semmelweis's handwashing protocol, his findings were met with resistance and skepticism from the medical community. Many doctors were reluctant to accept the idea that they themselves could be the source of infection. Semmelweis's abrasive personality and confrontational approach further alienated his colleagues. As a result, his work was largely ignored and dismissed during his lifetime.

Impact on Medical Practice

The suppression of Semmelweis's discovery delayed the adoption of hand hygiene practices in medicine, contributing to unnecessary suffering and deaths from preventable infections. It was only decades later, with the acceptance of germ theory by scientists like Louis Pasteur and Joseph Lister, that the importance of handwashing in preventing infections was widely recognized.

The Tragic Case of Rosalind Franklin

Contributions to DNA Research

Rosalind Franklin was a brilliant X-ray crystallographer whose work was crucial to the discovery of the DNA double helix. Her famous Photograph 51 provided critical evidence of the helical structure of DNA. However, Franklin's contributions were not fully recognized during her lifetime.

Suppression and Overshadowing

James Watson and Francis Crick, who are often credited with the discovery of the DNA double helix, used Franklin's data without her permission to build their model of DNA. While Watson and Crick, along with Maurice Wilkins, were awarded the Nobel Prize in 1962, Franklin's contributions were largely overshadowed and unacknowledged. Franklin had died of ovarian cancer in 1958, and Nobel Prizes are not awarded posthumously.

Impact on Scientific Recognition

The suppression and marginalization of Rosalind Franklin's work highlight the broader issue of gender bias in science. Franklin's case underscores the importance of recognizing and crediting all contributors to scientific discoveries, regardless of gender or other biases.

Cold Fusion: Promise and Controversy

The Fleischmann-Pons Experiment

In 1989, electrochemists Martin Fleischmann and Stanley Pons announced that they had achieved cold fusion—nuclear fusion at room temperature. This breakthrough promised a virtually limitless and clean energy source, potentially transforming the global energy landscape.

Scientific Controversy and Skepticism

The initial excitement surrounding cold fusion quickly turned to skepticism and controversy. Many scientists were unable to replicate Fleischmann and Pons' results, leading to accusations of experimental errors and fraudulent claims. The scientific community largely dismissed cold fusion as pseudoscience, and the researchers faced significant professional and personal backlash.

Suppression and Marginalization

Despite some ongoing research and occasional positive results, cold fusion remains a marginalized field. Funding for cold fusion research has been scarce, and many scientists and institutions avoid the topic due to its controversial reputation. The suppression of cold fusion has prevented thorough exploration of its potential, leaving a promising avenue of research largely unexplored.

Impact on Energy Research

The suppression of cold fusion has had a lasting impact on energy research. If cold fusion were feasible, it could provide a clean, abundant energy source, reducing reliance on fossil fuels and addressing global energy needs. The marginalization of this research area highlights the potential cost of prematurely dismissing unconventional scientific ideas.

The Work of Wilhelm Reich

Orgone Energy and Controversial Theories

Wilhelm Reich was a psychoanalyst and scientist who proposed the existence of a universal life force called "orgone energy." He developed various devices, such as the orgone accumulator, which he claimed could harness this energy for therapeutic purposes. Reich's work was highly controversial and attracted both interest and skepticism.

Suppression by the FDA

In the 1950s, the U.S. Food and Drug Administration (FDA) launched an investigation into Reich's work, concluding that his claims were unscientific and fraudulent. The FDA obtained an injunction against the distribution of orgone-related materials and ordered the destruction of Reich's equipment and publications. Reich was later arrested for contempt of court and died in prison in 1957.

Impact on Alternative Medicine

The suppression of Wilhelm Reich's work underscores the challenges faced by alternative medical theories and treatments. While Reich's ideas remain controversial and unproven, the aggressive actions taken against him raise questions about the balance between regulation and scientific exploration.

Contemporary Examples of Suppression

Suppression of Alternative Energy Technologies

Renewable Energy Innovations

In the contemporary world, renewable energy technologies such as solar, wind, and geothermal power face various forms of suppression. Established energy industries, including fossil fuels and nuclear power, have significant financial and political influence, which they use to resist the adoption of alternative energy sources.

Case Study: The Solar Energy Industry

The solar energy industry has faced numerous obstacles, including restrictive regulations, inadequate funding, and opposition from traditional energy companies. Lobbying efforts by the fossil fuel industry have slowed the implementation of policies that would support the growth of solar power, such as subsidies and tax incentives. Additionally, misinformation campaigns have sought to undermine public confidence in the viability and efficiency of solar energy.

Impact on the Environment and Economy

The suppression of renewable energy technologies has significant environmental and economic implications. Continued reliance on fossil fuels contributes to climate change, environmental degradation, and public health issues. By delaying the transition to cleaner energy sources, the suppression of alternative technologies also hinders economic growth and job creation in emerging industries.

Suppression of Advanced Medical Research

Stem Cell Research

Stem cell research, which holds the potential to treat a wide range of diseases and injuries, has faced significant ethical and political opposition. Concerns about the use of embryonic stem cells have led to restrictive regulations and funding limitations in many countries, including the United States.

Impact on Medical Advancements

The suppression of stem cell research has slowed the development of promising therapies for conditions such as spinal cord injuries, Parkinson's disease, and diabetes. By restricting scientific exploration in this area, society risks missing out on potentially life-saving treatments and medical breakthroughs.

The Role of Whistleblowers and Investigative Journalism

Uncovering Suppression

Whistleblowers and investigative journalists play a crucial role in uncovering instances of scientific and technological suppression. By exposing hidden agendas and bringing suppressed information to light, they contribute to greater transparency and accountability.

Case Study: The NSA Surveillance Program

In 2013, former NSA contractor Edward Snowden leaked classified documents revealing the extent of the U.S. government's surveillance activities. Snowden's disclosures sparked a global debate about privacy, security, and government overreach. His actions highlighted the importance of whistleblowers in revealing hidden information and fostering public discourse.

Challenges and Risks

Whistleblowers and investigative journalists often face significant risks, including legal repercussions, professional ostracism, and personal threats. Despite these challenges, their work is essential for uncovering suppression and promoting a more open and informed society.

Conclusion

The suppression of scientific discoveries has profound implications for societal progress. By understanding the mechanisms and motivations behind suppression, we can better recognize its occurrence and address its consequences. Historical and contemporary cases highlight the need for a more inclusive and open environment for scientific inquiry and technological development.

In the following chapters, we will delve deeper into specific instances of suppressed scientific discoveries and technological innovations, providing detailed analyses and historical accounts. Through these explorations, we aim to uncover the hidden agendas behind acts of suppression and celebrate the resilience of those who have fought for transparency and progress. By shining a light on these stories, we hope to inspire a renewed commitment to fostering a culture of innovation and openness in our society.

| **23** |

Chapter 23: Technological Innovations Kept from the Public

Technological advancements have the power to transform societies, economies, and daily life. However, not all innovations reach the public domain. Various factors, including political, economic, and strategic interests, can lead to the suppression or delayed release of ground-breaking technologies. In this chapter, we explore notable examples of technological innovations that have been kept from the public, examining the reasons behind their suppression and the potential impact they could have had if they were widely accessible. By investigating these hidden stories, we aim to understand the complex interplay between innovation and power, and the implications for societal progress.

The Case of Free Energy Devices

Nikola Tesla and Free Energy

Nikola Tesla's vision of free energy remains one of the most tanta-lizing examples of suppressed technological innovation. Tesla believed that energy could be harnessed from the natural environment and transmitted wirelessly to provide free, unlimited power to everyone.

The Wardenclyffe Tower

Tesla's Wardenclyffe Tower project, initiated in the early 20th century, aimed to demonstrate his concept of wireless energy transmission. The tower was intended to transmit electrical energy without wires by tapping into the Earth's ionosphere. Tesla claimed that this technology could provide free energy to the entire world.

Economic Interests and Suppression

The potential implications of Tesla's free energy technology threatened established energy industries and financial interests. Financiers like J.P. Morgan, who initially funded Tesla's work, withdrew their support when they realized that widespread free energy would undermine their investments in conventional energy infrastructure. As a result, Tesla's project was abandoned, and his ideas were marginalized.

Impact on Society

If Tesla's free energy technology had been fully realized and implemented, it could have revolutionized the global energy landscape, reducing dependency on fossil fuels and eliminating energy costs. This innovation could have addressed energy poverty, driven economic growth, and significantly reduced environmental degradation.

The Suppression of Zero-Point Energy

Concept of Zero-Point Energy

Zero-point energy is the lowest possible energy that a quantum mechanical system may have, a concept arising from quantum physics. Some researchers theorize that this energy could be harnessed to provide a virtually limitless and clean power source.

Research and Developments

Over the decades, various scientists and inventors have claimed to develop devices capable of tapping into zero-point energy. These claims, however, often face significant skepticism from the mainstream scientific community and are rarely given serious consideration.

Barriers and Suppression

Several barriers contribute to the suppression of zero-point energy research, including scientific skepticism, lack of funding, and active discrediting by established energy interests. Prominent figures in the energy industry, fearing the disruption of their economic models, have been accused of suppressing research and patents related to zero-point energy.

Potential Impact

If zero-point energy technology were developed and made accessible, it could provide a revolutionary solution to global energy needs. It would offer a clean, abundant energy source, addressing both environmental and economic challenges associated with fossil fuels and renewable energy limitations.

Water-Powered Engines

Stanley Meyer's Water Fuel Cell

In the 1980s, inventor Stanley Meyer claimed to have developed a water fuel cell that could power a car using water as fuel. Meyer demonstrated his technology in a modified dune buggy, which he claimed could travel significant distances on a small amount of water.

Technical Claims and Controversy

Meyer's water fuel cell allegedly split water into hydrogen and oxygen through a process more efficient than conventional electrolysis. This hydrogen would then be burned to generate energy. Despite Meyer's demonstrations and patents, his claims were met with skepticism from the scientific community, and he was accused of fraud.

Legal and Financial Challenges

Meyer faced numerous legal challenges and financial difficulties, which some attribute to efforts by established energy interests to suppress his technology. Meyer died under mysterious circumstances in 1998, and his technology was never fully developed or independently verified.

Impact on Transportation and Energy

If Meyer's water fuel cell technology were viable, it could have had a transformative impact on transportation and energy. Vehicles powered by water could reduce reliance on fossil fuels, lower emissions, and provide a sustainable and cost-effective energy source.

The Philadelphia Experiment

Alleged Military Experiments

The Philadelphia Experiment is an alleged military experiment conducted by the U.S. Navy in 1943. According to conspiracy theories, the experiment aimed to render the USS Eldridge, a naval destroyer escort, invisible to radar and possibly to the naked eye using a technique called "electromagnetic field manipulation."

Claims of Time Travel and Teleportation

Some accounts of the Philadelphia Experiment suggest that the experiment caused the ship to teleport to another location and travel through time. These claims are largely based on anecdotal evidence and have been widely dismissed by mainstream science.

Suppression and Secrecy

Despite the lack of concrete evidence, the Philadelphia Experiment has become a focal point for discussions about suppressed military technologies and the potential capabilities of electromagnetic fields. The U.S. Navy has consistently denied the experiment took place, contributing to the aura of secrecy and speculation.

Potential Impact

If the claims surrounding the Philadelphia Experiment were true, the technology involved could have profound implications for military strategy, transportation, and our understanding of physics. However, the lack of credible evidence and the fantastical nature of the claims make it a controversial and highly speculative topic.

Advanced Propulsion Technologies

Electrogravitics and Anti-Gravity Research

Electrogravitics is a field of research that explores the possibility of manipulating gravity using electrical energy. Some researchers believe that anti-gravity propulsion systems could revolutionize transportation and aerospace technology.

Claims of Suppression

Various inventors and researchers, including Thomas Townsend Brown, have claimed to develop technologies capable of anti-gravity propulsion. These claims, however, have often been met with skepticism and suppression. Allegations include the confiscation of patents and research by government agencies and the discrediting of researchers.

Potential Impact on Aerospace

If anti-gravity propulsion technologies were viable, they could drastically reduce the cost and energy requirements of space travel, making it more accessible and opening new frontiers for exploration and commerce. Additionally, these technologies could revolutionize terrestrial transportation, leading to new forms of vehicles and infrastructure.

The Role of Intellectual Property and Patents

Patents as Tools of Suppression

Intellectual property laws and patents, while designed to protect inventors and promote innovation, can also be used to suppress technological advancements. Powerful entities may acquire patents for revolutionary technologies and then shelve them to prevent competition or protect existing interests.

Case Study: The Light Bulb Conspiracy

The "light bulb conspiracy," or Phoebus cartel, is a historical example of corporate suppression of innovation. In the 1920s and 1930s, major light bulb manufacturers formed a cartel to control the production and lifespan of light bulbs. By intentionally limiting the lifespan of bulbs, the cartel ensured ongoing demand and profits while stifling innovations that could have produced longer-lasting products.

Impact on Innovation

The misuse of intellectual property laws and patents to suppress technological advancements has significant implications for innovation and economic growth. By preventing the development and dissemination of new technologies, such practices hinder societal progress and maintain the status quo.

The Role of Whistleblowers and Investigative Journalism

Uncovering Suppression

Whistleblowers and investigative journalists play a crucial role in uncovering instances of technological suppression. By exposing hidden agendas and bringing suppressed information to light, they contribute to greater transparency and accountability.

Case Study: The NSA Surveillance Program

In 2013, former NSA contractor Edward Snowden leaked classified documents revealing the extent of the U.S. government's surveillance activities. Snowden's disclosures sparked a global debate about privacy, security, and government overreach. His actions highlighted the importance of whistleblowers in revealing hidden information and fostering public discourse.

Challenges and Risks

Whistleblowers and investigative journalists often face significant risks, including legal repercussions, professional ostracism, and personal threats. Despite these challenges, their work is essential for uncovering suppression and promoting a more open and informed society.

Conclusion

The suppression of technological innovations has profound implications for societal progress. By understanding the mechanisms and motivations behind suppression, we can better recognize its occurrence and address its consequences. Historical and contemporary cases highlight the need for a more inclusive and open environment for technological development.

In the following chapters, we will delve deeper into specific instances of suppressed technological innovations, providing detailed analyses and historical accounts. Through these explorations, we aim to uncover the hidden agendas behind acts of suppression and celebrate the resilience of those who have fought for transparency and progress. By shining a light on these stories, we hope to inspire a renewed commitment to fostering a culture of innovation and openness in our society.

| 24 |

Chapter 24: The Impact of Suppression on Progress

The suppression of scientific discoveries and technological innovations has far-reaching consequences, affecting not only the individuals directly involved but also society as a whole. These acts of suppression can delay progress, hinder economic growth, and perpetuate social inequities. By examining the broader impact of suppression, we gain insight into the complex interplay between power, innovation, and societal advancement. This chapter explores the multifaceted effects of suppressing scientific and technological breakthroughs, providing detailed analyses of historical and contemporary examples to illustrate the profound implications for human progress.

Economic Consequences of Suppression

Stifling Innovation and Economic Growth

The suppression of technological innovations can have significant economic repercussions. By hindering the development and dissemination of new technologies, suppression stifles innovation and limits economic growth.

Case Study: The Electric Car

The history of the electric car provides a stark example of how suppression can impact economic progress. In the early 20th century, electric vehicles (EVs) were a viable alternative to gasoline-powered cars. However, the rise of the internal combustion engine, supported by powerful oil interests, led to the decline of EVs. For decades, electric car technology was marginalized, delaying advancements that could have reduced reliance on fossil fuels and spurred economic growth in the renewable energy sector.

Impact on Industries and Job Creation

The suppression of innovative technologies can also affect industries and job creation. By maintaining the status quo, powerful interests can prevent the emergence of new industries and the economic opportunities they provide. The delayed adoption of renewable energy technologies, for example, has limited the growth of green jobs and the development of a sustainable energy economy.

Technological Stagnation

Suppressing technological innovations can lead to technological stagnation, where progress is slowed or halted. This stagnation can prevent societies from addressing critical challenges and seizing new opportunities for advancement.

Case Study: Renewable Energy Technologies

The suppression of renewable energy technologies by established energy interests has contributed to technological stagnation in the energy sector. Despite the urgent need to transition to sustainable energy sources to combat climate change, the dominance of fossil fuels has slowed the development and adoption of renewable technologies. This stagnation has hindered efforts to reduce greenhouse gas emissions and mitigate the impacts of climate change.

Social and Cultural Consequences

Perpetuation of Social Inequities

The suppression of scientific discoveries and technological innovations can perpetuate social inequities by limiting access to knowledge and resources. Innovations that could benefit marginalized communities are often suppressed, maintaining existing power structures and inequalities.

Case Study: Medical Innovations

The suppression of medical innovations can have severe consequences for public health and social equity. For example, the marginalization of stem cell research has delayed the development of treatments for diseases that disproportionately affect underserved populations. By restricting access to cutting-edge medical technologies, suppression exacerbates health disparities and undermines efforts to achieve health equity.

Impact on Education and Knowledge Dissemination

Suppressing scientific discoveries can also impact education and the dissemination of knowledge. When groundbreaking ideas are marginalized or dismissed, they are less likely to be incorporated into educational curricula and public discourse. This limits opportunities for learning and stifles intellectual curiosity.

Case Study: Evolution and Climate Science

The suppression of scientific theories such as evolution and climate change in educational settings has significant implications for public understanding and engagement with science. In some regions, ideological opposition to these theories has led to their exclusion from school curricula, depriving students of a comprehensive science education. This undermines efforts to foster scientific literacy and critical thinking skills.

Political and Ideological Consequences

Maintaining Power and Control

The suppression of scientific and technological advancements is often driven by political and ideological motivations. By controlling the flow of information and innovation, powerful entities can maintain their dominance and suppress dissent.

Case Study: Galileo and Heliocentrism

The persecution of Galileo Galilei by the Catholic Church is a historical example of how ideological opposition can lead to the suppression of scientific discoveries. Galileo's support for the heliocentric model of the solar system, which contradicted the Church's geocentric view, led to his trial and house arrest. The suppression of heliocentrism delayed the acceptance of a scientific theory that is now fundamental to our understanding of the universe.

Impact on Democratic Governance

Suppressing scientific and technological innovations can undermine democratic governance by limiting transparency and accountability.

When governments and powerful interests control the dissemination of information, it becomes difficult for citizens to make informed decisions and hold authorities accountable.

Case Study: Government Surveillance Programs

The suppression of information about government surveillance programs, such as those revealed by Edward Snowden, highlights the tension between national security and democratic accountability. By keeping surveillance activities secret, governments can undermine public trust and infringe on civil liberties. Whistleblowers and investigative journalists play a crucial role in exposing such activities and promoting transparency.

Environmental Consequences

Delayed Environmental Protection and Sustainability

The suppression of environmental science and sustainable technologies can have dire consequences for the planet. By hindering the development and adoption of sustainable practices, suppression exacerbates environmental degradation and undermines efforts to protect natural resources.

Case Study: Climate Change Denial

The suppression of climate science by fossil fuel interests and political actors has significantly delayed efforts to address climate change. Despite overwhelming scientific consensus on the causes and impacts of climate change, misinformation campaigns and lobbying efforts have obstructed policy actions aimed at reducing greenhouse gas emissions. This delay has intensified the global climate crisis, increasing the severity of its impacts on ecosystems and human communities.

Impact on Biodiversity and Ecosystems

Suppressing scientific research and technological innovations related to environmental conservation can also impact biodiversity and ecosystems. By delaying the implementation of sustainable practices, suppression contributes to habitat destruction, species extinction, and ecological imbalances.

Case Study: The DDT Controversy

The controversy surrounding the pesticide DDT highlights the tension between technological innovation and environmental protection. While DDT was initially hailed as a breakthrough for controlling insect-borne diseases, its widespread use had devastating effects on wildlife and ecosystems. The suppression of scientific evidence about the environmental impacts of DDT delayed regulatory actions, exacerbating its harmful consequences.

Ethical and Moral Consequences

Compromising Scientific Integrity

The suppression of scientific discoveries and technological innovations can compromise the integrity of the scientific community. When researchers face pressure to conform to established interests or risk suppression, it undermines the principles of scientific inquiry and intellectual honesty.

Case Study: Lysenkoism in the Soviet Union

The case of Lysenkoism in the Soviet Union illustrates how political ideology can compromise scientific integrity. Trofim Lysenko's rejection of Mendelian genetics in favor of his own theories was supported by the Soviet government, leading to the persecution of geneticists and the suppression of legitimate scientific research. This political interference delayed advancements in biological science and had long-lasting consequences for Soviet agriculture.

Impact on Public Trust in Science

Suppressing scientific discoveries can erode public trust in science and scientific institutions. When people perceive that scientific information is being manipulated or suppressed, it undermines confidence in the scientific process and the credibility of researchers.

Case Study: Vaccine Misinformation

The spread of misinformation about vaccines, often driven by ideological and economic interests, has contributed to vaccine hesitancy and public distrust in medical science. This suppression of accurate scientific information about vaccines' safety and efficacy has had significant public health consequences, including outbreaks of preventable diseases.

The Role of Whistleblowers and Investigative Journalism

Uncovering Suppression

Whistleblowers and investigative journalists play a crucial role in uncovering instances of scientific and technological suppression. By exposing hidden agendas and bringing suppressed information to light, they contribute to greater transparency and accountability.

Case Study: The Pentagon Papers

In 1971, Daniel Ellsberg leaked the Pentagon Papers, a classified report detailing the U.S. government's deception regarding the Vietnam War. The publication of the Pentagon Papers by The New York Times and other newspapers was a landmark moment for investigative journalism, highlighting the importance of transparency and the role of the press in holding authorities accountable.

Challenges and Risks

Whistleblowers and investigative journalists often face significant risks, including legal repercussions, professional ostracism, and personal threats. Despite these challenges, their work is essential for uncovering suppression and promoting a more open and informed society.

Conclusion

The suppression of scientific discoveries and technological innovations has profound and far-reaching consequences for societal progress. By understanding the mechanisms and motivations behind suppression, we can better recognize its occurrence and address its consequences. Historical and contemporary cases highlight the need for a more inclusive and open environment for scientific inquiry and technological development.

In the following chapters, we will continue to explore the influence of secret societies and government cover-ups on scientific and technological suppression. Through these explorations, we aim to uncover the hidden agendas behind acts of suppression and celebrate the resilience of those who have fought for transparency and progress. By shining a light on these stories, we hope to inspire a renewed commitment to fostering a culture of innovation and openness in our society.

PART IX

THE GLOBAL ELITE AND THEIR HIDDEN AGENDAS

Throughout history, the concept of a powerful global elite orchestrating events from behind the scenes has captivated the public imagination. These elites are often perceived as a small group of influential individuals and organizations that wield disproportionate power over global politics, economics, and social developments. While some dismiss these ideas as mere conspiracy theories, there is substantial evidence that suggests the existence of coordinated efforts by powerful entities to shape world events to their advantage. In Part IX of "Hidden Agendas: Exposing the Dark Secrets," we delve into the murky world of the global elite, exploring their origins, motivations, methods, and the profound impact they have on global society and individual freedoms.

The Concept of the Global Elite

Historical Roots

The notion of a ruling elite is not new; it has roots in ancient civilizations where power was concentrated in the hands of monarchs, aristocrats, and high priests. Over time, as societies evolved and became more complex, so did the structures of power. The modern concept of a global elite emerged in the 20th century, influenced by economic globalization, technological advancements, and the rise of transnational organizations.

Definitions and Characteristics

The global elite can be broadly defined as a small group of individuals and institutions that hold significant influence over global affairs. They typically include political leaders, corporate executives, financial magnates, media moguls, and influential think tanks. Characteristics of the global elite include:

- **Wealth and Economic Power**: Control over vast financial resources and major corporations.
- **Political Influence**: Ability to shape policies and decisions at national and international levels.
- **Networked Influence**: Extensive networks that span across borders, allowing for coordinated efforts.
- **Access to Information**: Privileged access to critical information and decision-making processes.

Theoretical Frameworks

Several theoretical frameworks help explain the existence and actions of the global elite:

- **Elite Theory**: Suggests that a small minority, consisting of members of the economic elite and policy-planning networks, holds the most power and that this power is independent of democratic elections.
- **C. Wright Mills' "The Power Elite"**: Describes a relatively small group of people who hold dominant positions in the major

institutions of society and whose decisions have significant consequences.

- **Globalization Theory**: Examines how global processes of economic integration and political interdependence have led to the emergence of a global elite.

Origins and Evolution of the Global Elite

Early 20th Century Foundations

The foundations of the modern global elite were laid in the early 20th century, as industrialization, urbanization, and the expansion of international trade created new centers of power. Key historical events and developments include:

- **The Rise of Multinational Corporations**: Companies like Standard Oil and U.S. Steel became powerful entities with significant influence over national and international policies.
- **The Formation of Central Banks**: Institutions like the Federal Reserve System in the United States centralized control over monetary policy, impacting global financial markets.
- **World War I and II**: These conflicts reshaped global power dynamics, leading to the creation of international institutions such as the League of Nations and later the United Nations.

Post-World War II Expansion

The end of World War II marked a significant expansion of the global elite's influence, driven by the establishment of key international organizations and agreements:

- **Bretton Woods Institutions**: The International Monetary Fund (IMF) and the World Bank were established to oversee global economic stability and development, often influencing national policies.

- **The United Nations**: Created to promote international cooperation, the UN became a platform for the global elite to shape international norms and policies.
- **NATO and Other Alliances**: Military alliances like NATO consolidated the power of Western elites and ensured their dominance in global security affairs.

Late 20th and Early 21st Century Consolidation

In the late 20th and early 21st centuries, globalization and technological advancements further consolidated the power of the global elite:

- **Neoliberal Economic Policies**: The adoption of neoliberal policies in many countries facilitated the concentration of wealth and power in the hands of a few.
- **The Digital Revolution**: Advances in technology and communication created new avenues for influence and control, particularly through the control of information and media.
- **Transnational Organizations**: Groups like the Bilderberg Group, the Trilateral Commission, and the World Economic Forum emerged as platforms for elites to coordinate their agendas.

The Mechanisms of Control and Influence

Economic Control

The global elite exert significant control over the global economy through various mechanisms:

- **Financial Institutions**: Banks, investment firms, and hedge funds managed by elites influence global financial markets and economic policies.
- **Corporate Power**: Major multinational corporations control vast resources, labor markets, and supply chains, shaping global economic trends.
- **Trade Agreements**: Elites influence the creation and enforcement of international trade agreements, often prioritizing corporate interests over national sovereignty and public welfare.

Political Influence

Political power is another critical tool for the global elite:

- **Lobbying and Campaign Contributions**: Elites use their wealth to influence political campaigns and policy decisions through lobbying and donations.
- **Think Tanks and Policy Planning**: Organizations like the Council on Foreign Relations (CFR) and the Brookings Institution produce research and policy recommendations that shape government decisions.
- **International Institutions**: Elites hold influential positions in organizations like the IMF, World Bank, and UN, guiding global governance and policy-making.

Media and Information Control

Control over media and information is crucial for maintaining influence:

- **Media Ownership**: Many major media outlets are owned or controlled by elite interests, shaping public perception and discourse.

- **Censorship and Propaganda**: Elites can suppress dissenting voices and promote narratives that align with their interests.
- **Digital Platforms**: The rise of social media and digital platforms has given elites new tools to influence public opinion and behavior.

Social and Cultural Influence

Elites also exert control through cultural and social channels:

- **Philanthropy and NGOs**: Elite philanthropy, while often seen as altruistic, can also serve to advance specific agendas and influence social policies.
- **Educational Institutions**: Elites fund and influence prestigious universities and research institutions, shaping the education and training of future leaders.
- **Cultural Production**: Control over film, music, and other cultural industries allows elites to shape societal values and norms.

Hidden Agendas and Strategic Goals

Economic Dominance

One of the primary goals of the global elite is to maintain and expand their economic dominance:

- **Market Control**: Elites seek to control key industries and markets, ensuring their continued profitability and influence.
- **Resource Extraction**: Control over natural resources, such as oil, minerals, and water, is crucial for maintaining economic power.

- **Financial Stability**: Elites aim to stabilize financial markets to protect their investments, often at the expense of broader economic equity.

Political Stability and Control

Political stability and control are also key objectives:

- **Regime Change**: Elites may support or orchestrate regime changes to install governments that are more amenable to their interests.
- **Surveillance and Security**: Expanding surveillance and security measures ensures control over populations and prevents dissent.
- **Legal and Regulatory Influence**: Shaping legal and regulatory frameworks to favor elite interests while limiting accountability and transparency.

Social Engineering and Cultural Hegemony

Elites often engage in social engineering to maintain cultural hegemony:

- **Population Control**: Policies and initiatives aimed at controlling population growth and demographics to align with elite interests.
- **Behavioral Influence**: Utilizing psychology and behavioral science to influence public behavior and attitudes.
- **Cultural Narratives**: Promoting cultural narratives that reinforce elite dominance and discourage resistance.

Impact on Global Society and Individual Freedoms

Erosion of Democracy

The concentration of power in the hands of a global elite undermines democratic processes:

- **Voter Disenfranchisement**: Efforts to suppress voter participation and influence electoral outcomes.
- **Policy Capture**: Policymaking that prioritizes elite interests over the public good, leading to increased inequality and social unrest.
- **Lack of Accountability**: Limited mechanisms for holding elites accountable for their actions and decisions.

Economic Inequality

The actions of the global elite contribute to growing economic inequality:

- **Wealth Concentration**: Increasing concentration of wealth in the hands of a few, leading to disparities in income and opportunities.
- **Labor Exploitation**: Practices that exploit labor and suppress wages, particularly in developing countries.
- **Barriers to Social Mobility**: Policies and practices that entrench social and economic hierarchies, limiting opportunities for upward mobility.

Restrictions on Freedom and Privacy

The drive for control and stability often results in restrictions on individual freedoms and privacy:

- **Surveillance State**: Expanding surveillance measures that infringe on privacy and civil liberties.
- **Censorship and Information Control**: Efforts to control the flow of information and suppress dissenting voices.
- **Restriction of Freedoms**: Laws and policies that restrict freedom of expression, assembly, and movement.

Environmental Impact

The pursuit of economic and political dominance by the global elite has significant environmental consequences:

- **Resource Exploitation**: Unsustainable extraction of natural resources leading to environmental degradation.
- **Climate Change**: Contributions to climate change through industrial activities and resistance to environmental regulations.
- **Environmental Justice**: Disproportionate impact of environmental harm on marginalized communities and developing countries.

Conclusion

The influence of the global elite on world events and individual freedoms is profound and multifaceted. By examining their origins, mechanisms of control, and hidden agendas, we gain a deeper understanding of the challenges and consequences of concentrated power. The actions of the global elite have significant implications for democracy, economic equity, social justice, and environmental sustainability.

In the following chapters, we will explore specific examples and case studies that illustrate the impact of the global elite on various aspects of society. Through these detailed analyses, we aim to uncover the hidden agendas behind their actions and highlight the importance of fostering a more transparent, equitable, and just world. By shining a light on these hidden dynamics, we hope to inspire a renewed commitment to protecting individual freedoms, promoting democratic governance, and ensuring sustainable development for all.

Chapter 25: The Concept of the Global Elite

The notion of a global elite—a small, powerful group of individuals and institutions that influence and control significant aspects of global politics, economics, and society—has been a topic of intrigue and controversy for decades. This chapter delves into the concept of the global elite, examining its historical roots, characteristics, and the mechanisms through which it exerts control. By exploring the evidence and theories surrounding this elusive group, we aim to provide a comprehensive understanding of its role in shaping world events and its impact on global society.

Historical Roots of the Global Elite

Ancient and Medieval Origins

The idea of a ruling elite is as old as civilization itself. In ancient times, monarchs, high priests, and aristocrats wielded significant power, controlling resources, and shaping societies according to their interests. These early elites often justified their dominance through divine right or hereditary privilege.

Feudal Systems and Aristocracy

During the medieval period, feudal systems further entrenched the power of elites. Landowning nobility and monarchs exercised control over vast territories and populations. The aristocracy maintained their status through a combination of military might, political alliances, and economic control.

Emergence of Capitalism and Industrialization

The advent of capitalism and the Industrial Revolution in the 18th and 19th centuries marked a significant shift in the structure of the elite. Wealth and power became increasingly tied to industrial and financial success. Prominent industrialists, bankers, and entrepreneurs emerged as new elites, often referred to as "captains of industry" or "robber barons."

Characteristics of the Global Elite

Wealth and Economic Power

The global elite is characterized by its immense wealth and economic influence. This group controls significant financial resources, major corporations, and key industries, giving them considerable leverage over global economic trends.

- **Top 1% Wealth Concentration**: The richest 1% of the world's population holds more wealth than the rest combined. This concentration of wealth allows the elite to exert disproportionate influence over economic policies and practices.
- **Corporate Control**: Major multinational corporations, often owned or controlled by the elite, dominate global markets and

supply chains. These corporations have the power to shape labor markets, trade policies, and consumer behavior.

Political Influence

The global elite wields significant political power, often influencing or directly participating in the decision-making processes of governments and international institutions.

- **Lobbying and Campaign Contributions**: Elites use their financial resources to lobby politicians, fund campaigns, and shape legislation. This ensures that policies align with their interests.
- **Think Tanks and Policy Institutes**: Organizations like the Council on Foreign Relations (CFR), the Brookings Institution, and the American Enterprise Institute (AEI) produce research and policy recommendations that guide government actions and public discourse.

Networked Influence

One of the defining features of the global elite is its extensive network of relationships that span across national borders and institutions. These networks facilitate coordinated efforts to shape global events and policies.

- **Interlocking Directorates**: Members of the elite often serve on the boards of multiple corporations, think tanks, and non-profits, creating a web of interconnected influence.
- **Exclusive Clubs and Gatherings**: Elite gatherings such as the Bilderberg Group, the Trilateral Commission, and the World Economic Forum (WEF) provide platforms for networking and strategy formulation.

Access to Information and Decision-Making

The global elite benefits from privileged access to critical information and decision-making processes, allowing them to stay ahead of trends and influence outcomes effectively.

- **Insider Knowledge**: Access to insider information from governments, financial markets, and corporations gives the elite a strategic advantage.
- **Policy Advisory Roles**: Many elites hold advisory roles in governments and international institutions, directly influencing policy decisions.

Theoretical Frameworks

Elite Theory

Elite theory posits that a small, cohesive group of people holds the most power in society, regardless of democratic processes. This theory suggests that elites are able to shape society to their benefit, often at the expense of the broader population.

- **C. Wright Mills' "The Power Elite"**: Mills argued that the power elite consists of individuals who hold top positions in the military, corporate, and political spheres. These elites are able to coordinate their efforts to maintain their dominance.
- **Gaetano Mosca and Vilfredo Pareto**: These early sociologists argued that societies are always governed by a minority elite, who use their resources and influence to maintain control over the majority.

Globalization Theory

Globalization theory examines how the processes of economic integration and political interdependence have led to the emergence of a global elite. This perspective highlights the transnational nature of elite power and the ways in which global networks facilitate elite control.

- **Economic Globalization**: The integration of global markets has created opportunities for elites to expand their influence across borders, leveraging international trade and investment to their advantage.
- **Political Globalization**: International institutions and agreements, such as the United Nations, the World Trade Organization (WTO), and various trade agreements, provide platforms for elites to coordinate their efforts on a global scale.

Origins and Evolution of the Modern Global Elite

Early 20th Century Foundations

The foundations of the modern global elite were laid in the early 20th century, as industrialization, urbanization, and the expansion of international trade created new centers of power.

- **The Rise of Multinational Corporations**: Companies like Standard Oil and U.S. Steel became powerful entities with significant influence over national and international policies.
- **The Formation of Central Banks**: Institutions like the Federal Reserve System in the United States centralized control over monetary policy, impacting global financial markets.
- **World War I and II**: These conflicts reshaped global power dynamics, leading to the creation of international institutions such as the League of Nations and later the United Nations.

Post-World War II Expansion

The end of World War II marked a significant expansion of the global elite's influence, driven by the establishment of key international organizations and agreements.

- **Bretton Woods Institutions**: The International Monetary Fund (IMF) and the World Bank were established to oversee global economic stability and development, often influencing national policies.
- **The United Nations**: Created to promote international cooperation, the UN became a platform for the global elite to shape international norms and policies.
- **NATO and Other Alliances**: Military alliances like NATO consolidated the power of Western elites and ensured their dominance in global security affairs.

Late 20th and Early 21st Century Consolidation

In the late 20th and early 21st centuries, globalization and technological advancements further consolidated the power of the global elite.

- **Neoliberal Economic Policies**: The adoption of neoliberal policies in many countries facilitated the concentration of wealth and power in the hands of a few.
- **The Digital Revolution**: Advances in technology and communication created new avenues for influence and control, particularly through the control of information and media.
- **Transnational Organizations**: Groups like the Bilderberg Group, the Trilateral Commission, and the World Economic Forum emerged as platforms for elites to coordinate their agendas.

Mechanisms of Control and Influence

Economic Control

The global elite exerts significant control over the global economy through various mechanisms.

- **Financial Institutions**: Banks, investment firms, and hedge funds managed by elites influence global financial markets and economic policies.
- **Corporate Power**: Major multinational corporations control vast resources, labor markets, and supply chains, shaping global economic trends.
- **Trade Agreements**: Elites influence the creation and enforcement of international trade agreements, often prioritizing corporate interests over national sovereignty and public welfare.

Political Influence

Political power is another critical tool for the global elite.

- **Lobbying and Campaign Contributions**: Elites use their wealth to influence political campaigns and policy decisions through lobbying and donations.
- **Think Tanks and Policy Planning**: Organizations like the CFR and the Brookings Institution produce research and policy recommendations that shape government decisions.
- **International Institutions**: Elites hold influential positions in organizations like the IMF, World Bank, and UN, guiding global governance and policy-making.

Media and Information Control

Control over media and information is crucial for maintaining influence.

- **Media Ownership**: Many major media outlets are owned or controlled by elite interests, shaping public perception and discourse.
- **Censorship and Propaganda**: Elites can suppress dissenting voices and promote narratives that align with their interests.
- **Digital Platforms**: The rise of social media and digital platforms has given elites new tools to influence public opinion and behavior.

Social and Cultural Influence

Elites also exert control through cultural and social channels.

- **Philanthropy and NGOs**: Elite philanthropy, while often seen as altruistic, can also serve to advance specific agendas and influence social policies.
- **Educational Institutions**: Elites fund and influence prestigious universities and research institutions, shaping the education and training of future leaders.
- **Cultural Production**: Control over film, music, and other cultural industries allows elites to shape societal values and norms.

Hidden Agendas and Strategic Goals

Economic Dominance

One of the primary goals of the global elite is to maintain and expand their economic dominance.

- **Market Control**: Elites seek to control key industries and markets, ensuring their continued profitability and influence.

- **Resource Extraction**: Control over natural resources, such as oil, minerals, and water, is crucial for maintaining economic power.
- **Financial Stability**: Elites aim to stabilize financial markets to protect their investments, often at the expense of broader economic equity.

Political Stability and Control

Political stability and control are also key objectives.

- **Regime Change**: Elites may support or orchestrate regime changes to install governments that are more amenable to their interests.
- **Surveillance and Security**: Expanding surveillance and security measures ensures control over populations and prevents dissent.
- **Legal and Regulatory Influence**: Shaping legal and regulatory frameworks to favor elite interests while limiting accountability and transparency.

Social Engineering and Cultural Hegemony

Elites often engage in social engineering to maintain cultural hegemony.

- **Population Control**: Policies and initiatives aimed at controlling population growth and demographics to align with elite interests.
- **Behavioral Influence**: Utilizing psychology and behavioral science to influence public behavior and attitudes.
- **Cultural Narratives**: Promoting cultural narratives that reinforce elite dominance and discourage resistance.

Impact on Global Society and Individual Freedoms

Erosion of Democracy

The concentration of power in the hands of a global elite undermines democratic processes.

- **Voter Disenfranchisement**: Efforts to suppress voter participation and influence electoral outcomes.
- **Policy Capture**: Policymaking that prioritizes elite interests over the public good, leading to increased inequality and social unrest.
- **Lack of Accountability**: Limited mechanisms for holding elites accountable for their actions and decisions.

Economic Inequality

The actions of the global elite contribute to growing economic inequality.

- **Wealth Concentration**: Increasing concentration of wealth in the hands of a few, leading to disparities in income and opportunities.
- **Labor Exploitation**: Practices that exploit labor and suppress wages, particularly in developing countries.
- **Barriers to Social Mobility**: Policies and practices that entrench social and economic hierarchies, limiting opportunities for upward mobility.

Restrictions on Freedom and Privacy

The drive for control and stability often results in restrictions on individual freedoms and privacy.

- **Surveillance State**: Expanding surveillance measures that infringe on privacy and civil liberties.
- **Censorship and Information Control**: Efforts to control the flow of information and suppress dissenting voices.
- **Restriction of Freedoms**: Laws and policies that restrict freedom of expression, assembly, and movement.

Environmental Impact

The pursuit of economic and political dominance by the global elite has significant environmental consequences.

- **Resource Exploitation**: Unsustainable extraction of natural resources leading to environmental degradation.
- **Climate Change**: Contributions to climate change through industrial activities and resistance to environmental regulations.
- **Environmental Justice**: Disproportionate impact of environmental harm on marginalized communities and developing countries.

Ethical and Moral Consequences

Compromising Scientific Integrity

The suppression of scientific discoveries and technological innovations can compromise the integrity of the scientific community. When researchers face pressure to conform to established interests or risk suppression, it undermines the principles of scientific inquiry and intellectual honesty.

Case Study: Lysenkoism in the Soviet Union

The case of Lysenkoism in the Soviet Union illustrates how political ideology can compromise scientific integrity. Trofim Lysenko's rejection of Mendelian genetics in favor of his own theories was supported by the Soviet government, leading to the persecution of geneticists and the suppression of legitimate scientific research. This political interference delayed advancements in biological science and had long-lasting consequences for Soviet agriculture.

Impact on Public Trust in Science

Suppressing scientific discoveries can erode public trust in science and scientific institutions. When people perceive that scientific information is being manipulated or suppressed, it undermines confidence in the scientific process and the credibility of researchers.

Case Study: Vaccine Misinformation

The spread of misinformation about vaccines, often driven by ideological and economic interests, has contributed to vaccine hesitancy and public distrust in medical science. This suppression of accurate scientific information about vaccines' safety and efficacy has had significant public health consequences, including outbreaks of preventable diseases.

Conclusion

The influence of the global elite on world events and individual freedoms is profound and multifaceted. By examining their origins, mechanisms of control, and hidden agendas, we gain a deeper understanding of the challenges and consequences of concentrated power. The actions of the global elite have significant implications for democracy, economic equity, social justice, and environmental sustainability.

In the following chapters, we will explore specific examples and case studies that illustrate the impact of the global elite on various aspects of society. Through these detailed analyses, we aim to uncover the hidden agendas behind their actions and highlight the importance of fostering a more transparent, equitable, and just world. By shining a light on these hidden dynamics, we hope to inspire a renewed commitment to protecting individual freedoms, promoting democratic governance, and ensuring sustainable development for all.

Chapter 26: Organizations and Their Agendas

The concept of a global elite is often associated with powerful organizations that operate behind the scenes to influence global events. These organizations, composed of influential individuals from various sectors, have significant sway over political, economic, and social developments. This chapter delves into some of the most prominent organizations alleged to be part of the global elite, examining their origins, agendas, and methods of operation. By exploring the intricate web of connections and influence, we aim to uncover the hidden agendas that drive these organizations and their impact on global society.

The Bilderberg Group

Origins and Purpose

The Bilderberg Group was founded in 1954 by Dutch statesman Joseph Retinger, with the support of Prince Bernhard of the Netherlands. The group's purpose is to foster dialogue and cooperation between Europe and North America on political, economic, and social issues. The inaugural meeting was held at the Hotel de Bilderberg in the Netherlands, from which the group takes its name.

Membership and Meetings

The Bilderberg Group's membership includes influential politicians, business leaders, academics, and media figures from Europe and North America. Meetings are held annually, with attendees selected by a steering committee. These gatherings are conducted under strict secrecy, with no press coverage or public statements.

Agendas and Influence

While the Bilderberg Group claims that its meetings are informal discussions that do not result in binding decisions, critics argue that the group wields significant influence over global policy. Topics discussed at Bilderberg meetings often reflect pressing global issues, and the participants' positions of power enable them to implement the ideas and strategies formulated during these gatherings.

Secrecy and Controversy

The lack of transparency surrounding Bilderberg meetings has fueled suspicion and conspiracy theories. Critics contend that the group's secrecy undermines democratic accountability and allows a small elite to shape global policies without public scrutiny. Allegations of the group's involvement in orchestrating significant geopolitical events have persisted for decades.

The Trilateral Commission

Origins and Objectives

The Trilateral Commission was founded in 1973 by David Rocke-feller, Zbigniew Brzezinski, and other prominent leaders from North America, Europe, and Japan. The commission aims to foster closer cooperation among these regions to address global challenges and promote stability and prosperity.

Membership and Structure

The Trilateral Commission's membership includes influential figures from politics, business, academia, and media. The commission is divided into three regional groups: North America, Europe, and Asia-Pacific, each with its own leadership and members. The groups meet separately and collectively to discuss and formulate policies.

Agendas and Influence

The Trilateral Commission focuses on a wide range of global issues, including economic policy, international security, and environmental sustainability. The commission's reports and recommendations often shape global policy debates and influence the actions of governments and international organizations.

Criticism and Conspiracy Theories

Critics of the Trilateral Commission argue that it represents the interests of a global elite seeking to consolidate power and influence. Conspiracy theories suggest that the commission is part of a larger network of secret societies working towards a New World Order. These theories often allege that the commission's members use their positions to manipulate global events for their benefit.

The Council on Foreign Relations (CFR)

Origins and Purpose

The Council on Foreign Relations (CFR) was founded in 1921 in New York City, following the end of World War I. The organization's primary purpose is to promote a better understanding of foreign policy and international affairs among policymakers and the public.

Membership and Activities

The CFR's membership includes prominent leaders from government, business, academia, and media. The organization conducts research, publishes reports, and hosts events on a wide range of global issues. The CFR's influential publication, "Foreign Affairs," is widely read by policymakers and scholars.

Agendas and Influence

The CFR plays a significant role in shaping U.S. foreign policy and international relations. The organization's reports and recommendations often inform government decisions and public discourse. The CFR's extensive network of members and connections enables it to exert considerable influence over global affairs.

Criticism and Controversy

Critics argue that the CFR represents the interests of a global elite and promotes policies that benefit the wealthy and powerful at the expense of the broader population. Conspiracy theories suggest that the CFR is part of a larger effort to establish a global government and undermine national sovereignty.

The World Economic Forum (WEF)

Origins and Mission

The World Economic Forum (WEF) was founded in 1971 by German economist Klaus Schwab. The WEF's mission is to improve the state of the world by engaging business, political, academic, and other leaders in collaborative efforts to address global challenges.

Annual Meetings and Membership

The WEF is best known for its annual meeting in Davos, Switzerland, which brings together influential leaders from around the world to discuss pressing global issues. The organization's membership includes major corporations, political leaders, and thought leaders from various fields.

Agendas and Initiatives

The WEF focuses on a wide range of issues, including economic development, environmental sustainability, technology, and global governance. The organization's initiatives and reports often shape global policy debates and influence the actions of governments and international organizations.

Criticism and Controversy

The WEF has faced criticism for its perceived elitism and lack of transparency. Critics argue that the organization's meetings and initiatives primarily serve the interests of the wealthy and powerful, rather than addressing the needs of the broader population. Conspiracy theories suggest that the WEF is part of a larger effort to establish a global technocratic government.

The Bilderberg Group: Specific Agendas and Influences

Economic Globalization

One of the primary agendas of the Bilderberg Group is to promote economic globalization. The group supports policies that facilitate free trade, deregulation, and the integration of global markets. By advocating for these policies, the Bilderberg Group aims to create a more interconnected and interdependent global economy.

Case Study: The Eurozone

The Bilderberg Group has been credited with playing a role in the creation of the Eurozone. Meetings in the 1990s included discussions on European economic integration, and several key figures involved in the establishment of the euro attended Bilderberg meetings. The group's support for a unified European currency aligns with its broader agenda of economic globalization.

Political Integration and Global Governance

The Bilderberg Group also advocates for greater political integration and global governance. The group supports the strengthening of international institutions and the development of multilateral approaches to global challenges.

Case Study: European Union Expansion

The Bilderberg Group has been linked to efforts to expand the European Union (EU) and strengthen its political institutions. The group's discussions on European integration have influenced the EU's enlargement and the development of its governance structures. By promoting political integration, the Bilderberg Group aims to create a more cohesive and coordinated global political order.

Technological Advancements and Control

The Bilderberg Group recognizes the transformative potential of technology and advocates for policies that support technological innovation and control. The group promotes the development of advanced technologies, such as artificial intelligence (AI) and biotechnology, while also emphasizing the need for regulatory frameworks to manage their impact.

Case Study: Digital Privacy and Surveillance

The Bilderberg Group has discussed issues related to digital privacy and surveillance, reflecting its interest in controlling the implications of technological advancements. The group's support for surveillance technologies and data control aligns with its broader agenda of maintaining influence over global developments.

The Trilateral Commission: Specific Agendas and Influences

Economic Policy and Neoliberalism

The Trilateral Commission has been a strong advocate for neoliberal economic policies, which emphasize free markets, deregulation, and privatization. The commission supports policies that promote economic growth and integration, often at the expense of social welfare and environmental sustainability.

Case Study: Structural Adjustment Programs

The Trilateral Commission has influenced the development and implementation of structural adjustment programs (SAPs) by international financial institutions like the IMF and the World Bank.

These programs, which often include austerity measures and market liberalization, reflect the commission's neoliberal agenda and have had significant social and economic impacts on developing countries.

International Security and Military Cooperation

The Trilateral Commission also focuses on issues related to international security and military cooperation. The commission supports policies that strengthen alliances and promote collective security.

Case Study: NATO Expansion

The Trilateral Commission has been linked to efforts to expand NATO and enhance its capabilities. The commission's support for NATO expansion aligns with its broader agenda of promoting international security and military cooperation among its member regions.

Environmental Sustainability

The Trilateral Commission has increasingly emphasized the importance of environmental sustainability in its policy recommendations. The commission advocates for policies that address climate change, protect natural resources, and promote sustainable development.

Case Study: Climate Change Agreements

The Trilateral Commission has supported international climate change agreements, such as the Paris Agreement, which aim to reduce greenhouse gas emissions and mitigate the impacts of climate change. The commission's advocacy for environmental sustainability reflects its recognition of the global nature of environmental challenges and the need for coordinated action.

The Council on Foreign Relations (CFR): Specific Agendas and Influences

U.S. Foreign Policy

The CFR plays a significant role in shaping U.S. foreign policy. The organization's reports and recommendations often inform government decisions and public discourse on international relations.

Case Study: The Iraq War

The CFR was influential in shaping the debate on U.S. policy toward Iraq in the lead-up to the 2003 invasion. Several CFR members, including prominent policymakers and analysts, supported the case for military intervention. The organization's influence on the Iraq War reflects its broader impact on U.S. foreign policy decisions.

Global Economic Governance

The CFR also focuses on issues related to global economic governance. The organization advocates for policies that promote economic stability, growth, and integration.

Case Study: Global Financial Crisis

During the global financial crisis of 2008-2009, the CFR played a key role in analyzing the causes and consequences of the crisis and recommending policy responses. The organization's reports and discussions on financial regulation and economic recovery influenced government actions and international cooperation.

Human Rights and Democracy Promotion

The CFR emphasizes the importance of human rights and democracy promotion in its policy recommendations. The organization advocates for policies that support democratic governance and protect human rights worldwide.

Case Study: Arab Spring

The CFR was actively involved in analyzing and responding to the Arab Spring uprisings in the Middle East and North Africa. The organization's reports and recommendations on supporting democratic transitions and addressing human rights abuses influenced U.S. policy and international responses to the events.

The World Economic Forum (WEF): Specific Agendas and Influences

Fourth Industrial Revolution

The WEF has been a leading advocate for the Fourth Industrial Revolution, which involves the integration of advanced technologies such as AI, robotics, and the Internet of Things (IoT) into various sectors of the economy.

Case Study: Industry 4.0 Initiatives

The WEF's initiatives on Industry 4.0 aim to promote the adoption of advanced technologies in manufacturing and other industries. The organization's reports and recommendations on the Fourth Industrial Revolution have influenced government policies and corporate strategies, driving technological innovation and economic transformation.

Global Health and Pandemics

The WEF focuses on global health issues, including pandemic preparedness and response. The organization advocates for policies that strengthen healthcare systems and improve global health security.

Case Study: COVID-19 Response

During the COVID-19 pandemic, the WEF played a key role in facilitating discussions and collaborations on pandemic response and recovery. The organization's initiatives, such as the COVID Action Platform, brought together governments, businesses, and international organizations to address the crisis and develop strategies for future health emergencies.

Sustainable Development and Climate Action

The WEF emphasizes the importance of sustainable development and climate action in its policy recommendations. The organization advocates for policies that promote environmental sustainability and address climate change.

Case Study: Sustainable Development Goals (SDGs)

The WEF has been a strong supporter of the United Nations' Sustainable Development Goals (SDGs), which aim to address global challenges such as poverty, inequality, and climate change by 2030. The organization's initiatives and partnerships related to the SDGs have influenced government policies and corporate actions to promote sustainable development.

Conclusion

The influence of organizations such as the Bilderberg Group, the Trilateral Commission, the Council on Foreign Relations, and the

World Economic Forum is profound and multifaceted. These organizations play significant roles in shaping global policies and agendas, often operating behind the scenes and beyond the reach of democratic accountability. By examining their origins, structures, and specific agendas, we gain a deeper understanding of the complex interplay between power, influence, and global governance.

In the following chapters, we will explore specific examples and case studies that illustrate the impact of these organizations on various aspects of society. Through detailed analyses, we aim to uncover the hidden agendas behind their actions and highlight the importance of fostering a more transparent, equitable, and just world. By shining a light on these hidden dynamics, we hope to inspire a renewed commitment to protecting individual freedoms, promoting democratic governance, and ensuring sustainable development for all.

| **27** |

Chapter 27: Impact on Global Society and Individual Freedoms

The actions and agendas of the global elite have profound and far-reaching impacts on global society and individual freedoms. These impacts manifest in various ways, influencing economic policies, political structures, social norms, and environmental practices. Understanding these influences is crucial for comprehending the challenges faced by democratic governance, economic equity, and social justice. This chapter delves into the specific effects of elite influence, examining how their actions shape global society and affect individual freedoms. Through detailed analyses and case studies, we aim to uncover the hidden dynamics at play and their implications for the future.

Economic Inequality and Wealth Concentration

Global Wealth Disparities

The concentration of wealth among the global elite has led to significant economic inequalities worldwide. The richest 1% of the global population holds more wealth than the rest combined, creating vast disparities in income and opportunities.

Impact on Economic Mobility

Economic inequality hampers social mobility and perpetuates cycles of poverty. The elite's control over key industries and financial markets often leads to policies that favor their interests, limiting opportunities for the broader population.

Case Study: The Gig Economy

The rise of the gig economy, characterized by short-term contracts and freelance work, highlights the growing economic disparities. While the gig economy offers flexibility, it often lacks job security, benefits, and fair wages. The elite, who own and control the platforms that drive the gig economy, benefit from reduced labor costs and increased profits, exacerbating income inequality.

Political Influence and Democratic Erosion

Undermining Democratic Processes

The global elite's influence over political processes poses significant challenges to democratic governance. Through lobbying, campaign contributions, and control over media narratives, the elite can shape policies and electoral outcomes to align with their interests.

Case Study: Citizens United v. FEC

The 2010 U.S. Supreme Court decision in Citizens United v. Federal Election Commission allowed for unlimited corporate spending on political campaigns. This ruling has led to increased influence of wealthy individuals and corporations in politics, undermining the democratic principle of equal representation.

Policy Capture and Regulatory Favoritism

The concept of policy capture refers to the elite's ability to influence regulatory and legislative frameworks to favor their interests. This often results in policies that prioritize corporate profits over public welfare, environmental protection, and social equity.

Case Study: Financial Deregulation

The deregulation of financial markets in the late 20th and early 21st centuries, influenced by elite lobbying, contributed to the global financial crisis of 2008. Policies that favored financial institutions and reduced oversight allowed for risky practices that ultimately led to economic collapse, affecting millions of people worldwide.

Restrictions on Civil Liberties and Privacy

Surveillance and Data Privacy

The elite's control over technology and information has significant implications for privacy and civil liberties. Governments and corporations often collaborate to expand surveillance capabilities, collecting vast amounts of data on individuals.

Case Study: Edward Snowden and NSA Surveillance

In 2013, Edward Snowden, a former NSA contractor, leaked classified documents revealing the extent of U.S. government surveillance programs. These programs, which collected data on millions of people without their knowledge, highlighted the tension between national security and individual privacy. The revelations sparked global debates about the balance between security and civil liberties.

Censorship and Information Control

The elite's influence over media and digital platforms allows them to control the flow of information, shaping public perception and suppressing dissenting voices. This control can limit freedom of expression and restrict access to diverse viewpoints.

Case Study: Social Media Censorship

Major social media platforms, often owned or influenced by elite interests, have faced criticism for their role in censoring content and shaping public discourse. Algorithms that prioritize certain types of content over others can skew public perception and limit exposure to alternative viewpoints. Additionally, instances of content removal and account suspensions for political reasons have raised concerns about the power of tech giants to influence democratic processes.

Environmental Degradation and Climate Change

Resource Exploitation

The elite's pursuit of economic dominance often leads to the unsustainable extraction of natural resources, contributing to environmental degradation and loss of biodiversity. Policies that prioritize short-term profits over long-term sustainability exacerbate these issues.

Case Study: Amazon Deforestation

Deforestation in the Amazon rainforest, driven by agricultural expansion and resource extraction, has significant environmental impacts.

Elite interests in agribusiness and mining often drive these activities, leading to habitat destruction, climate change, and the displacement of indigenous communities.

Climate Change Denial and Delay

The elite's influence over political and economic systems has also contributed to delays in addressing climate change. By funding climate change denial campaigns and lobbying against environmental regulations, elite interests have hindered global efforts to mitigate climate change.

Case Study: Fossil Fuel Lobbying

The fossil fuel industry, heavily influenced by elite interests, has been a major force in climate change denial and delay. Lobbying efforts by oil and gas companies have obstructed the implementation of policies aimed at reducing carbon emissions and transitioning to renewable energy sources. This delay has exacerbated the impacts of climate change, affecting ecosystems and human communities worldwide.

Social Engineering and Cultural Hegemony

Shaping Public Opinion and Social Norms

The elite's control over media, education, and cultural institutions allows them to shape public opinion and social norms. By promoting certain values and narratives, they can influence societal attitudes and behaviors.

Case Study: Media Ownership and Bias

The concentration of media ownership in the hands of a few elite corporations has significant implications for public discourse. Media bias, influenced by the interests of owners and advertisers, can shape public perception on critical issues such as politics, economics, and social justice. This control over information can limit democratic engagement and perpetuate existing power structures.

Population Control and Social Policies

Elite interests often drive policies related to population control and social engineering. These policies can include efforts to control population growth, influence reproductive rights, and shape family structures.

Case Study: China's One-Child Policy

China's One-Child Policy, implemented in 1979, aimed to control population growth in response to economic and environmental concerns. While the policy was driven by government interests, it also reflected broader elite agendas related to resource management and social engineering. The policy had significant social and demographic impacts, including gender imbalances and human rights abuses.

Resistance and Movements for Change

Grassroots Movements and Activism

In response to elite influence and its negative impacts, grassroots movements and activism have emerged as powerful forces for change. These movements often advocate for economic justice, environmental sustainability, and democratic accountability.

Case Study: The Occupy Movement

The Occupy Movement, which began in 2011 with Occupy Wall Street, protested against economic inequality and the influence of the global elite. The movement's slogan, "We are the 99%," highlighted the disparities between the wealthy elite and the broader population. While the movement faced challenges in achieving concrete policy changes, it succeeded in raising awareness and sparking global discussions about economic justice.

Whistleblowers and Investigative Journalism

Whistleblowers and investigative journalists play a crucial role in exposing elite influence and holding powerful entities accountable. By revealing hidden information and bringing suppressed stories to light, they contribute to greater transparency and public awareness.

Case Study: The Panama Papers

The Panama Papers, a massive leak of documents from the law firm Mossack Fonseca, revealed the secretive financial dealings of wealthy individuals and organizations. The investigation exposed the use of offshore accounts to hide wealth and avoid taxes, highlighting the need for greater transparency and accountability in global finance.

Policy Reforms and Democratic Innovations

Efforts to counter elite influence also include policy reforms and democratic innovations aimed at increasing transparency, accountability, and public participation in decision-making processes.

Case Study: Participatory Budgeting

Participatory budgeting is a democratic process that allows citizens to directly decide how to allocate public funds. By involving community members in budget decisions, participatory budgeting promotes transparency and accountability, empowering individuals to influence policies that affect their lives. This approach has been successfully implemented in various cities worldwide, demonstrating its potential to enhance democratic governance.

Conclusion

The influence of the global elite on global society and individual freedoms is profound and multifaceted. From economic inequality and political influence to environmental degradation and social engineering, the actions of the elite shape many aspects of our lives. Understanding these impacts is crucial for addressing the challenges they pose and fostering a more just, equitable, and sustainable world.

As we conclude this exploration of the global elite and their hidden agendas, it is essential to recognize the power of collective action and democratic engagement in challenging elite influence. By supporting grassroots movements, advocating for policy reforms, and promoting transparency and accountability, we can work towards a future where power is more equitably distributed and individual freedoms are protected.

In the final chapter, we will reflect on the key themes and findings of this book, highlighting the importance of continued vigilance and action in uncovering and addressing hidden agendas. By shining a light on these issues, we hope to inspire a renewed commitment to protecting democracy, promoting social justice, and ensuring sustainable development for all.

CONCLUSION

UNVEILING HIDDEN AGENDAS AND SHAPING THE FUTURE

As we conclude this in-depth exploration of hidden agendas, suppressed information, and the influence of the global elite, it is crucial to reflect on the key themes and findings that have emerged. This book has delved into the intricate and often opaque world of powerful entities and their impact on global society. From the suppression of scientific discoveries and technological innovations to the manipulation of political and economic systems, we have uncovered the complex mechanisms through which elites maintain their dominance. In this final chapter, we summarize our key insights, reflect on the broader implications for democracy and societal progress, and discuss the steps we can take to foster a more transparent, equitable, and just world.

Key Themes and Findings

The Pervasiveness of Suppression

Throughout our exploration, a recurring theme has been the pervasive nature of suppression—whether of scientific discoveries, technological advancements, or dissenting voices. Suppression serves as a tool for powerful entities to maintain control and prevent challenges to their authority.

Historical and Contemporary Examples

We have examined historical and contemporary examples of suppression, from the persecution of innovators like Nikola Tesla and Ignaz Semmelweis to the marginalization of modern-day advancements in renewable energy and medical research. These cases illustrate how suppression delays progress and deprives society of potential benefits.

Mechanisms of Suppression

The mechanisms of suppression are diverse and multifaceted, including censorship, discrediting, legal obstacles, and economic pressures. Understanding these mechanisms is essential for recognizing and addressing instances of suppression in various contexts.

The Role of the Global Elite

The global elite—comprising influential individuals and organizations—plays a central role in shaping world events and maintaining existing power structures. Their influence extends across political, economic, and social spheres, often operating behind the scenes to further their interests.

Economic and Political Influence

The elite's economic and political influence is evident in their control over key industries, financial institutions, and policy-making processes. Through lobbying, campaign contributions, and control over media narratives, they shape policies and electoral outcomes to align with their interests.

Cultural and Social Engineering

Beyond economic and political spheres, the elite also exerts control through cultural and social channels. By shaping public opinion, social norms, and educational content, they maintain cultural hegemony and influence societal values and behaviors.

Impact on Global Society and Individual Freedoms

The actions of the global elite and the suppression of innovation have profound implications for global society and individual freedoms. These impacts manifest in various ways, from economic inequality and environmental degradation to restrictions on civil liberties and democratic erosion.

Economic Inequality

The concentration of wealth among the elite has led to significant economic disparities, limiting opportunities for the broader population and perpetuating cycles of poverty. This inequality hampers social mobility and undermines efforts to achieve economic justice.

Environmental Consequences

The pursuit of economic dominance by the elite often results in unsustainable resource extraction and environmental degradation. Delays in addressing climate change and resistance to environmental regulations exacerbate these issues, affecting ecosystems and human communities worldwide.

Civil Liberties and Privacy

The elite's control over technology and information has significant implications for privacy and civil liberties. Expanding surveillance capabilities and information control threaten individual freedoms and democratic accountability.

Challenges to Democratic Governance

The concentration of power in the hands of a global elite poses significant challenges to democratic governance. By undermining democratic processes, influencing policy decisions, and shaping public perception, the elite erodes the principles of equal representation and accountability.

Reflecting on Broader Implications

The Need for Vigilance and Action

Uncovering and addressing hidden agendas requires vigilance and collective action. Whistleblowers, investigative journalists, activists, and informed citizens play crucial roles in exposing suppression and holding powerful entities accountable.

Supporting Whistleblowers and Investigative Journalism

Whistleblowers and investigative journalists often face significant risks in their efforts to reveal hidden information. Supporting their work through legal protections, funding, and public recognition is essential for promoting transparency and accountability.

Grassroots Movements and Democratic Engagement

Grassroots movements and democratic engagement are powerful tools for challenging elite influence and advocating for social justice. By mobilizing communities, raising awareness, and advocating for policy reforms, these movements can drive meaningful change.

Promoting Transparency and Accountability

Transparency and accountability are fundamental principles for ensuring that power is exercised responsibly and in the public interest. Strengthening mechanisms for transparency, such as open government initiatives and robust regulatory frameworks, is crucial for fostering a more equitable and just society.

Policy Reforms and Institutional Changes

Policy reforms and institutional changes are necessary to address the root causes of suppression and elite influence. These reforms should aim to promote economic equity, environmental sustainability, and democratic governance.

Economic Policies for Equity

Reforming economic policies to address inequality and promote social mobility is essential for creating a more inclusive economy. This includes progressive taxation, fair labor practices, and social safety nets that support vulnerable populations.

Environmental Sustainability

Addressing environmental challenges requires policies that promote sustainable resource management, reduce carbon emissions, and protect ecosystems. International cooperation and strong regulatory frameworks are key to achieving environmental sustainability.

Democratic Innovations

Innovations in democratic governance, such as participatory budgeting and citizen assemblies, can enhance public participation and ensure that decision-making processes are more inclusive and accountable. These innovations can help bridge the gap between citizens and policy-makers, fostering a more responsive and representative democracy.

Conclusion: Shaping the Future

The journey of uncovering hidden agendas and understanding the influence of the global elite is a continuous process. As we move forward, it is essential to remain vigilant, informed, and engaged in efforts to promote transparency, equity, and justice.

Empowering Individuals and Communities

Empowering individuals and communities to participate actively in democratic processes and advocate for their rights is crucial for building a more just and equitable society. Education, access to information, and opportunities for civic engagement are key components of this empowerment.

Building Alliances and Solidarity

Building alliances and fostering solidarity among diverse groups is essential for addressing the complex and interconnected challenges posed by elite influence and suppression. Collaborative efforts across social, economic, and political spheres can drive meaningful change and create a more inclusive and sustainable future.

Inspiring a Renewed Commitment

In closing, we hope that this exploration of hidden agendas and the influence of the global elite has inspired a renewed commitment to protecting democracy, promoting social justice, and ensuring sustainable development for all. By shining a light on these issues and fostering a culture of transparency and accountability, we can work towards a future where power is more equitably distributed and individual freedoms are protected.

Call to Action

We encourage readers to continue their own research, engage in informed discussions, and support efforts to uncover and address hidden agendas. By staying vigilant and actively participating in the democratic process, we can collectively shape a more just, equitable, and sustainable world.

Final Thoughts

The challenges posed by the global elite and their hidden agendas are significant, but they are not insurmountable. Through collective action, informed advocacy, and a commitment to democratic principles, we can build a future that prioritizes the well-being of all individuals and communities. Let us move forward with determination and hope, striving for a world where transparency, equity, and justice prevail.

ADDITIONAL RESOURCES AND REFERENCES

The appendix of "Hidden Agendas: Exposing the Dark Secrets" serves as a comprehensive guide to further your understanding of the topics discussed in this book. It includes a curated list of recommended books, documentaries, scholarly articles, declassified government documents, and credible websites. These resources provide additional insights, evidence, and perspectives on the complex issues of suppression, elite influence, and hidden agendas. Whether you are a curious reader, a student, or a researcher, this appendix will equip you with the tools to delve deeper into the subjects covered in this book.

Books

"The Power Elite" by C. Wright Mills

A seminal work that explores the structure and influence of the elite in American society, focusing on the intersections of military, corporate, and political power.

"Confessions of an Economic Hit Man" by John Perkins

An insider's account of how economic hit men manipulate countries' economies for the benefit of global elites, detailing the strategies and consequences of these actions.

"Tragedy and Hope: A History of the World in Our Time" by Carroll Quigley

A comprehensive historical analysis that reveals the role of secret societies and elite groups in shaping global events.

"Dark Money: The Hidden History of the Billionaires Behind the Rise of the Radical Right" by Jane Mayer

Investigates the influence of wealthy individuals and their foundations on American politics, uncovering the networks and strategies used to sway public policy.

"Superclass: The Global Power Elite and the World They Are Making" by David Rothkopf

Examines the global elite, their connections, and their influence on world events, offering a detailed look at how this group operates.

"The New Confessions of an Economic Hit Man" by John Perkins

An updated version of Perkins' original work, including new chapters that discuss recent developments and continuing economic manipulation by the elite.

"The Shock Doctrine: The Rise of Disaster Capitalism" by Naomi Klein

Explores how global elites exploit crises to implement controversial policies and economic reforms that benefit their interests.

"Merchants of Doubt: How a Handful of Scientists Obscured the Truth on Issues from Tobacco Smoke to Global Warming" by Naomi Oreskes and Erik M. Conway

Investigates how a small group of scientists with ties to elite interests has misled the public on various health and environmental issues.

Documentaries

"The Corporation" (2003)

Directed by Mark Achbar and Jennifer Abbott, this documentary examines the modern corporation, its power, and its influence on society and the environment.

"Inside Job" (2010)

Directed by Charles Ferguson, this documentary provides a comprehensive analysis of the global financial crisis of 2008, exposing the systemic corruption of the financial industry.

"The Panama Papers" (2018)

Directed by Alex Winter, this documentary details the investigation and impact of the Panama Papers leak, revealing how elites use offshore accounts to hide wealth and avoid taxes.

"Citizenfour" (2014)

Directed by Laura Poitras, this documentary follows Edward Snowden as he leaks classified information about NSA surveillance programs, highlighting issues of privacy and government overreach.

"13th" (2016)

Directed by Ava DuVernay, this documentary explores the intersection of race, justice, and mass incarceration in the United States, revealing how elite interests have shaped these systems.

"An Inconvenient Truth" (2006)

Directed by Davis Guggenheim, this documentary features Al Gore's campaign to educate the public about the dangers of climate change, emphasizing the role of elite interests in climate denial.

"Food, Inc." (2008)

Directed by Robert Kenner, this documentary examines the industrialization of food production and its impact on health, the environment, and worker rights, highlighting the influence of elite corporations.

"The Social Dilemma" (2020)

Directed by Jeff Orlowski, this documentary explores the dangerous human impact of social networking, with tech experts sounding the alarm on their own creations.

Scholarly Articles

"The Rise of the Global Elite" by Chrystia Freeland (The Atlantic, 2011)

Analyzes the increasing influence of the global elite and its impact on global inequality and governance.

"Globalization and the Transnational Capitalist Class" by Leslie Sklair (International Sociology, 2001)

Examines the emergence of a transnational capitalist class and its role in shaping globalization processes.

"The Theory of the Transnational State: A Decade of Controversies" by William I. Robinson (International Critical Thought, 2016)

Explores the concept of the transnational state and its implications for understanding global power dynamics.

"The Financialization of the American Economy" by Greta R. Krippner (Socio-Economic Review, 2005)

Investigates how financialization has transformed the American economy and the role of elite interests in this process.

"Elite Networks and the Rise of Global Cities" by Saskia Sassen (Urban Studies, 2001)

Discusses how elite networks have contributed to the rise of global cities and their impact on urban development and inequality.

"The Power Elite Revisited: The New American Ruling Class" by G. William Domhoff (Critical Sociology, 2006)

Revisits C. Wright Mills' concept of the power elite, examining its relevance and manifestations in contemporary American society.

"Climate Change and the Global Elite: Understanding the Politics of Environmental Governance" by Matthew Paterson (Global Environmental Politics, 2001)

Analyzes the role of the global elite in shaping climate change policies and environmental governance.

"Neoliberalism and the End of Liberal Democracy" by Wendy Brown (Theory & Event, 2003)

Explores how neoliberal policies promoted by elite interests have undermined liberal democratic principles and institutions.

Declassified Government Documents

CIA MK-Ultra Documents

Declassified documents related to the CIA's MK-Ultra program, which involved covert mind control and behavioral modification experiments.

NSA Surveillance Documents (Edward Snowden Leaks)

Classified documents leaked by Edward Snowden revealing the extent of NSA surveillance programs and their implications for privacy and civil liberties.

Operation Northwoods Documents

Declassified documents detailing a proposed false flag operation by the U.S. Department of Defense to justify military intervention in Cuba.

Church Committee Reports

Reports from the U.S. Senate Select Committee to Study Governmental Operations with Respect to Intelligence Activities, which investigated abuses by the CIA, FBI, and NSA.

Operation Paperclip Documents

Declassified documents related to Operation Paperclip, a secret program that recruited former Nazi scientists to work for the U.S. government after World War II.

The Pentagon Papers

Classified documents leaked by Daniel Ellsberg revealing the U.S. government's deception regarding the Vietnam War.

Project Blue Book Files

Declassified documents from the U.S. Air Force's Project Blue Book, which investigated UFO sightings and related phenomena.

The Pike Committee Report

A report by the U.S. House of Representatives Select Committee on Intelligence, which investigated CIA and FBI covert activities and their impacts.

Credible Websites

The Intercept

An online publication dedicated to investigative journalism, founded by Glenn Greenwald, Laura Poitras, and Jeremy Scahill. The Intercept focuses on issues of government and corporate transparency, civil liberties, and justice.

WikiLeaks

A non-profit organization that publishes classified, censored, or otherwise restricted information from anonymous sources, with a focus on government and corporate misconduct.

ProPublica

An independent, non-profit newsroom that produces investigative journalism in the public interest, covering topics such as politics, health care, education, and the environment.

The Center for Investigative Reporting (CIR)

A non-profit news organization that conducts in-depth investigative reporting on issues of social justice, transparency, and accountability.

The National Security Archive

An independent non-governmental research institute and library located at George Washington University, which collects and publishes declassified documents obtained through the Freedom of Information Act (FOIA).

Freedom of the Press Foundation

An organization that supports and defends public-interest journalism, focusing on issues of press freedom, transparency, and accountability.

The Electronic Frontier Foundation (EFF)

A non-profit organization that defends civil liberties in the digital world, advocating for privacy, free expression, and digital rights.

OpenSecrets

A non-profit organization that tracks money in U.S. politics and its effects on elections and public policy, providing data on campaign contributions, lobbying, and dark money.

Conclusion

The appendix of "Hidden Agendas: Exposing the Dark Secrets" offers a wealth of resources for readers who wish to further explore the complex issues discussed in this book. By delving into the recommended books, documentaries, scholarly articles, declassified government documents, and credible websites, readers can gain a deeper understanding of the hidden agendas that shape our world

These resources provide valuable insights and evidence, empowering individuals to engage critically with the information and advocate for greater transparency, accountability, and justice.

Demetri Welsh is a passionate researcher and writer dedicated to uncovering the hidden truths that shape our world. With a keen interest in history, conspiracy theories, and suppressed knowledge, Demetri has spent years delving into the shadows of our past and present to bring untold stories to light. His work is characterized by meticulous research, compelling narratives, and a commitment to challenging mainstream narratives.

Demetri's journey began with a fascination for lost civilizations and secret societies, which soon expanded to include government cover-ups, religious control mechanisms, and the global elite's hidden agendas. His unique ability to weave together historical facts, declassified documents, and controversial theories has earned him a reputation as a thought-provoking and fearless author.

In "Hidden Agendas: Exposing the Dark Secrets," Demetri invites readers to join him on an eye-opening exploration of the mysteries that have been kept from us. His goal is not only to reveal these secrets but also to inspire others to question the world around them and seek the truth for themselves.

When he's not writing, Demetri enjoys engaging with fellow truth-seekers, exploring ancient sites, and continuing his quest for knowledge. He believes that understanding our hidden history is the key to shaping a more informed and empowered future.

Stay connected with Demetri Welsh on his journey to uncover the unknown and challenge the status quo. Join the conversation and become part of a community dedicated to seeking the truth and exposing the dark secrets that influence our world.